LIVING WITH
HONOR

Staff Sergeant
Salvatore A. Giunta

With Joe Layden

THRESHOLD EDITIONS

New York   London   Toronto   Sydney   New Delhi

Threshold Editions
A Division of Simon & Schuster, Inc.
1230 Avenue of the Americas
New York, NY 10020

First Threshold Editions hardcover edition December 2012

THRESHOLD EDITIONS and colophon are trademarks of Simon & Schuster, Inc.

For information about special discounts for bulk purchases, please contact Simon & Schuster Special Sales at 1-866-506-1949 or business@simonandschuster.com.

The Simon & Schuster Speakers Bureau can bring authors to your live event. For more information or to book an event, contact the Simon & Schuster Speakers Bureau at 1-866-248-3049 or visit our website at www.simonspeakers.com.

Designed by Joy O'Meara

Manufactured in the United States of America

10   9   8   7   6   5   4   3   2   1

Library of Congress Cataloging-in-Publication Data

Giunta, Salvatore A. (Salvatore Augustine), 1985–
   Living with honor / by Salvatore A. Giunta ; with Joe Layden.—1st Threshold Editions hardcover ed.
       p.   cm.
   1. Giunta, Salvatore A. (Salvatore Augustine), 1985–   2. Afghan War, 2001— Campaigns—Afghanistan—Korangal Valley.   3. Afghan War, 2001—Personal narratives, American.   4. Medal of Honor—Biography.   5. Soldiers—United States—Biography.   I. Layden, Joe.   II. Title.
   DS371.4123.K67G58 2012
   958.104'742—dc23
   [B]   2012030594

ISBN 978-1-4516-9146-7
ISBN 978-1-4516-9153-5 (ebook)

For my wife, Jennifer, and our daughter, Lillian.

It is my earnest hope—indeed the hope of all mankind—that from this solemn occasion a better world shall emerge out of the blood and carnage of the past, a world founded upon faith and understanding, a world dedicated to the dignity of man and the fulfillment of his most cherished wish for freedom, tolerance and justice.

—GENERAL DOUGLAS MacARTHUR

If I die in a combat zone, box me up and ship me home.

—TIM O'BRIEN

CONTENTS

PROLOGUE

November 16, 2010
Washington, D.C.

How's this for surreal? I'm standing at the front of a crowded room in the White House, an arm's length from the president of the United States, listening to a disembodied voice recite the formal narrative that accompanies the presentation of the Medal of Honor.

> *The president of the United States of America, authorized by act of Congress, March 3, 1863, has awarded in the name of Congress, the Medal of Honor, to then Specialist Salvatore A. Giunta, United States Army.*
>
> *Specialist Salvatore A. Giunta distinguished himself conspicuously by gallantry and intrepidity at the risk of his life above and beyond the call of duty in action with an armed enemy in the Korengal Valley, Afghanistan, on October 25, 2007. While conducting a patrol as team leader with Company B, Second Battalion (Airborne), 503rd Infantry Regiment, Specialist Giunta and his team were navigating through harsh terrain when they were ambushed by a well-armed and well-coordinated insurgent force. While under heavy enemy fire, Specialist Giunta immediately sprinted toward cover and engaged the enemy. Seeing that his squad leader had fallen and be-*

lieving that he had been injured, Specialist Giunta exposed himself to withering enemy fire and raced toward his squad leader, helped him to cover, and administered medical aid.

While administering first aid, enemy fire struck Specialist Giunta's body armor and his secondary weapon. Without regard to the ongoing fire, Specialist Giunta engaged the enemy before prepping and throwing grenades, using the explosions for cover in order to conceal his position. Attempting to reach additional wounded fellow soldiers who were separated from the squad, Specialist Giunta and his team encountered a barrage of enemy fire that forced them to the ground. The team continued forward and upon reaching the wounded soldiers, Specialist Giunta realized that another soldier was still separated from the element. Specialist Giunta then advanced forward on his own initiative. As he crested the top of a hill, he observed two insurgents carrying away an American soldier. He immediately engaged the enemy, killing one and wounding the other. Upon reaching the wounded soldier, he began to provide medical aid, as his squad caught up and provided security.

Specialist Giunta's unwavering courage, selflessness, and decisive leadership while under extreme enemy fire were integral to his platoon's ability to defeat an enemy ambush and recover a fellow American soldier from the enemy. Specialist Salvatore A. Giunta's extraordinary heroism and selflessness above and beyond the call of duty are in keeping with the highest traditions of military service and reflect great credit upon himself, Company B, Second Battalion (Airborne), 503rd Infantry Regiment, and the United States Army.

I'm a kid from Hiawatha, Iowa, a former "sandwich artist" at Subway who enlisted in the Army in part because I wanted to serve my country. Well, let's be honest, it was also because I wanted one of those free T-shirts they were handing out at the recruiting center.

Now, just a few short years later, I can hear the words describing what I did, and I know exactly what they represent: I remember every minute, every second, of that awful day in the Korengal Valley. And yet—even now—it still seems almost impossible to comprehend. Two of my friends and comrades were killed that day; three others were seriously wounded. But here I am, receiving the highest honor presented by the U.S. military—the first living person to receive the Medal of Honor since the conclusion of the Vietnam War.

I am proud—make no mistake about that. But even as President Obama places the medal around my neck, pride is merely one of several conflicting emotions. This whole event seems bittersweet, joyous and at the same time almost unbearably painful. I can feel the price of it all now—that little piece of fabric with the star on it, which these people are watching the president bestow on me, cost two people their lives and cost five others life-changing wounds. And here I am, with no scars, no injuries, standing up there receiving all of this adulation. I honestly don't know how to handle it. But I have no choice, so I do the best I can.

There is no handbook for something like this. You just sort of let it wash over you. And you try to get it right in your head.

I've come a long way since the day they first told me I'd been recommended for the Medal of Honor. That day, all I could say was "Fuck you," because that's what I really felt. A medal? For what? My buddies died that day. There is nothing to celebrate. I did what any of my fellow soldiers would have done, got lucky, and lived through it. For that you want to give me a seat at such a prestigious table? No, thanks.

But standing there, I get it now. I look out from the stage and see my wife and family. I see the other guys who were with me on the mountainside that night. I see the parents of those who didn't make it out: Sergeant Josh Brennan and Specialist Hugo Mendoza. I see all the brass in the audience, and there, in the front row, eight of the surviving Medal of Honor recipients from previous wars. I can't help but be moved beyond words. I can't help but understand: This isn't for me.

It's for all of us.

The president clasps the medal around my neck, and I can feel the weight of it now. We embrace for a moment—the president and me.

Blinking back tears, I turn to face the audience, and applause fills the room. But I know it's not for me alone. I know I am part of something bigger, something vast and still incomprehensible. I look at my mom and dad. I look at Brennan's parents, and I look at Mendoza's.

And I try to communicate to Brennan and Mendoza wordlessly:

This is for you . . . and for everyone who has fought and died. For everyone who has made the ultimate sacrifice. I am not a hero. I'm just a soldier.

I think they understand. I hope they do.

October 25, 2007

There was the sound of a single bullet, and then . . . a deafening barrage of gunfire and explosions.

There were, literally, thousands of bullets in the air at once, and more tracers streaking across the sky than there were stars overhead.

It was a miracle that most of us weren't killed instantly . . .

PART ONE

Before Afghanistan

CHAPTER 1

I should probably warn you at the outset that there is nothing very inspirational or heroic about the early part of my life. There is no military tradition in my family, no long gray line of service that inspired my enlistment. To the best of my knowledge, I have only two relatives who served in the military: a grandfather who did two years in the Navy during World War II, and an uncle on my mother's side who retired after twenty-one years of service, also in the Navy. Although I'm sure they were decent men who served their country honorably, neither one really inspired me, simply because I never really knew either of them. I suppose my uncle might have had some wisdom to impart, or at least some practical information about what it's like to serve in the military, but I rarely had a chance to speak with him. Practically speaking, there wasn't much need for a Navy man to spend time in Iowa, where I grew up. In recent years we've gotten to know each other a bit, but when I was a kid he was just someone whose name we invoked from time to time. Both he and his job were a mystery.

Our family history is a fairly typical American story, although maybe a bit more colorful than most. Three generations back, Augustine Giunta emigrated from Termini Imerese, a small Sicilian port city of maybe seventy thousand people located roughly twenty kilometers from Palermo.

My great-grandfather Augustine first came to the United States with one of his brothers, Anthony, when he was just fourteen years old in 1892. Augustine worked in Chicago at markets until he was twenty-eight years old, sending money back to his mother in Italy and traveling back to see her from time to time. When he went back to Italy, he would work as a sheepherder, making five cents a month. In 1905, he married Josephine Pusateri and together they emigrated to the United States, arriving first at Ellis Island and then moving to McHenry, Illinois— roughly sixty miles northwest of Chicago. They soon opened an ice cream parlor in the Chicago area.

As I understand it, being a Sicilian in America at that time was a rather difficult and complicated matter. Sicily, of course, had its own issues with organized crime and the pressure it exerted. Some people were marrying into their own families in a desperate attempt to preserve lineage and avoid the corrupting influence of the Mafia. Others simply pulled up roots and left their homeland. The Giunta family became fractured around the turn of the century: Some stayed in Sicily and some came to America. But even among those that immigrated, there was disagreement over how the family name would be represented in the New World.

There was, of course, a thriving criminal element in Chicago at the time, and because of this Augustine and Josephine figured it wasn't a safe place to raise a family. Augustine decided they would move to Dubuque after hearing the town announced at the train station in Chicago and then taking the train there to see what it had to offer. Among the first things he saw were some Italian storefronts, and the decision was made on the spot. During the move from McHenry to Dubuque, there was a train wreck in which all of the family's ice cream parlor glassware broke. Lacking the funds to purchase new equipment, Augustine and his brother Sam bought a horse and wagon and in 1913 began delivering produce door-to-door. By 1928 they had opened Giunta Brothers Produce in an open-market area of Dubuque. Business went so well that the family (which by this time included Augustine's two sons, Salvatore and Vince) opened a second Giunta Brothers Produce store in Clinton, Iowa, in 1940. That store, unfortunately, burned down in 1963, and due to a combination of financial problems and the growing popularity of large supermarkets, the family produce store gradually went out of business, prompting my great-grandfather to reconsider the merits of a being a small business owner.

Having now visited Termini Imerese, I can't help but be filled with admiration for my great-grandfather. To think of that journey—from a coastal city in Sicily to Chicago and finally to Dubuque, Iowa—well, you don't do something like that unless you have a sturdy set of balls. I can only imagine the disorientation the Giuntas must have felt while passing through the great, sweeping cornfields of eastern Iowa. But I guess they figured it was worth the risk.

Family history gets a little fuzzy after that. I was named after my grandfather, Salvatore, who held a number of different jobs in addition to serving in the Navy. I do know he was stationed for a while in Australia, and that he suffered from a variety of health problems, most notably emphysema, and from what I hear he was a good and honest man. But my dad didn't talk about him that much, and I always got the sense that Salvatore Giunta was not a strong, visible father figure in his kids' lives. At least, not in the manner that my father was involved in our lives. But I suppose that's a generational difference.

My father, Steven Giunta, is Iowa born and raised. He grew up in Dubuque, went to school in Chicago, came back home, and eventually got a job as a lab technician for Abbott Laboratories, covering a territory that stretched across the eastern portion of the state. I was born in Clinton, Iowa, and we spent a few years there before we moved to Cedar Rapids, which gave Dad the opportunity to get home more often.

My mother is of Irish descent; her maiden name was Rosemary Judge. There's actually some Irish blood in my father's family as well, so despite having a name like Salvatore Giunta, I'm more Irish than Italian. It's a volatile mix, but a good one, in my opinion. You get the Irish and the Italians together, and nobody backs down from a fight.

Looking back on it, I was blessed with a remarkably stable and nurturing upbringing. I didn't always see it that way at the time, unfortunately, but I know better now. Before getting married, my mother had worked as a security guard at the Quad Cities Generating Station, a nuclear power plant located in Cordova, Illinois. I never saw this part of her life and couldn't imagine it, frankly—the idea of my mom wearing a uniform, carrying a gun, and escorting truck drivers from the front gate to their destination within the plant was almost beyond comprehension. That part of her life had long since passed by the time I came along. And for the next several years she was a stay-at-home mom, raising three kids while my father worked, and re-entering the workforce only when all of her children were in school.

I have two younger siblings, a brother named Mario and a sister named Katie. We're all lucky to have been raised in this environment. Cedar Rapids was a city of perhaps a hundred thousand people when I was growing up—big enough to be interesting, but not overwhelming. We lived in a pleasant suburban subdivision where the doors were never locked and you knew all your neighbors. Mom was actively involved in everything we did, from teaching arts and crafts to arranging play dates with other kids. It was idyllic.

Best of all, we lived right across the street from the city's municipal golf course. I wasn't a country club kid—we didn't have that kind of money. Nevertheless, thanks to the city of Cedar Rapids, I became an avid golfer. A youth golf membership at the muni was ridiculously cheap. For a hundred bucks you could golf every day, all summer long, quitting only when your hands blistered or you grew bored or frustrated. It was easily the best deal in town. As a result, from roughly the age of nine, golf became my passion. I'd get up in the morning, throw my bag over my shoulder, and meet a few of my friends on the first tee. Sometimes we'd stay there all day long.

Golf was the first sport that really captured my attention, which is interesting when you consider that it's such a contemplative, finicky sport, and I was by nature a hyperactive and even somewhat reckless boy. But time and circumstance and proximity allowed me to get serious about it. Golf also encouraged me to learn the fine art of bullshitting, a skill that comes in handy to this day. There were times I'd show up in the clubhouse alone, eager to play a round, only to find that I'd been assigned to a foursome with three strangers, some of whom were older than my parents. I learned to introduce myself, and to act like I belonged there. I tried always to be respectful, because I knew that, unlike me, most of them had paid some fairly serious money for the privilege of golfing. I'd listen thoughtfully to their conversations, choosing carefully any words I might contribute. Last thing I wanted was for them to think I was some punk kid. Fortunately, my game spoke for itself. At that time, when I was golfing virtually every day, I could outshoot a lot of grown-ups, and my skill on the course gave me confidence in social interactions.

Golf helped me fine-tune interpersonal skills like shaking hands or looking someone in the eye when I spoke. I could do twenty-seven holes a day; sometimes thirty-six holes. Then I could walk home, jump on my bike, and ride a mile or two to hang out with my buddies. How many boys have that sort of freedom and fun when they're nine or ten years old?

Yeah . . . I was lucky.

Like most kids in Iowa, I was introduced to wrestling at an early age as well. While wrestling is an overlooked or forgotten sport in most parts of the country, it continues to be practiced with an almost religious fervor in the Hawkeye State. I was in first grade the first time I wrestled, weighed maybe fifty pounds. I got into it because all of my cousins wrestled, and it was Iowa, and the sport just seemed to be out there in the atmosphere, taking up space and demanding interest. Within a few years, though, I'd learned how to golf and my interest in wrestling ebbed and flowed from that point forward. I liked the physicality of the sport, the intensity of one-on-one battle, but golf was more convenient, more fun. And I was better at it.

Golf gets into your blood, in ways both good and bad. As a grown man I golf only recreationally, more for the peacefulness and tranquility it offers than for any desire to master the game or shoot a particular score. I like being outdoors; I like the smell of a freshly clipped green, and the feel of the earth giving slightly beneath my feet. When I golf I am reminded of how much I love nature and the outdoors, and how much I have to be grateful for. In the beginning, though, I was a competitor and a student of the game. For maybe five years I soaked up every lesson I could learn, spent hours on the driving range and putting green. I was calm and focused, determined to absorb everything around me. I'd find myself in a foursome with better golfers and start taking mental notes. It was a healthy, productive obsession.

And then it wasn't.

I golfed so much, and became so familiar with my home course, that I began to expect perfection. The slightest deviation—a single bad approach shot or three-putted green—could mess up an entire round. By the time I hit the teenage years, I had become a volatile and unpredictable golfer—your basic club-throwing, cursing, red-faced maniac. And that's when I quit. Golfing was no longer fun; it was an exercise in frustration. I'd started out playing for economic reasons, falling in love with the game because it was enjoyable and a good way to spend time with my buddies, and now I cared only about shooting a great score. If I didn't par the first three holes, I'd want to turn around, march back to the clubhouse, and start all over again. I sought perfection, and perfection just isn't possible. Not in golf; not in life. There are things you can't control.

Fortunately, other sports are more forgiving. Eighth grade was the first year I could play football for my school team, and I fell for it almost as quickly as I had fallen for golf, although in a very different way, and for very different reasons. How can I put this without sounding like a knucklehead? I guess I can't, so I'll just say it:

I liked to hit people.

It kind of surprised me that I felt that way, as I'd never been a particularly big or tough kid. Even now, I'm only five-foot-nine, maybe 175 pounds. And I don't think of myself as being especially aggressive or temperamental by nature. With adolescence, though, I was flooded with testosterone, and it was in need of some proper channeling. Football was the most obvious and healthy option. Anyway, the competition for golf in Cedar Rapids was intense. If I wanted to excel at something, football provided a much wider path. That realization, combined with my growing annoyance with the sport of golf, and the satisfaction I felt whenever I had a chance to put on a helmet and collide with another boy, led me to football. Truth is, while I still enjoy golf to this day, I also enjoy flattening someone to the ground once in a while. No point in denying who and what we are.

——

Something happened to me around middle school. For a while I was a reasonably engaged and successful student, but then things began to change. School lost its appeal and quickly became merely something I was required to attend, several hours of forced inactivity made tolerable only by the presence of middle-school girls. I'm not proud to say this, but by the time I reached high school, here's the way I looked at it: *I know I need a diploma in order to do anything with my life, and all my friends are here anyway, so . . . I guess I'll keep going.*

If dropping out had been an acceptable option, I might have quit school at the age of sixteen, but it wasn't an option. Not in my house. So I continued to float through school, getting Cs and Bs without a whole lot of effort, never striving for anything more than that (even though I was capable), never missing class often enough or causing sufficient trouble to get tossed out or even suspended. I went to school for my own reasons—which had nothing to do with academics—and figured I had control of the situation. I didn't lack confidence or capability, that's for sure, but I was not, by any stretch of the imagination, a serious student. I didn't exert myself, didn't study, didn't lose a moment's sleep about how I would perform on a given test or lab. I'd just sit in class, half-listening, half-daydreaming, and then I'd take the test and generally do well enough to avoid calling attention to my performance.

And that was fine with me.

It was not acceptable to my parents, however. I'm a new father myself now, so I have a completely different perspective on a lot of things that occurred while I was growing up, but at the time I just didn't understand why my mother and father were so exasperated by my lack of academic effort. That I was a perfectly competent but indifferent student was a source of unending irritation and frustration to them, as it would be for any parent. I would never go so far as to call myself "smart," but certainly I was capable of more in the classroom than I had demonstrated. I was a classic underachiever, and what parent wouldn't find that disappointing?

"What's the big deal?" I'd say. "It's not like I'm flunking out."

This often provoked a lecture about responsibility and the importance of setting goals and having some greater purpose in life, some focus and ambition . . . none of which I wanted to hear. As a result, my parents and I engaged in a running battle, one that stretched out over the course of some five years, ultimately ending with a fracturing of our relationship—particularly between my father and me.

The thing is, I wasn't a troublemaker, so I usually felt the criticism was unwarranted. I would show up to class, be quiet and respectful while the teacher was talking, speak only when I was called upon, and simply try to avoid embarrassment or trouble. Granted, my mind would often be a hundred miles away (or at least a few rows away, depending on where the pretty girls were seated), but I wasn't a bad kid. I didn't get detention and I wasn't disrespectful to teachers; I didn't get into fights with other students. I knew where the line was and I tried very hard not to cross it. This was true throughout middle school and high school, and, to a great extent, even while I was in the Army. It's a valuable skill—knowing when to pull back from the abyss of stupidity. Despite my best efforts to underwhelm them, most of my teachers actually liked me. I think they saw me for what I was: a nice enough kid, sociable to a fault, who would rather have been somewhere else.

Football provided structure and engagement for a while. I played safety and wide receiver, preferred the former because I got to hit more than get hit. By the end of my sophomore year, though, I had given up the sport in favor of less structured and wholesome pursuits. I had a group of buddies, and we would pass the time by lifting weights, playing ball at the Y, drinking beer . . . the stuff kids do when they have no real direction or ambition. I had a girlfriend, too, at the time. As has been the case throughout my life (including my marriage), she was an example of me outkicking my coverage: A senior, two years older than me, Abby was intelligent and pretty and as driven as I was directionless. I'm not sure what she saw in a sophomore, but then I don't claim to have any great insight into the female mind. My parents were ambivalent about our relationship. They were naturally concerned about the age difference, but couldn't deny that in every other way Abby was a positive influence and a terrific role model. She was a good girl, popular with her classmates, admired and respected by teachers. She was in the school orchestra, which by definition made her a smart and motivated student. If not for the fact that she was eighteen and I was sixteen, they wouldn't have had any reason to complain.

As it turned out, the difference in our ages proved too formidable a hurdle. Abby went off to the University of Iowa the following year. I chased her to Iowa City on weekends (and sometimes even during the week), driving my '96 Dodge Stratus forty-five miles down the highway for the chance to spend a few hours with her. The idea of their sixteen-year-old son running around unchecked in a college town did not sit well with my parents, of course, but there wasn't much they could do about it except let the relationship run its course. Which it did, in fairly short order.

———

I can honestly say that military service wasn't even on my personal radar until about a week before I actually enlisted. I was not a particularly ambitious or zealous kid, not really politically or militarily aware. There was one current-events class I enjoyed at Kennedy High School, a language arts class called Perspectives. It involved a lot of discussion and debate about topics in the news, and I kind of liked that. Still, it felt somewhat abstract and distant. Like many other kids of my generation,

I felt no strong connection to or interest in politics until the morning of September 11, 2001.

Like most people, I can vividly recall exactly where I was when I heard the news. It was chemistry class, second period. I was a sixteen-year-old junior, wandering aimlessly through another school day, working halfheartedly on a lab assignment, trying to figure out the density of different liquids, when word filtered down to our classroom. Something about a terrible accident in New York City; a plane crashing into one of the Twin Towers. Suddenly every television set in the school was lit up, and every classroom had suspended normal teaching activities to focus on this tragedy half a continent away. At that point that morning, no one knew what had happened yet. The news commentators—like everyone else—were working under the assumption that the jet had gone wildly off course and experienced some sort of catastrophic failure, resulting in a collision with one of the towers. It wasn't until the second plane hit that the unfathomable became real: This wasn't an accident—it was a terrorist attack, intentional, willful, coordinated, and almost incomprehensibly lethal.

To those of us watching, it was our first view of evil.

We didn't do any work the remainder of that school day. We just watched in stunned silence as events unfolded in real time. I remember feeling a weird and almost inexplicable mixture of repulsion, anger, and energy. I was just a kid, but I was an easily excited kid. Although generally lazy and unmotivated when it came to schoolwork, I could be hyperactive to the point of annoyance if something caught my attention. I'd slog through the day at school, but as soon as the final bell rang, my motor would shift into gear, and I'd be going a hundred miles an hour. Even as I sat there quietly, trying to be respectful of the horror endured by the victims of 9/11, thinking about their friends and families, I felt like I wanted to jump out of my skin. I wanted to be there. Better yet, I wanted to be wherever it was that these fuckers called home, laying waste to everything they held dear.

It was primitive, unfocused, animalistic.

I wanted revenge.

Not long before 9/11 I had read a book about the Vietnam War, and the sacrifices that had been made by the men who fought there, and how underappreciated they were. The book resonated to some extent, but more on a visceral level than a psychological level: *Hey, war sounds kind of cool!* I didn't get it then, and I wouldn't get it for quite some time to come. War is not cool, of course. It is brutal and inhuman and tragic on multiple levels. It's also sometimes necessary. All I knew then, as I watched the Twin Towers fall, was that someone had to pay for what was happening to the United States. And I wanted in on the deal. To a great extent, I think this was true of the entire country. Even though there had been other military actions since Vietnam—Desert Storm had brought us into Kuwait and Iraq in the 1990s, and by the start of a new decade we had established a presence in Afghanistan as well—it took a historic terrorist attack to galvanize the nation to such an extent that we were not only prepared for war, but eager for it.

So, yeah, the sixteen-year-old kid in that classroom wanted to jump out of his seat, run out of school, enlist in the Army, and get a gun in his hand as quickly as possible. I wanted to shoot someone in the face for attacking the United States, and for doing it in such a cowardly way. Admittedly, though, it was a fleeting moment of rage, fueled primarily by adolescent adrenaline. In the coming weeks and months, the images of 9/11 fell into the back of my mind, losing clarity and provocation with the passage of time; as they receded, so, too, did my bloodlust. I had smaller, more personal things to worry about—like graduating from high school, which was still nearly two years down the road, and still far from guaranteed.

———

After taking a few years off from wrestling, I returned to the mat late in the fall of my junior year, hoping to earn a spot on the varsity team. Unfortunately, right before the season started, I suffered what would prove to be a career-ending injury. It happened in a preseason tournament, when my opponent executed a single-leg takedown. I knew it was bad before I even hit the ground. I felt something pop in my knee—one of those weird sensations that doesn't just hurt like hell, but also demands attention simply by virtue of how unusual it feels. When I looked down, I could see that my kneecap was in the wrong place, sort of pushed to the side, out of its normal track. The orthopedic surgeon popped it back into place the next day, but made it clear that I wouldn't be wrestling any time soon. I was placed in a straight-leg immobilizer for several weeks and continued to feel the effects of the injury for some time to come. Rather than work my butt off trying to rehabilitate the leg in time to salvage a few weeks at the end of the season, I decided to direct my energy elsewhere. After all, it was winter in Iowa; if you're not on the wrestling or basketball or swimming team, there's not a lot else for a high-school kid to do. So I decided to get a job.

In theory, this seemed like an admirable display of maturity and initiative.

In reality it was a big mistake.

See, the job was at a Krispy Kreme doughnut shop. And not just any old Krispy Kreme, but a production facility, where they make thousands of doughnuts a day. I'd stand there all day, bored out of my mind, watching the doughnuts slide off the line, hot and sticky and tantalizingly fragrant. More times than I can remember I'd just grab a doughnut and pop it into my mouth. Sometimes, in fact, one wasn't enough. I'd grab five or six glazed doughnuts at a time, squish them into a solid little doughnut ball, and devour it in one bite. That's like two thousand calories and a hundred grams of fat—in one mouthful!

This was a bad time for me. When I got hurt right before wrestling season I was in great shape. Stood about five-foot-eight, weighed maybe 145 pounds. Six months later I had ballooned to an unfathomable 220 pounds. It looked like there were two people stuffed into my body. I was abusing myself—eating too much, drinking too much, not working out, feeling sorry for myself. Abby broke up with me, citing, among other things, a sudden lack of physical attraction. (Who could blame her?) Most of my buddies were playing sports, so I didn't see them quite as much. And home life? Well, that had become a toxic situation.

I'll take most—if not all—of the blame for the deterioration of my relationship with my parents. Mom was more tolerant of my aimlessness and belligerence, so we managed to at least keep the lines of communication open. But my relationship with my father completely fell apart. When I was sixteen years old, I thought my dad was the stupidest man I'd ever met in my entire life. I couldn't see why I had to listen to him or take his advice or follow his rules. What did we fight about? You might better ask what *didn't* we fight about. Every interaction was cause for antagonism and verbal jousting. Simply put, I was an idiot: drinking, hanging out with the boys, chasing girls, ignoring my schoolwork . . . getting fat and lazy.

My father had been a hard and diligent worker his whole life, so he naturally and understandably found my lack of initiative and my self-destructive tendencies somewhat disturbing. I didn't want to hear it, though. I figured as long as I wasn't being brought home by the cops, I wasn't doing anything wrong. And that wasn't true, of course. It's not the right way to look at life. But at that point in time, that's the way I saw things: through a very narrow and selfish prism.

Only when I became smarter and older (which went hand in hand with me, by the way) did I come to realize that my father's advice and concern came from an honest and respectful place—a place of love. I'm a father now, so I get that. I can just imagine the way he felt at night, staying up and worrying when he knew I was out drinking with my friends, driving home, and generally just behaving irresponsibly and selfishly. I can imagine how much I must have hurt him when I lashed out at him and insulted him and refused to even negotiate. I understand now that while he wasn't a perfect man, he had my best interests at heart. He had life experience; I had none. Hell, I was the one being stupid and rigid. I look back on it today and I just feel so apologetic, so . . . ashamed.

I don't mean to imply that I was a budding criminal or anything like that. A lot of activities that occupied my time fell under the heading of Normal Stupid Adolescent Behavior. When I joined the military I was suddenly surrounded by kindred spirits—kids who had gotten sidetracked in one way or another, maybe didn't fit in at school, or had gotten into some trouble. Most of these guys had not been as fortunate as I was in regard to their family or socioeconomic background. A number of them had been raised near the poverty line; many came from broken homes. I was lucky by comparison. I'd come from an affluent area and had been raised by two loving parents. In some ways I led a double life while growing up. I'd go out and raise a little hell, treat my parents poorly, and then behave respectfully and maturely around other people, like my teachers and coaches and employers. I figured (incorrectly) that one canceled out the other.

Being a good person in one setting does not give you a free pass to be an asshole in others.

It's interesting, though: I ran into a lot of people in the Army, especially the infantry, with similar stories. The job no doubt attracts a certain personality type, one that craves action and confrontation and risk. Adrenaline junkies, I guess. While some of us have had difficulty with authority and discipline, we ironically embrace a culture in which, from the moment you sign up, someone is in your face, screaming at you, barking orders, telling you when you can tie your shoes or take a shit. Maybe "embrace" isn't the right word. When you join the Army, you either accept the culture or you wash out. You learn to survive. I got sucked in by a recruiting pitch and soon found myself in a world unlike anything I'd ever experienced. And while it seemed at first to be a place of maddening illogic, where rules were established for no apparent reason and punishment was dispensed with glee, eventually I learned otherwise.

The Army brought me for the first time into a world with an unyielding moral compass; a world in which breaking the law results in the law breaking you right back—swiftly and without discussion. It taught me for the very first time that responsibility is a real thing and that authority matters. And you will respect it.

But, as I said, those were not the reasons why I signed up. I did not enlist in the Army to better myself. I did not enlist because I wanted to learn the value of respecting authority, or to force myself to behave in a certain manner. No, no, no. Those were secondary things that came with enlisting in the military—fringe benefits, I suppose you could call them. I signed up to fight for my country; to jump out of planes, shoot guns, and kill people. I signed up for the T-shirt. That's just the truth of it.

But I got much more than I bargained for, in ways both good and bad.

———

I should also tell you that Jared was my inspiration.

Remember Jared? The guy who lost a hundred pounds by adopting a diet composed mainly of Subway sandwiches and later became (and remains) a popular Subway spokesperson? I was thinking about Jared when I swapped my job at Krispy Kreme for a position at Subway late in the fall of my senior year. Everything about Subway was an improvement. At Krispy Kreme I worked the assembly line; at Subway I was a sandwich "artist." Instead of scarfing down mounds of hot, greasy doughnuts, I'd eat one six-inch sub, loaded with veggies, every shift. And I started working out again. Like crazy. Pretty soon I was down to 185 pounds and feeling good about myself.

That's when I heard the commercial.

It came over the radio one night in April of 2003, a simple little advertisement by the Army, promising a free T-shirt to anyone who stopped by the local recruiting center. I went in the very next day, not so much because I had any burning desire to join the Army, but because I thought it would be neat to have an Army T-shirt.

I'm not kidding.

I went in for the free T-shirt and came out with a sense of curiosity. The recruiter did not feed me a line of bullshit. He very quietly and matter-of-factly said that we were a country at war.

"We're in Afghanistan," he said. "We're in Iraq. And we need men and women to fight these battles."

Then he sort of shrugged.

"If you want to make a difference, this is your chance. You can do this if you want to do it."

He paused, smiled.

"Or you can be a pussy and not do it."

I have to give the guy credit—he knew how to push the right buttons. Dispense with the flag-waving and rah-rah rhetoric. Just go straight for the gut: question my manhood. It worked, too. For the next few days I chewed on his challenge. Beyond the visceral attraction of being a soldier—this guy was airborne infantry, which sounded exciting—I found that the notion of serving my country (a higher purpose, to be sure) began to resonate.

I was eighteen years old, and at that age there's not a lot you can do to change the world. I liked the idea of trying to have an impact on something important. It made sense to me that the Army offered that opportunity. If nothing else, the Army offered a guaranteed paycheck and a job that would entail significantly more action than working at Subway . . . as well as a chance to jump out of planes, shoot guns, and see the world. It promised an adventure, and it sure delivered on that promise.

It took about a week for me to make the decision. I'd already accumulated enough credits to graduate, so most of my time was spent working and working out. I had no intention of going to college. Whether I had the required brainpower was irrelevant; I wanted no part of school at that time. I wanted to get out of the Midwest, do something exciting, serve my country.

So I signed up. I'd like to say I asked my parents for their permission, because they probably deserved to be involved in the process. At the time, though, we were essentially estranged—I'd moved into an apartment with some friends and had little contact with my mother and no contact with my father. Frankly, I didn't really care one way or another how my parents felt. Our relationship now is much different than it was

then (thank goodness), but during that period in our lives there was no chance of reconciliation. I wouldn't listen to my father, and if I wasn't going to listen, then I wasn't going to live under his roof. It was a hard thing for my mom to accept, of course. She wanted peace in the family. But the truth is, I was a crappy teenager; I was up to no good, and I wanted to be up to no good. I'm not proud of that, but I own up to it. There's no point in whitewashing it. It's part of who I am, and what I was before I went into the Army.

Did I know what I was getting into? Not really. The recruiter's pitch had nothing to do with daily life in the Army, or with trying to carve out a career path; it was all about trying to get people to enlist. When I found out there were jobs you could sign up for, I was actually surprised. I just figured they'd give me a gun and send me to Iraq. The complexity of training and education I was about to undergo did not factor into my decision at all. I suppose that's true of many guys who enlist. Along the way I took a competency test to determine which jobs were best suited to my skill set, and I did pretty well. They told me I could choose almost any job in the Army. The recruiter was a member of the airborne infantry, and I kind of liked the sound of that: They were the ones jumping out of planes and getting into the heat of battle. In the abstract, at least, it seemed interesting. I figured if I was going to join the Army, I might as well feel like a soldier. I didn't want to sit behind a desk and stare at a computer screen all day. I wanted to get out there and do the job.

Not that I really understood the job. In retrospect, I might have asked a few more questions.

What I knew about the military, or thought I knew about the military, could be summed up by what I saw on the cover of *Time* magazine when I visited the recruiting center. It was a picture of a soldier kneeling in the mud, a parachute draped behind him, mortars hanging off his uniform. The photo was snapped shortly after the soldier and his unit, the 173rd Airborne Brigade, nicknamed the Sky Soldiers, had dropped into Iraq on March 26, 2003. To me, that was the face of war: strong, tough, triumphant. I wanted to be part of it. I could do almost any job the Army had to offer, but I had one plan: I wanted to be like that guy on the cover of *Time*; I wanted to do what they did on the television commercials. I wanted to jump out of planes and shoot guns and spit and swear and kill bad guys.

Spitting and swearing almost always comes with those first two things, so I felt pretty confident that everything would fall right into place. See, the thing about the infantry is that it attracts fighters. There are a lot of people in the U.S. Army, but not a lot who are guaranteed to see combat duty. Some people enlist as a way to subsidize their education or simply because they have limited options. Maybe they want to learn computer skills or engineering. Maybe they want to become a medic.

I wanted to join for one reason: to learn how to shoot my weapon more proficiently, and with greater accuracy, than the person I was shooting at, so that I could kill him and then move on and kill some of his friends, because they were all enemies of the United States. If that sounds barbaric, well, it was exactly what the infantry wanted: people who were eager to fight.

Practically speaking, that was the only skill the infantry was interested in teaching. It was the only one that mattered.

I was a good learner.

CHAPTER 2

The thing is that I'm not a quitter, but there is one hole in my resume.

Seven months passed between the day I enlisted and the day I arrived at Fort Benning, Georgia, in November 2003, to begin basic training. Had I not elected to join the airborne infantry, that gap likely would have been much shorter, but there were so many people enlisting in the military at that time, and such a large number who were interested in really joining the fight and becoming part of the infantry, that a logjam had been created. If I was determined to earn a spot in the airborne infantry, I'd have to wait my turn. So I got a job working behind the counter at General Nutrition Center, which was convenient and cool, as most of my free time was devoted to working out—lifting weights, running—and preparing for basic training. For the first time in memory I was excited about doing something with my life, and I was determined to be properly prepared.

Unfortunately, there is no way to be prepared for basic training. Oh, sure, some people have a better idea than others—usually because they have a sibling in the military service, or because a parent has served at some time. But even those guys are generally stunned by the sudden and total shock to the system that comes with leaving the comfort of your home and being thrown into a barracks with a hundred other men, and having your every move dictated by someone else.

For me, the disorientation and anxiety of *What the hell have I gotten myself into?* set in the moment I arrived at Fort Benning and was told by a screaming drill instructor to drop my bag, fall to the ground, and begin doing push-ups. This did not subside until probably the end of the second week of basic training. As anyone who has been through the process can attest, basic training is immersion therapy on an epic scale, so thorough and overwhelming that within a fairly short period of time you can't even remember what your previous life was like.

It's part of the process, of course: the breaking down and building back up, the eroding of ego and selfishness. Like just about anyone else who goes through basic training, I didn't like it; nor did I understand it. I was a fairly strong-willed kid with very specific reasons for having enlisted in the military. I hadn't signed on for the privilege of being verbally abused. I had no real interest in learning responsibility and maturity. For the first two weeks all I could think was *Is this shit really necessary?* It's shocking to have every moment of your life dictated, and to have someone you don't know—someone you'd never even seen just a few days earlier and whose background and qualifications are basically a mystery—suddenly put in a position of such authority and control that you can't even take a crap or pick your nose without permission.

It felt like some weird, masochistic summer camp.

In reality, though, it was something else entirely.

Drill sergeants are in fact skilled professionals, highly trained and adept at what they do. I know now that they have one of the most important and challenging jobs in the Army: indoctrinating new soldiers, the vast majority of whom are just a few months out of high school and completely unprepared for what lies ahead. For some new enlistees there is a way to soften the blow. It's called the debt program, and it encourages new soldiers to use the time between enlistment and basic training to slowly adapt to the ways of the military through a series of seminars and other training opportunities. It was an ideal opportunity for me, since I had seven months to kill. I could have filled that time by going to the recruiting station, talking with officers or other enlisted men, taking classes, playing paintball and other military exercises. It made a lot of sense and certainly would have been beneficial for me.

But I wasn't interested in, didn't understand, and didn't care about the stepping-stones. As abstract and distant as it might have been, the war in Iraq—or the war in Afghanistan, which at the time was far overshadowed by our involvement in Iraq—was all I cared about. I was still in America, and the fighting was someplace else. I wasn't interested in filling those seven months with additional training. In fact, I wasn't even interested in training at all. I wanted to sign on the dotted line and wake up the next morning in Afghanistan or Iraq. I was that eager, that naïve. I had no illusions about being a career military man. I didn't aspire to become an officer. If we had not been a country at war, I never would have joined in the first place. It seemed to me that the thing you could do to make the most difference in the Army—or anywhere else, for that matter—was to go do the dirty work. The "practice" dirty work? That didn't interest me in the least. Nor did I want anyone to tell me how to do the dirty work.

Just put me there and let me do it, all right?

If that sounds bullheaded and immature, well, that's what I was. Frankly, that's the type of personality the infantry routinely attracts . . . and seeks. In combat you want soldiers who are aggressive and confident. The trick is molding them into competent, skilled fighters before putting them in harm's way. I wake up every morning knowing I am lucky to be alive—there is no small element of chance in what determines whether you survive two tours of duty in Afghanistan. But I also understand that I would not be here today without the training and preparation I received at the hands of the U.S. Army. As frustrating and demeaning and difficult (and at times downright boring) as it might have been, every ounce of that preparation served a purpose.

Sports is the perfect analogy, and it's no secret that a great many soldiers were athletes before entering the military. You practice for a few weeks, and then you have a game, and the practice permits execution within the framework of the contest. The difference, though, aside from the obvious fact that the stakes are much higher, is that the football player has a game every week. The drudgery of practice is interrupted on a regular basis by the fun and challenge of competition; rewards come at regular and anticipated intervals, and thus validate the suffering of practice and training.

Not so in the military.

I can't imagine what it's like in peacetime, when the training exists as an end unto itself. I mean, obviously war is not a good thing. But for the infantryman, combat is not something to be avoided or dreaded. It is craved. It justifies his existence.

And an infantryman can wait a long time for that justification.

I went through basic training and Airborne School, and then spent nearly an entire year overseas, training some more, before I went to Afghanistan. That's basically a year and a half of intense preparation, getting ready for something that I'd never been tested on along the way. And you know what? That's exactly how it should have been. I can see that now; at the time, though, I could not understand why everyone above me seemed to be keeping such a tight grip on the reins.

All I kept thinking was *Why the hell are they holding me back? Can't they just let me do my job?*

———

Something happens after the first few weeks of basic training—after you get your mind around the concept of sleep deprivation and constant verbal abuse and punishment meted out in the form of push-ups and sit-ups for seemingly every offense imaginable, no matter how small (because punishment is simply part of the training). You settle into a routine and begin to form a bond with the other men in your unit. Once I understood how everything worked, and how we all were going to be treated the same, it dawned on me that we had quite a bit in common.

Most of us had been average students in high school, at best. Many had experienced problems with their families. We talked about some of this stuff because circumstances encouraged us to share our stories. It's not the same bond you form in combat, obviously, but it's the bond of people experiencing some sort of hardship together, knowing you depend on them and they depend on you, and once that bond is formed, people start opening up, and differences are outweighed by similarities, and by the fact that you are all there together, living under one roof, suffering through basic training, working toward a common goal.

The Army is an impressively deep melting pot, tossing together young men and women from different parts of the country, and from different religious and ethnic backgrounds, and demanding that they not only get along, but treat each other with respect and dignity. Everyone brings certain preconceptions and biases to the table, but the Army pretty quickly compels you to move beyond those feelings, and not merely by cutting off your hair and putting you all into identical uniforms and treating each of you with the same degree of contempt. It does this by forcing you to live with one another and work with one another, and rely on one another for success and (in combat) survival.

Each new enlistee in basic training is assigned a partner, a "battle buddy," with whom you share various responsibilities and duties. You're expected to look out for each other, and to make sure the other person doesn't screw up too badly. Battle buddies are assigned alphabetically, without regard to any other factor. You don't like black guys? Too bad. Never worked with a white guy? Get over it. My battle buddy was a kid named Gibson. I can't recall his first name—in basic training, the last name is all that appears on your uniform, and it's all anybody uses when addressing a fellow soldier. Gibson and I could not have had less in common, at least on the surface. He was a Haitian kid from Miami, Florida. I was a white boy from the Midwest. I had never met anyone from Haiti, could barely even understand him when he spoke. Circumstances, though, dictated that we be in close proximity several hours a day. At first we just fumbled around, trying to get past our cultural differences, but pretty quickly we came to be friends. And we started telling each other about our respective backgrounds.

"You know, I've never had a white friend before," Gibson said to me one day.

"That's okay. I've never had a Haitian friend."

The truth was, I'd never even had a friend who wasn't just like me. Like most suburban school districts, my high school had been remarkably homogeneous—roughly 95 percent Caucasian. There was another high school in Cedar Rapids that was considerably more diverse, but it was on the other side of town and played no role in my life. My friendship with Gibson represented my first experience with another culture. Not just appearance, but language as well. The color of someone's skin has never mattered to me one bit, but to not understand the words coming out of his mouth . . . well, that's a more complicated issue, especially when you're relying on each other to get through basic training. But Gibson and I dealt with it, and we got past it.

Regardless of how you feel about the military, there's no denying that it is one of the most egalitarian of American institutions. It gathers people from all over and unites them in the pursuit of a given mission. And it continually stirs the pot, creating strikingly incongruous groups in which few people share the same ancestral background. Discussion of these differences is somewhat cautious and respectful in basic training, simply because everyone is so timid and existing in an atmosphere of pressure and anxiety. Once you're assigned to a unit, though, and the walls of formality come down, almost everything is fair game: race, religion, socioeconomic background. When it comes to your buddies—especially in combat—there are virtually no limitations or restrictions to ball-busting. Best friends have the best burns on you, and they do hit close to home sometimes. But it takes a while to achieve that level of comfort and camaraderie.

In basic training it's all about fitting in and not screwing up. I was good at that. Just as in high school, I figured out how to find the gray area—that middle level where no one really notices what you're doing. You don't want to stand out in basic training, because standing out— even in a positive way—can make your life difficult. You don't want to show up your fellow soldiers; and you sure as hell don't want to exhibit any sort of incompetency, which will incur the wrath of the drill sergeant and make life miserable for everyone around you. My physical training scores were high. I could shoot better than most people, hike better than most. But I wasn't the best. And I didn't make a big deal out of it. I didn't have a loud mouth. When everybody was quiet, I was quiet. I figured out right away that it wasn't necessarily a good thing if the drill sergeant knew my name; that there were two types of soldiers who stood out in basic training: loudmouths and fuckups.

I kept my mouth shut.

And I didn't fuck up. Not more than most, anyway.

———

I also attended Airborne School at Fort Benning. Not to diminish the experience, but frankly it was easy. I'd never done anything like that, never even gone skydiving with my buddies. For some reason, though, it came naturally to me. Don't get me wrong—I was nervous as hell the first time I leaned into the open door of a plane at twelve hundred feet, but it wasn't a crippling sort of fear. It was more like the kind of thing you'd feel before boarding a particularly nasty roller-coaster. I wasn't consumed by it. It was more like *I'm ready—let's go!* Airborne training, for me, was the start of a lifelong love affair with skydiving. It's a hobby even today, though I'm no longer in the military. I even went skydiving with the Golden Knights, the Army's elite performing and demonstration team, a couple of times in January 2011, which was quite a thrill. Basically, if someone offers me a chance to jump, I'll do it.

The next logical step was Ranger training. The United States Army Ranger School at Fort Benning is an arduous two-month session in which qualified candidates are taught skills in leadership, survival, and small-unit tactics. It is generally considered one of the most demanding and intense training schools offered by any of the branches of the U.S. military. Some people confuse Ranger School with Ranger Battalion or the 75th Ranger Regiment. While there is overlap among the ranks, the two are in fact separate and distinct entities. The 75th is a light infantry unit with a relatively small and unique membership, fighting under the authority and guidance of the U.S. Special Operations Command. Each of the Ranger battalions is also a distinct fighting unit. While Ranger School is a requirement for all soldiers in the 75th Ranger Regiment or Ranger Battalion, not everyone who completes Ranger School goes on to join either of those groups.

The work is roughly the same for all Rangers, but the deployment is different. Ranger Battalion has more money, more assets. There are Rangers throughout the U.S. Army who are not part of Ranger Battalion. Regardless of placement, though, all graduates of Ranger School receive a Ranger Tab, and there is no question that it is considered one of the more prestigious adornments found on a soldier's uniform. It signifies toughness, skill, fitness, courage.

I wanted a Ranger Tab.

Unfortunately, so did a lot of other guys in the Army in the early to middle portion of the decade. My performance in basic training had been strong. I scored very well on the physical training test—primarily push-ups, sit-ups, and a timed run—and I was rated an "expert" based on my marksmanship scores. I was one of only a small handful of men in the company to be promoted from E-1 to E-2 before the conclusion of basic training, so that put me on the fast track to Airborne School; near the conclusion of Airborne, I was asked whether I'd be interested in attending Ranger School.

Hell, yeah!

As with almost every process in the military, though, Ranger School proved to be more complicated and bureaucratic than it appeared on the surface. All Ranger School candidates are required to complete the Ranger Indoctrination Program, a monthlong torture session intended to weed out those who aren't really Ranger material. I went to RIP straight from Airborne School in April of 2004, full of confidence, ready to tackle anything the Army could throw my way.

Or so I thought.

In the end, it wasn't any of the nightmarish physical challenges that prevented me from becoming a Ranger.

It was the boredom.

See, once I got to RIP, or what was supposed to be RIP, I discovered once more that the Army had been doing a very good job of recruitment—in certain areas, anyway. Just as I'd waited seven months after enlistment for a chance to join the airborne infantry, I'd now have to wait for a loosening of the logjam that had been created at Ranger School. So, instead of RIP, I was placed in something known as RIP Hold—a way station for candidates awaiting an opening in Ranger School. RIP Hold wasn't even that difficult, but it was just about the worst experience I had in the military, in part because of the crushing tedium, but also because of my own impatience. I'd just come off Airborne School, which had been fun and exciting and challenging in all the right ways; it had made me feel like a soldier, like I was ready to ship off to Afghanistan or Iraq and get the job done (which I wasn't, of course). Then, suddenly, I was at RIP Hold, ostensibly preparing for some elite assignment within the Army, but actually just biding my time until a space opened up. To fill that time, the Army put me to work in a variety of stultifying ways, the worst of which involved kitchen duty—"KP," as it used to be known. Endless hours spent mopping floors, cleaning dishes, emptying trash cans. And training. Lots and lots of mindless physical training. Hundreds, even thousands of push-ups and sit-ups a day. A barrage of yelling and insults and orders that seemed to have no bearing on whether I would be a successful member of the Army Rangers.

In all candor, I couldn't believe what I had gotten myself into, and it seems even stranger in retrospect. Most Army bases today don't even employ military personnel in the dining halls, or not many of them, anyway. Instead, they have private civilian contractors. Occasionally, when you deploy to a remote place, you might run into a military cook, but if it's too remote, you'll be eating nothing but MREs (Meals Ready to Eat). Nevertheless, there I was, at RIP Hold, pulling eight or ten hours of KP, doing all the shitty jobs the cooks did not want to do.

After two weeks at RIP Hold, with no indication that placement in the actual indoctrination program was imminent, I'd had enough. I had come here to be a Ranger, not a glorified kitchen bitch. I was legitimately worried that if I stayed there long enough, I might end up working in the kitchen for the duration of my enlistment. That wouldn't have happened, obviously, but I had no patience. There were more than two hundred candidates for Ranger School in line ahead of me, and I was no longer willing to wait my turn.

Those two weeks did something that basic training could not; something that even two tours of duty in Afghanistan could not: They broke my spirit. I didn't need the Ranger Tab anymore. I didn't even want it. I don't mean to disparage the Rangers or their proud history. But at that time, for me, it just no longer seemed all that important. RIP was voluntary; all I had to do was withdraw and I'd likely be assigned to an airborne infantry unit. I'd still get to jump out of planes and shoot guns. I'd still get to fight.

Ranger training typically involves a few months of complete detachment from the outside world, but since we weren't officially part of Ranger School, or even RIP, there were fewer restrictions on our activities. We were allowed to possess and use cell phones, for example. One day, after sweeping up the dining hall, I pulled out my phone and called home. Given the fact that I was completely estranged from my father, and that my relationship with my mother had been strained considerably, this wasn't the easiest thing to do; it involved swallowing my pride to some extent. But I needed to talk with someone I trusted, someone I loved, and my mom was that person.

"I know this is what I said I wanted to do," I told her. "I know I made a commitment to be a Ranger. But this sucks, and it's not what I thought it would be."

Mom listened, offered little in the way of feedback. I told her I was going to withdraw from RIP and that I would probably be sent back to the regular Army.

There was a long pause before she responded.

"Sal, I didn't make your decision to join the Army, and I'm not making your decisions for you now. Just do what you think is right . . . and don't look back."

"Okay, Mom. Thanks."

I knew that would be her response; I just needed to hear it from her. And yet, I was filled with a sense of uncertainty and even remorse about what I was going to do. I had friends who had signed up for Ranger School. We had committed together. This was what we all wanted, to be among the hard chargers . . . the door kickers.

The Army Rangers.

So why didn't I want it anymore?

The next day, when I went into my staff sergeant's office, I had a sick feeling in my stomach. As quickly as possible, I stammered out the words, without explanation or any attempt to justify my decision.

"Sergeant, I don't want to be here anymore."

Predictably, for the next several minutes, he chewed my ass out.

"You're quitting? What the fuck are you taking about? You're not even in the program yet!"

"Yes, Sergeant. I know that."

At first he seemed disappointed, almost surprised, but as the conversation went on, it became apparent that he was actually relieved to be rid of me. I guess he figured that if I was the type to quit while I was in RIP Hold, just because I hated sweeping floors and cleaning dishes, then I wasn't exactly Ranger material.

"Get the fuck out of here!" he finally said, waving dismissively.

And so I left.

But as I said, I'm not a quitter. I wasn't the greatest student in high school, but I got through. I even graduated early. At every job I held, I always was a diligent worker. To that point, at least, the Army had reinforced in my mind the importance of tenacity and commitment and hard work. I didn't feel good about leaving RIP Hold. I still don't feel good about it, even now, eight years later, after all I've been through. It would be wrong to say I regret anything that came about as a result of that decision; too many things about my life have been phenomenal as a result of what happened afterward. But it represents unfinished business. I'd like to have a Ranger Tab. I wish I could have completed Ranger School and gone on to have exactly the same military career and experiences I had—taking into account the good and the bad, the heartbreaking and the life-affirming. But I don't regret the decision to leave RIP Hold. My life has been a blessing and I consider myself to be a fortunate man.

If that's the only hole on my resume, I can live with it.

——

It took about a week to separate from RIP Hold. During that time I trained with a group of maybe fifty soldiers waiting for assignment. We had all been successful in basic training and Airborne School, but had, for one reason or another, opted out of Ranger training. Some had made it through a portion of RIP; others, like me, had quit while in RIP Hold. Regardless, our commonality was that we were airborne infantry, and we were about to be shipped out. The only question was, where would we be going?

One morning the sergeant began calling off names and separating us into three different groups. He stood in front of us, clipboard in hand, and delivered the news we'd been waiting to hear.

The first group, he said, would be going right down the road to Kelly Hill, which was part of Fort Benning.

The second group was shipping out to Korea.

Finally there was the third group. My group.

The sergeant tucked his clipboard under his arm and began shaking his head.

"All you motherfuckers get down and start doing push-ups!" he screamed.

Oh, shit . . . what does this mean?

I couldn't figure it out. Ten guys were staying in Georgia, which wasn't very exciting. Fifteen or twenty were going to Korea, which would have been cool. There were only a few other options, and I didn't want to start thinking about them, or get my hopes up. So I hit the ground and began pumping out push-ups as the sergeant walked among our ranks.

"You miserable little pieces of shit! Here I've been waiting my entire career to go to Italy, and you fuckers get to go on your first assignment!? Gimme a fuckin' break!"

We all froze in mid push-up.

Oh, man! This is awesome!

"Did I tell you to stop?" The sergeant's voice barely registered, even though he was screaming. "Keep going!"

I didn't care. I could have done push-ups for the next hour, without a break. I was that excited, that pumped. We all were. Of all the places the U.S. Army could send you—of all the crappy bases both home and abroad—we were going to Vicenza, Italy. What an incredible break!

"All right, get on your feet," the sergeant shouted, almost spitting his words. "Grab your gear and get the fuck out of my sight."

We scrambled quickly, before anyone could change their minds.

Italy . . .

Occasionally guys would talk about where they hoped to be assigned, but it wasn't something you focused on. Most people in the infantry simply hoped to be deployed to one of the current hot spots as quickly as possible, to get in on the fight. That's all I wanted. The truth, though, was that Italy represented the best of both worlds: a chance to see combat quickly (since troops stationed in Vicenza typically deployed directly to Iraq or Afghanistan) and to spend time in one of the most beautiful countries on earth while preparing for that deployment; the country of my ancestors. The Army had promised me an adventure, a chance to see the world. But that really hadn't factored into my enlistment. I wanted to fight. But I have to admit that when I found out we were going to Italy, I couldn't believe my good fortune.

Not that I knew much about the country. Heritage notwithstanding, Italy was as foreign to me as it was to most Americans. I knew that my family came from Sicily and that Italian people spoke with a weird accent and drank lots of wine. I'd seen *The Godfather*. I'd eaten at the Olive Garden. And that was about the extent of my meager knowledge of Italian history and culture. In other words, I was clueless. But I could not possibly have cared less. Here is what mattered: I was going to be stationed in Vicenza for a minimum of three years. I was virtually guaranteed to be deployed to either Iraq or Afghanistan during that time. I would see war, in all its glory and horror.

And I would do all of this as a member of the 173rd Airborne Brigade, the same unit represented by the soldier I had seen on the cover of *Time* magazine one year earlier. I was airborne infantry. The 173rd was based in Vicenza. There was no other option. If I was going to Italy, I'd be assigned to the 173rd. The thought of it made the hair stand up on the back of my neck. The 173rd wasn't just any Army unit; it was *the* Army unit. Soon, I'd be joining their ranks. Whatever residual disappointment or shame I might have felt about my Ranger experience evaporated with that realization.

"Pack your bags, assholes!" the sergeant barked.

I'd never been so happy to be insulted.

The moment orders were issued, my time at RIP Hold officially ended. We were told to get our gear and report to the duty station. I had two weeks of leave time, so I went back to Iowa to see some friends. I spent only a little time at my parents' house, and even then I reconnected only with my mother and my brother and sister. My father and I did not talk. Not a single word passed between us. So much damage had been done that I doubted we'd ever have any sort of relationship again.

And, quite honestly, I didn't care.

CHAPTER 3

Holy crap . . . We're flying!

That's the first thing that entered my mind as I looked at the speedometer on our transport van and saw the needle fluttering north of the 120 mark. We'd just arrived in Italy after a nine-hour flight and now we were rolling down the highway, a dozen soldiers heading to Caserma Ederle, the U.S. Army base in Vicenza. We were all tired and disoriented, a state compounded by the fact that this big, lumbering van was somehow running like a Maserati.

I gripped the handrests and shook my head in disbelief. Listening to the engine groan, I wondered what I'd gotten myself into.

The van rocked as tiny cars swept past us on the left and right, apparently preparing for takeoff into orbit. Eventually I glanced over the driver's shoulder once again. This time, though, I spotted something else on the speedometer . . . two tiny letters, in bright orange: *km*.

I laughed quietly under my breath and eased back into my seat. We weren't traveling at 120 miles per hour; we were traveling at 120 *kilometers* per hour, which translated to a much saner and more logical 75 mph. That's how naïve I was when I first showed up. What did I know about the metric system? What did I know about Italy? What did I know about combat? Not much. Like everyone else arriving at Caserma Ederle, I was basically an empty vessel.

Once on the base we fell into formation and were quizzed about physical training scores by the sergeant major. Based on the numbers we reported, each of us was assigned to a particular company. A brigade typically consists of four battalions; each battalion consists of four to five companies; each company is further divided into four platoon units of thirty to forty men. Four of us were told to report to Battle Company. So we grabbed our gear, jogged a distance of maybe a football field to where Battle Company's training area was located, and reported to our new boss, First Sergeant Howe.

"On the ground!" he shouted. "Push-ups! Now! And don't stop until I give the order!"

It occurred to me then that perhaps life in Italy wasn't going to be markedly better, or even different, than it had been at Fort Benning, Georgia. Eventually, though, I came to understand that there was in fact a method to the madness, that the endless degradation and discomfort served a purpose.

While I'd never been much of a student, I took the time to do some additional research on the 173rd Airborne Brigade; the more I read, the more impressed I became. First activated in 1915, during World War I, the 173rd had a long and storied combat tradition, most notably during the Vietnam War, when more than six thousand brigade members received Purple Hearts. Following a period of peacetime deactivation, the 173rd was reactivated in 2000 to support American military efforts in the Middle East, particularly in the fight against terrorism. I already knew that it was soldiers from the 173rd who had made the first combat jump into Iraq a year earlier; what I hadn't realized is that many of those soldiers had been deployed to Kosovo in the months prior. They just packed their gear and went directly from one hot spot to another, without complaint or question.

When you show up on a military base, raw and ready but utterly lacking in experience, you can instantly tell when you're dealing with combat veterans. Almost nowhere else in the world in 2003 and 2004 could you look at a group of twenty-year-old American men and know that they had all been involved in combat. But you could do that with the 173rd, which had just returned from a tour in Iraq. On their jump wings was a little gold star, representative of a combat jump. If you weren't in the 173rd, you didn't have one of those stars, and the impact of that tiny adornment was significant. I remember looking at it and thinking that it represented everything I was training to accomplish, everything I hoped to do. In peacetime, soldiers train for years without ever getting an opportunity to test their skills and knowledge, to measure their courage and strength. But these guys, the men of the 173rd Airborne Brigade, had been through it all in the last eighteen months. And here they were, walking among us every day.

These were young men who knew about combat and fear and getting shot at. They knew the job. Every single soldier at every level understood the prestige of being a member of the 173rd. If there was any doubt, the point was hammered home on a daily, if not hourly, basis. There were standards established by the brigade, and we were expected to live up to them. And a big part of the process involved endless training and repetition. You have to put in your time with the 173rd to be part of such an elite group. It's about more than just being assigned. You have to earn the privilege with sweat and patience and performance.

The message is imparted in many ways, some more obvious than others. It's discussed during training and it's shared through something akin to osmosis, by merely hanging around the men who have returned. But it's also conveyed in a more primal way.

Through push-ups and sit-ups.

That might sound silly, but it actually works rather well. In the military it's important to be proud of your unit, proud of what you are doing. If you are part of an elite group, you'd better be elite, and you'd better live up to those standards. And you frequently hear this while you are doing push-ups. I didn't get it at first, but I get it now. When you are cranking out push-ups for no apparent reason, and someone is screaming at you despite the fact that you haven't done anything wrong, you start to question the wisdom of the entire experience. You start to think, *I just want to help, and you're not letting me help!* That's only natural. But when the soundtrack to the pain changes, and you start hearing about the hardships endured by the men of the 173rd—from the relative inconvenience of sleep deprivation and shitty food, to the sometimes fatal consequences of knocking down doors in Iraq—you can't help but get the message. Hearing the experiences of the men who served before you, along with the history of the unit, somehow acts as an anesthetic. It motivates as it dulls the pain. In fact, by comparison, it really isn't pain at all.

It's a minor inconvenience.

You lower your nose to the ground for the one hundredth time, your arms trembling, your breathing labored, and you just want to stay there—prone and comfortable. But you don't. You keep going, pushing through it, because you realize, to your shame and embarrassment, that whatever you're feeling at that moment, it isn't shit compared to one second in Vietnam or Iraq. Who the hell are you to wallow in self-pity? No one is shooting at you. No one is threatening your existence. There is zero chance that a roadside IED (improvised explosive device) will take your life the next time you get in a truck. You are safe, warm, well-fed.

So stop whining.

Personally, I can't think of any better way to learn history. I know it helped me move from a place of self-pity to one of strength and respect and admiration. It helped, too, that we never did push-ups individually. We always did them as a group, so that we understood the camaraderie inherent in our mission. We'd hear stories while doing push-ups; we'd be quizzed about the tradition and exploits of the 173rd, as well as basic comprehension about our various duties, while pounding out push-ups. If we answered correctly, the push-ups would end.

For a while, anyway.

Eventually you get a chance to prove yourself in other ways—on the rifle range, in training exercises—but at the start there is no tangible proof that you belong, nor any opportunity to demonstrate proficiency. You simply put in the pain time. If that sounds primitive, well, so be it. In the Army they have a saying: "You'd better be smart or strong." If you happen to be smart *and* strong, good for you. Few people are blessed in that way, although certainly I met a few in the Army. Most of the guys in the 173rd possessed a certain kind of intelligence—instinct, street smarts, an ability to figure things out and survive. But I wouldn't say most of us were "smart" in the traditional sense of the word, in a bookish or scholarly way. Which was fine. If you weren't one of the smartest guys in the world, there was still a place for you in the 173rd, so long as you were one of the strongest. You had to bring something special to the table. After a few months in Italy I could get down and do a hundred, one-fifty, push-ups, nonstop, and then get up and be prepared to do it again, right away. And you know what? It made me feel stronger. It made me feel better about myself and my unit. It forced me to grow in ways I'd never considered, simply by encouraging me to question the limits of my own endurance.

That's a good thing in any walk of life, but in combat, it's a necessity.

"Up on your feet!" Sergeant Howe shouted. He was perched directly above one of the men, speaking only to him. The soldier scrambled to his feet as the rest of us continued to crank out push-ups. "Grab your gear. You're going to 3rd Platoon."

Still breathing heavily, pack slung over his shoulder, the soldier jogged off.

For the next couple of minutes, Sergeant Howe repeated this drill with each of us.

I was in mid-push-up, arms locked and trembling, sweating profusely, my heart pounding, when he came to me. I paused, knowing full well that I couldn't go down again, that if I tried to lower my body, my arms would give out and I'd be facedown in the dirt.

"All right, up!" he shouted.

I pulled my knees into my chest and stood in front of Sergeant Howe, trying not to wobble too badly.

"First Platoon," he said. "Get outta here."

I picked up my bag and slowly jogged off, officially a member now of the 173rd Airborne Brigade, Battle Company, First Platoon. It would be my home for the next seven years.

———

When you're one of the new guys in the company, bonding becomes just about the most important thing. Bonding with other new arrivals creates a team atmosphere and helps ease the sting of feeling like you're the stupidest guy in the world. If nothing else, at least you aren't the only one screwing up. At the platoon level, however, new soldiers sometimes arrive in solitary fashion, and in these cases you have no choice but to suffer the indignity of ignorance on your own while also leaning heavily on the more experienced members of the platoon—even if they've only been on base a few weeks longer than you have.

This was the situation I encountered upon arriving at Caserma Ederle. Other guys in First Platoon were new, but I was *really* new, and they were nice enough to take me under their wing. Of course, their generosity stemmed in large part from knowing that the more I screwed up, the more everyone in the platoon would suffer. So it was to their benefit to show me the ropes. That was the way the system worked, and it was an effective method for building camaraderie and teamwork. Bonding most often manifested itself through physical training, primarily because so much of our time each day was devoted to marching, running, calisthenics, and other physical pursuits. We'd have PT in the morning, followed by a lecture by a team leader—for example, there might be a discussion of weapon systems, and later we'd be quizzed on the material. Then we'd have more PT, and another lecture.

Days were full, and whatever downtime we had was usually spent in our rooms, hanging out with other members of the platoon. And as was the case with my Haitian friend in basic training, my first two roommates in Vicenza, Michael Chioke and Justin Berg, provided further evidence that the United States Army is nothing if not diverse.

Chioke had been born in Nigeria and emigrated with his family to the United States when he was just a boy. He was a couple of years older than me, and one of the more well-educated enlisted men I came across, having already completed a couple of years of college back home in Chicago. But Chioke neither looked nor sounded like anyone I'd ever known. Very dark skin, sharp features, maybe five-foot-nine, 140 pounds, and an accent so thick with some African dialect that I could barely understand a word he was saying. The second day I was there, I overheard Chioke talking on the phone. I tried to listen, but I could only pick up random words, here and there. And he was very animated, very loud. All I could think was, *This isn't English. This sounds like some terrorist shit! What's going on here?* It sounded unlike anything I'd ever heard in my entire life.

And then there was Berg, a stocky little guy from California, about five-foot-six, 150 pounds, rip-roaring and ready to kick ass. I didn't know what to make of Berg either. I'd always heard Californians were laid-back and cool. But Berg was exactly the opposite. He was very intense, always fidgeting and moving, hyperactive. And the music . . . Oh, man, I couldn't get my head around Berg's taste in music. I'd grown up in Iowa, so I was basically a fairly easygoing midwestern kind of guy. I liked classic rock: the Beatles, Rolling Stones, Led Zeppelin. My all-time favorite song is "You Can't Always Get What You Want" by the Stones. And the song that would run through my head on deployment, the song I used to sing to myself when I wanted to chill out and feel like I was in control of a situation that was, by any reasonable definition, uncontrollable, was "Hey Jude" by the Beatles. Given my age, this made me somewhat unusual among infantrymen. A lot of guys listened to rap or hip-hop or country music, just as they had back home in Iowa, but that never did much for me. All that whining and crying about your horse dying or your truck breaking down or whatever. Everyone seems so sad in country music. People are always leaving each other and breaking up and losing their jobs. I never cared for it.

But Berg's music—and he wasn't alone in favoring this—was utterly incomprehensible to me. I guess you'd call it speed metal or thrash. I'm not even sure, and I won't pretend to know, which bands he favored. I never listened to that stuff back home and I tuned it out overseas. All I know is, it was loud and fast and filled with anger.

"Jesus, Berg. Turn that shit down, will you?" I'd say.

"Aw, come on, man. Listen. This is awesome."

"Die-die-die! Hate-hate-hate!"

Not the exact words, but that's what it sounded like to me. And it was the soundtrack to Berg's life, playing constantly in our little room, driving me crazy. Sometimes I'd turn to Chioke for sympathy.

"Chioke . . . you must hate this crap. Right?"

Chioke would just shake his head and laugh.

"It's crazy-white-people music, man. These fuckers—they're all nuts. You just gotta go with it, dude."

He said it like I wasn't one of those crazy white people, which I guess was a compliment. But Chioke was a strange bird, too, just in a different sort of way. In the evening, at least, Chioke would listen to classical music, and somehow he managed to get not only me to listen to it, but Berg as well. We'd lie down at night, turn off the lights, and Chioke would put on some Beethoven. Then we'd all fall asleep to it. It was the strangest thing—three guys from completely different backgrounds listening to classical music, half a world from home, while preparing for the business of war. But Chioke, who was an awesome soldier, by the way, had a remarkable ability to compartmentalize his life; to be a fighter one moment and a scholar the next. I saw him at times in Afghanistan, out in the field, on deployment, in the shittiest of conditions, with an open book in his lap, reading or trying to solve dense, complicated mathematical problems.

"Dude," I'd say. "How can you focus on that stuff out here?"

"Gotta prepare, man. Ain't going to be here forever."

That was Chioke, always thinking about the future, trying to better himself. He's back in school now, letting the Army pay for his education. Smart guy. It took time for me to see that, though. Just as it took time for me to realize that Berg had his attributes, too. Both men were tough and tireless, and eager to fight on behalf of their country. They were just . . . *different.*

Not that we didn't have anything in common. Berg and I, for example, each had demonstrated questionable judgment in regard to body ink. He had a big eagle on his back, wings spread from one shoulder blade to the other. Sounds great, right? Very impressive and appropriate for an

American soldier. Berg's eagle, though, had the misfortune of looking less like an eagle than an oversized chicken. We busted his balls mercilessly about that for the better part of three years. Every time I'd see Berg shirtless, I'd start laughing.

"Man, that chicken sucks, Berg."

"It's not a chicken; it's an eagle. An American eagle! Can't you tell by the way it's ready to fly?"

Granted, the bird did have white feathers on its crown, like a bald eagle, and wings suitable for takeoff. Still, it just looked kind of . . . *chickenish*. Berg always said he was going to get the tattoo fixed someday, and eventually he did, adding an American flag in the grip of the bird's talons. Berg later took up mixed martial arts. I watched a video of one of his fights not long ago, and you could see the modified tattoo. Gotta admit—it looked slightly tougher, like a chicken ready to go to war.

I probably shouldn't talk about tattoos gone awry. I have only two on my body. The second and more recent is small and personal, just three letters imprinted on my calf while sitting on the side of a mountain during my second deployment to Afghanistan: DTV—Damn the Valley, a reference to Afghanistan's Korengal Valley. The first has little to no significance, and is, sadly, much larger. A swirling mass of tribal ink, it covers a big swath of my upper back. I got it when I was seventeen years old, simply because . . . well, because I could. I had tagged along with a friend of mine, a girl, when she got inked for the first time. While I was there, the guy running the tattoo shop kind of gave me a challenging look.

"How about you, buddy? You getting one, too?"

I looked at my friend. She smiled.

"Hell, yeah, I'm getting a tattoo."

They didn't ask my age, didn't seek parental consent. If I could pay for it, I could get a tattoo. That it wasn't legal, strictly speaking, made it all the more appealing, since I liked to think of myself then as the kind of guy who didn't need permission and cared little for rules and regulations. And what do I have to show for it? A massive and meaningless splatter of ink across my back, the kind of thing you end up with when the sum total of your preparation is five minutes spent thumbing through a tattoo catalogue:

"What's this?"

"Uhhh . . . I think it has something to do with the Aztecs."

"Cool . . . give me that one."

Most of the time now I forget that it's even on my body. If someone asks what it means, I tell them this:

"It means I was seventeen and stupid."

That's my story, and I'm sticking to it.

————

As much as I came to like and respect both Chioke and Berg, in those first few days I had no idea what to make of them. I can remember calling home and telling my mother that I felt as if I'd been transported not just to another country, but to a completely different planet. It was that disorienting. I didn't know my roommates, and both, quite candidly, seemed crazy as all hell. They were none too happy about having a new guy in their midst, screwing up and making things difficult for them, and they let me know it.

It's part of the acclimation process that the new guy gets picked on; that's just how it works. I'm not talking about hazing or anything like that. I'm simply referring to the natural resentment that occurs when others in your platoon suffer because of your mistakes. Chioke and Berg (and others) would find themselves on the ground, doing push-ups, because of something I'd done wrong, and naturally this made them unhappy. But there was no way around it. It was preordained that I'd mess up simply by virtue of being new and clueless. For a while it seemed as though everything I did was causing them pain, and they'd be up in my shit, either trying to offer assistance or merely expressing their dissatisfaction that I was such a fuckup. But that's the process. There is never enough time to do what you have to do; you are set up to fail so that you can then figure out how to adapt to your new surroundings. The truth, though, is that you cannot do it on your own. You have to rely on your fellow soldiers, your roommates in particular.

"What the fuck are you doing?" Chioke said to me one day as I applied black polish to my boots.

"Shining my shoes."

"Not like that," he said. "Don't be stupid."

"Okay, then show me how to do it! Please."

He did, and I got it right. Eventually there were other new guys and the focus shifted to them. And I came to think of Berg and Chioke as friends and brothers who were far more normal than they'd seemed to me in the beginning. Chioke, as I said, was introspective and studious. Berg, I learned, had a wife back in California; they're still married and raising a couple of kids. We were all just people, different in some ways, similar in others, tossed into the same turbulent boat.

———

Training in Italy came with unanticipated benefits, and an adventure of a totally different sort, for it was in Vicenza that I met my future wife. Coincidentally, Jennifer Mueller was also from my home state. A junior at the University of Iowa, Jen was on a twelve-week summer program called Camp Adventure. Like me, she got more than she bargained for. We met, clicked right away, and at first figured since the clock was running we'd have a little three-month fling and then go our separate ways. Three months turned into . . . forever.

Let me backtrack a bit. Within a few days of arriving in Italy, I found myself sitting in a lecture hall, attending a mandatory weeklong course known as Head Start. The object of the course was to impart some basic knowledge that would help us adapt to our new surroundings. It included an overview of Italian customs, culture, and laws, as well as an introduction to the Italian language. Obviously you can't become proficient in a foreign language in one week's time, but that wasn't the point or the objective. The Army simply hoped to give its soldiers enough information so that they could avoid going out into the streets at night and acting like big, dumb Americans. Not a bad idea, considering most of us were in fact big, dumb Americans.

I remember sitting in that class, so bored and uninterested that I could barely keep my eyes open. I had graduated high school early mainly because I was so completely sick of going to class. The last thing I wanted to do while I was in the Army was continue studying. I look back on it now and I can't believe that I wasted that week. It was such a great opportunity to learn something about the country of my ancestry. But I don't think I listened to a word. I had an Italian surname and I was old enough to drink legally. What more did I need? I was good to go.

One day while walking back from class, I heard someone call out my name.

"Hey, Sal!"

There were a couple of things about this that struck me as odd.

First of all, aside from the guys in my unit, I really didn't know anyone in Italy. And they knew me only as "Giunta." The Army, as I said, is a place of surnames, especially when you are new to a particular unit. People identify you by the name on your uniform, and nowhere on my uniform did the word "Sal" appear.

Second, the voice belonged to a female.

I turned around and saw a girl with whom I'd gone to high school. Her name was Tina.

"What are you doing here, Sal?" she said with a big smile.

I shrugged, sort of gestured to my own uniform, and laughed.

"Uh . . . I work here, Tina. I'm in the Army. What are you doing here?"

She explained that she'd come to Italy as part of Camp Adventure, a program sponsored by the University of Northern Iowa, in which American college students are sent to American military installations and embassies to work as summer camp counselors. There were roughly a dozen students in the program and they had been assigned to the

Child Development Center at Caserma Ederle. Most of those students were young women.

"Hey, there's a bowling alley on base," Tina said. "We're going there tonight. Want to hang out with us?"

I looked over her shoulder, to where several of her friends and fellow counselors were milling about.

"As a matter of fact, yes," I said. "I'd love to hang out."

So we went bowling that night. And several subsequent nights. I began spending a fair amount of time with Tina and her friends. They were all fun people, roughly my age, and from similar backgrounds. They were excited about being in Italy. They wanted to visit Verona and Venice; I wanted to see Verona and Venice. Within a couple of weeks I was spending most of my free time with them. Although our days were busy with training, we were allowed off base in the evening and on weekends, and I took full advantage of the opportunity. The 173rd was in a transitional phase at that time, with a large portion of the brigade having recently returned from Iraq. Many soldiers were preparing to leave the military or awaiting reassignment, and new men were arriving every day. A few months would be required to complete the cycle, after which our training would accelerate. For now, though, we were in a holding pattern, and I spent much of that period with the gang from Camp Adventure.

There were a few other Army guys who became part of this group, including Michael Mason, a member of Battle Company, Third Platoon. Michael also knew a couple of the girls from Camp Adventure, so we spent a lot of time together and became very good friends, both in Vicenza and on deployment. My primary focus, however, was a pretty, bright-eyed blond who had grown up in Dubuque, only a hundred miles or so from my hometown.

I fell for Jen hard and fast. She wasn't just attractive; she was whip-smart and funny and adventurous. Her dad was a successful business executive who had served in the Navy Reserves and one of her uncles had been a Marine during the Vietnam War. We simply started hanging out together with the rest of the group, and in time found ourselves increasingly more inclined to break off and spend time alone. We went on day trips together; then we went away for the weekend. I taught Jen how to drive a car with a manual transmission.

The thing is, there was a distinct timetable to our relationship; a clock ticking relentlessly in the background. We both knew that in twelve weeks' time, we'd be going in different directions. Camp Adventure would come to an end, Jen would leave Italy, and I'd be off on some training excursion, preparing seriously for the inevitable deployment that would follow.

About ten weeks in, Jen asked me a question not nearly as simple as it might have sounded.

"Do you like me, Sal?"

I didn't hesitate.

"Yes, I do. I absolutely do."

"Because . . . well . . . I'm thinking about taking the next semester off from school and just staying here."

I had no idea how we were going to make this work, or even if we could make it work. But it felt right, nevertheless. Before Jen left for the summer, she had an interview and got offered a job as a child and youth program assistant at the Child Development Center on post. All she had to do was go back to the States and obtain a work visa, which was easier than it sounds. At the end of August when Jen and the rest of the Camp Adventure interns had to leave, I didn't really know if I was going to see her again. She was going to go home, tell her parents of her new plans, and then return in a few weeks. It wasn't that I didn't trust her plan. I was just trying to protect myself so I didn't get disappointed or hurt.

It actually took a couple of months, but she made it work and came back just like she said she would. I could only imagine how that conversation went when she informed her mom and dad that she was taking a break from school to chase some guy she'd just met halfway around the world.

Oh, and by the way, he'd soon be going off to war.

CHAPTER 4

I had always been the kind of kid who enjoyed camping and other outdoor activities. I liked to fish and hunt, go off into the woods and set up my tent, eat by a fire, sleep beneath the stars, listen to the woods whisper on a clear summer night. To me, a wilderness experience was worth seeking, so when I found out that the 173rd would be spending a month in Germany, camping and training outdoors, my heart beat a little faster. Italy was great, but the training, on a day-to-day basis, had grown old and tiresome pretty quickly. I wanted to get my hands dirty; I wanted to feel like a soldier.

Germany offered that promise.

Near the end of the summer, word had filtered down that our next deployment might be to Afghanistan, rather than to Iraq. This dictated a rather dramatic change in tactical preparation, as the fight in Iraq had been primarily contested in urban settings. Afghanistan, I had heard, was completely different. Whereas Iraq is primarily flat and arid and stultifyingly hot, with most of the population located in urban centers, Afghanistan is a brutally mountainous country, its terrain unforgiving, its climate unpredictable, and its citizens spread out across a vast web of small and seemingly disconnected villages and towns. There are cities, of course, but military conflicts in Afghanistan historically have been contested (and won or lost) in the mountains. The Army by this point had come to the realization that the American military presence in Afghanistan would be on the uptick for some time to come, and if we were to have any hope of avoiding repeating the debacle experienced by the Soviet Union—and just about anyone else who had tried to establish a large military presence in Afghanistan—we would have to prepare vigilantly, providing troops an experience that would mimic as closely as possible the deplorable conditions soldiers could expect to encounter there.

You might not think of Germany as being a particularly challenging environment. But in the woods, where the entire 173rd was sent to train in October 2004, it can be a seriously unpleasant place. Within a couple of days I realized this would be unlike any camping trip I'd ever experienced. To that point, it was by far the most difficult thing I'd ever done. In fact, I'd never had a shittier time doing something that I thought I liked. Camping is great; communing with nature, surviving in the outdoors? All good. But when the camping trip goes on for weeks on end, in weather that vacillates between bad and horrible, and when you eat nothing but MREs and never get a chance to shower; when you're sleeping on rocks or marching through shin-deep mud for eight hours a day . . . well, that's nobody's idea of fun.

Which was exactly the point.

Living day to day in such relentlessly deplorable conditions has the weird effect of making you feel simultaneously less than human and more than human.

"You can't let the weather dictate your training," the Army would say. And while almost everyone bitched about the weather in Germany and the discomfort of spending a month outdoors in the rain and mud, we came to understand its value and its purpose. In combat, you have to be shit-hot no matter how horrible everything is around you. To use a sports analogy—and, yes, I know that seems to trivialize the grave consequences of war, but the truth is we used them all the time—you don't play to your surroundings. You play your game, and that game had better be one hundred percent all the time, regardless of terrain, climate, sickness, fatigue, or whatever.

Here, just for the sake of amplification, was a typical day in Germany: Go out and set up patrol bases; hike for a few hours, from one of the bases into the countryside; dig a hole, let it fill up with rain or mud (or both), then sit in that hole for twelve hours; return to the base; eat some MREs; and sleep for a few hours—never more than three or four hours at a stretch, because guard duty is a primary responsibility. The next day you go out and do it all over again. I had left Italy thinking, *Man, this is going to be awesome!* And it was exactly the opposite of awesome. It was much harder than I had envisioned, and yet, only those of us who hadn't experienced combat seemed to be aware of how truly unpleasant a trip it was.

"Man, this ain't shit compared to what it's going to be like in Afghanistan," some of the veterans would say. That, to me, was an eye-opener. I couldn't think of anything harder than this, couldn't recall a time when I'd had less sleep, or been more uncomfortable, or more pissed off, or just plain bored. And you know what? As bad as it was to have people shooting at me, trying to kill me, there were times in Afghanistan when I'd think, *Well, at least it's not Germany.*

That one month of raw wilderness camping really instilled in me the notion that in combat you never get to fight at full strength. Not us, not as Americans. And it's not merely about the environment or the climate. Our rules of engagement are very precise—and were even less lenient in 2004—dictating, above all else, that the U.S. Army does not start a fight. That wasn't our job in Iraq, and it wasn't our job in Afghanistan. This, obviously, is something of a political issue and I've never considered myself a particularly political man. My job as a soldier was to do whatever the Army asked of me, and I did it to the best of my ability, regardless of how I might have felt about the reasoning behind those orders or the overarching political and military ideology behind our involvement in the Middle East. These were (and are) nonissues to me. I don't aspire to any sort of political career; I didn't join the Army to become an officer bound by bureaucratic guidelines and ever-shifting political doctrine.

I joined to fight.

I didn't ask questions.

Our job in Afghanistan—and not many people understand just how enormously difficult and dangerous a job it was—could be distilled to terminology that sounded simple but was in fact incredibly complex:

Maintain order . . . protect the populace . . . resolve the fight. *Kill the bad guys.*

This all gets very dark and murky when the populace might be involved in the fight, or when village elders are accepting handouts from the Army and feigning cooperation during the daylight hours, and then either taking up arms or assisting the Taliban when the sun goes down. But that's the way it was; moral dilemmas notwithstanding, we had to get the job done, even if it meant giving the enemy the first shot. Often, even with that advantage, they'd wait to take their first crack at us. Whatever else they might be, the Taliban aren't stupid. They understand the power of the U.S. military. We have the strongest, most well-equipped and highly trained army in the world; no one can beat us when we're at one hundred percent.

So they wait until we're less than one hundred percent to attack.

Complicating matters in Afghanistan, and leveling the playing field somewhat, were the rules of engagement, which were actually more like "rules of response." It sounds crazy to say it, but a large part of our strategy was to draw contact—to establish outposts in areas known to be hospitable to the Taliban, and to march out from those areas in a seemingly masochistic effort to initiate combat. We'd wait for the crackle of gunfire, and then respond with lethal force.

But we were not allowed to initiate combat. Nor were we often allowed to invoke the full weight of our military—with air strikes, bombs, and the like—as the risk of collateral damage was deemed too great.

All of this information was presented in great detail during training, although the emphasis was on using our strength and technology and skill, rather than on how to exhibit the sort of restraint and diplomacy required every day, while on patrol or interacting with the Afghan people, many of whom did not exactly appreciate our presence in their country. The year before my first deployment was all about learning how to become an effective soldier, a killing machine; the actual deployments that followed were about long stretches of boredom and inactivity, punctuated by ferocious fighting, during which the tools polished during training proved invaluable. It's hard to see the value, though, when you're sitting in a mud-filled hole in the woods, thousands of miles from the fight.

———

A few days before the conclusion of our first camping trip, I ran into Michael Mason, who was in Germany with Third Platoon. We hadn't seen each other in a while, as most of our training was done at the platoon level, so we spent a few minutes catching up, commiserating about the horrible weather and how much we were looking forward to returning to Italy.

"Hey, I heard Jen is back," Michael said.

"Really? I didn't know that." This was true. Jen and I hadn't communicated since the day she left Italy in August.

Michael smiled. I don't know how he knew this, but he did. I didn't even have a phone with me in Germany, so there was nothing I could do but wait until I got back to Vicenza.

Three days later, following a fifteen-hour bus ride, we arrived at Caserma Ederle. I went straight to the wall locker in my room, pulled out my cell phone, and prepared to dial. Funny thing, though—as soon as it powered up, before I even had a chance to punch in a number, the phone started ringing.

It was Jen.

"I'm back," she said.

"Yeah, me too."

From that moment on, with the exception of deployments, we were basically inseparable. Jen was not merely someone I found attractive and smart and fun to hang out with. She was someone I could talk to, someone with whom I could share my crappy stories, my dreams and aspirations . . . as well as my frustrations. I could talk to her about anything.

That would change in time, of course—there were stories I didn't share with Jen, scary stories about war and combat, things she didn't need to know—but for now I felt like I could tell her anything.

I don't think I fully realized then the full weight of what Jen had done—putting her life on hold like that for me. We'd only known each other a few months, and yet she was willing to take a semester off in order to spend time with me and see where our relationship might go. But as I came to know Jen, I saw that it was in fact exactly in keeping with her personality. She was an impulsive, adventurous girl, the kind who made decisions based on what she felt was right, and not on what other people might think of those decisions. She was independent and strong-willed. Still is, as a matter of fact. Now that we're married, we butt heads occasionally because we're both fairly stubborn and temperamental (that Irish-Italian thing), but I feel extremely fortunate to have met Jen, and to somehow have convinced her that I was worth a lifetime investment. She's one of the most motivated and positive people I have ever met. Good and exciting ideas come to Jen in a way that they don't come to me. Usually someone has a good idea, and I just, you know, pick up on it, and repeat it. I'm the kind of guy who hears someone else's great idea and says, "Yeah, let's run with that." Jen actually produces those ideas.

"Want to go to Alaska?" she asked me not long ago.

"Ummm. Sure."

Next thing I knew, Jen had done all the research and planned a trip that would involve halibut fishing, something I'd always wanted to try. That's just the kind of person she is. The world doesn't have to be a big, intimidating place. It's actually a fairly small place, and Jen wants to see as much as she can. Whether it's taking a three-week yoga trip to India, halibut fishing in Alaska, or leaving school for a semester to hang out with some guy she'd just met in Italy, that's Jen.

She's an explorer.

From a logistical standpoint, Jen's return was a bit of a challenge, in that she no longer lived on the base. Instead, she was sharing an apartment in town with another young woman. Before long I had basically moved in with Jen. Technically speaking, the Army would not have approved of this arrangement, but as long as I was able to get back on base before morning duties, no one really cared. Chioke used to bust my balls about Jen—"You come all the way to Italy, man, to fall in love with a girl from Iowa. What the fuck's wrong with you?"—but he liked Jen, and he liked having a little extra room to kick back when I wasn't around. He and Berg had the place to themselves most of the time, which made the living arrangement much more comfortable for everyone.

Shortly after we moved in together, I had an interesting conversation with Jen's father. Dan Mueller was an executive with John Deere whose international responsibilities occasionally brought him to Austria. I don't know if he actually had business there at this time, or if he was just checking up on me. I would certainly understand if that was the case. I mean, looking back on it, I wouldn't be too keen on my little daughter moving overseas and taking some time off of school with one year left just so she could spend time with some guy I've never met. Regardless, we ended up going with him to Innsbruck, which was only about three hours north of Vicenza, and spending a couple of days together.

Although not physically imposing—he's only a little bigger than I am—Dan was an interesting guy with a formidable presence. Part of that no doubt arose from the fact that he was Jen's father, and I wanted to make a continued good impression (we'd met once before, but hadn't spent much time together). But that's not giving him enough credit. There was something in his demeanor that indicated he was a man accustomed to being taken seriously; a man accustomed to being in charge. Things generally went well on that trip, until the very end, when we were all saying our good-byes.

"Sal, you know, I like you . . ." he said quietly, letting the words trail off, a clear indication that something much more important and probably unnerving was about to follow. "But I love my daughter. She means everything in the world to me."

He paused, glanced over at Jen.

"I may not be the biggest guy, or the strongest guy," he went on.

"But if you hurt my daughter, I will pay people to come over here and hurt you."

At first I didn't respond, just stood there motionless, trying to be cool, thinking, *Holy shit!* Jen, who had heard every word, seemed surprised but unconcerned. She later told me that her father had never reacted this way to any of her boyfriends.

You haven't really been tested as a suitor for a woman's affections until you've been threatened with bodily harm by her father. And I knew he wasn't kidding. He knew exactly what he was doing. If you're going to threaten someone, make it an honest, viable threat. I was nineteen years old and in great physical condition. I was a soldier in the 173rd Airborne Brigade. Dan could have threatened to kick my ass personally, but that wouldn't have held much weight, and he knew it. So, instead, he did something much more impressive and meaningful.

He promised to farm out the job to someone, or several people, who could do it well. I got the message, loud and clear. I looked at his face, tried to measure his intent. He didn't smile, didn't laugh; he was dead serious. Everything about his demeanor and tone indicated that this conversation—right here, right now, in a parking garage in Austria—was the primary reason for our meeting. It was so devoid of emotion or pretense or bluster. It was all so matter-of-fact:

If you do this, here's what's going to happen. And I won't lose a moment's sleep over it.

I had no intention of hurting Jen. I loved her then as I love her now. But how do you get that point across to a man who has just met you, and understandably doesn't trust you? Now that I have a baby daughter, and I can look forward as easily as I can look back, I don't have much of a problem with what Dan said. I get it completely, and I actually admire him for it. I have time to figure out how I will handle my daughter's first date, her first boyfriend, her first broken heart. I hope to exhibit some restraint and common sense. But I can easily imagine saying some outlandish shit to anyone who might be trying to enter her life on a permanent basis.

I didn't even try that day to convince Dan of my honorable intentions; frankly, it didn't seem worth the effort. Only time and continued good behavior would do the trick. Several years passed before we talked about that conversation again. It happened while we were in Mexico with our families, preparing for our wedding. We were at the hotel bar one night, and I shared the story. We all laughed. Jen just dismissed it with a wave of the hand.

"I can't believe you took that seriously," she said.

I looked at Dan. He smiled.

We both knew better than to say anything else.

———

Training is one thing, but training with live ammunition in your weapon, and living, breathing human beings all around you, is quite another. It gets your attention.

The second trip to Germany involved not merely camping and tactical preparation, but serious, intense weapons training. Blanks were replaced by live rounds as we spent hours each day at the range, drilling and firing. I was a private first class; my job—SAW gunner. SAW is an acronym for Squad Automatic Weapon, which at the time was the M249 light machine gun, a mass-casualty-producing rifle that could fire up to nine hundred rounds per minute. Each person in the squad had a specific job. For two of us, that job was to master the M249. In combat, we were told, the M249 would be our bread and butter. Under no circumstances would we put it down. For the SAW gunner, everything else was secondary. For example, someone armed with an M4 automatic weapon might sling his rifle momentarily to grab a grenade or rocket, because the rocket trumps the M4. But the rocket doesn't trump the M249, so the SAW gunner would never sling his weapon in favor of something else. It was made very clear to me during training that the SAW was my partner, that it should never leave my hands, and if we were in a fight, it should be fired—relentlessly, lethally, and with as much accuracy as I could muster.

I remember vividly the first time I shot my gun with one of my buddies about ten feet in front of me. This was a key component of our training, and something you might not take into consideration when thinking about combat: the fact that it isn't just the enemy you have to worry about; it's friendly fire as well. We trained endlessly and diligently to prepare ourselves for the complex challenges of combat, the idea being that if we were somewhat anesthetized to the sound of gunfire and disciplined enough to hold our ground, then the chance of someone getting shot by one of his panic-stricken fellow soldiers was greatly reduced. I'd never fired a weapon under these conditions before. My experience was limited to target practice in basic training or hunting with a rifle back home in Iowa. But now, out there on the range, with one of my friends just a few feet ahead of me, I had to squeeze the trigger and calmly find my mark.

That was more than a little scary.

It was then that I realized something strange about the sound of gunfire going overhead. It isn't at all what you might expect. See, there's a difference between a gun being fired behind you and a gun being fired in front of you; and different still is the sound produced by a gun being fired at you. It has something to do with the way the explosion comes from the barrel of the gun. If someone is shooting at you, and the bullets are coming close, you hear two distinct sounds: a pop, and then a crack. The crack sounds worse, but it's actually the pop you have to worry about. A popping sound means a gun has been discharged; a crack means the bullet has already passed by.

Either way, it tends to get your attention.

Frankly, I found it invigorating. And I discovered that I was pretty good at it.

There was one day when we were doing a live training exercise in something known as a shoot house. The idea, basically, was to simulate conditions American soldiers could expect to find in Iraq and, to a somewhat lesser degree, Afghanistan, when entering a local residence deemed hostile. Basically, you'd kick in the door and begin searching the house while at the same time being confronted by a series of potential targets. The tricky part was that some of the targets were "friendly" (women and children, for example, or other unarmed civilians, or American soldiers), while other targets were "unfriendly" (armed males who clearly were not American soldiers). In Afghanistan, I would soon discover, the line between friendly and unfriendly was so blurred that it frequently became indistinguishable. Combatants did not wear uniforms or anything else that made them readily identifiable. They did not always carry weapons. Generally, we considered any Afghan male of service age to be a potential enemy soldier; given that economic circumstances, combined with hatred of Americans and coercion by the Taliban, resulted in the recruitment of virtually anyone between roughly the ages of twelve and sixty, this made for an incredibly complicated moral dilemma.

In training, though, it was a challenging but not complex matter: Shoot the bad guys; don't shoot the good guys (including your fellow soldiers). The idea was to instill restraint into a situation that was, by its very nature, impulsive, violent, and lethal. One of the most admirable traits of a U.S. soldier fighting in the war on terror is his ability to compartmentalize, to put fear in one place, hatred in another, and morality in yet another. He balances all of these things to a degree that most people would find unfathomable, in an effort to do his job to the best of his ability. The survival instinct is a powerful thing. When you walk into a quiet building that might be a simple family residence, or might be a virtual clubhouse for the Taliban, there is a heightened sense of awareness. Every fiber of your being is focused on getting out alive; somehow, you have to channel that instinct in such a way that you avoid making a terrible mistake and injuring or killing innocent civilians.

The shoot house was designed to mimic this scenario, and while there is nothing quite like the real thing, it did a reasonably good job of providing a glimpse of what we could expect in Afghanistan. We went in with live rounds, too, which certainly raised the stakes a bit. Bullets, we learned, don't actually bounce off walls the way they do in movies; they sort of follow the walls, channeling and funneling their way along until they hit something soft. Like the ground. Or human flesh. So, when you entered the shoot house, it was a good idea to keep some distance off the wall, simply to avoid being hit by a stray bullet.

The first time I went through the shoot house with other members of my squad, I felt surprisingly confident. It's hard to explain, but everything seemed to slow down for me. I could see which targets were friendly and which were hostile. I felt no sense of panic, only exhilaration. But when the exercise ended, the company commander walked through the house, inspected our performance, and then pulled me aside.

"Giunta, follow me."

There was no emotion in his voice. As was usually the case with guys who had been in the Army for a while, he seemed adept at revealing nothing. Naturally, I presumed the worst. I'd been carrying the heaviest, baddest gun, firing the most bullets. One of them undoubtedly had hit the wrong target.

Oh, shit. This is Bad News Bears.

We walked through the house together, me trailing the company commander, watching silently as he inspected each room, each wall, each target. My heart was in my throat. This guy was the big boss, and if I had messed up badly enough for him to be brought in, then I must have really failed miserably. As we exited the house he turned to face me. He didn't smile, didn't scowl. He just spoke calmly.

"This is the best shooting I've ever seen. Well done, Giunta."

I tried to remain calm, but that single line of validation did wonders for my confidence. It seemed I had found my niche in the Army. I ended up winning an award for my proficiency with the SAW. I was the best in the entire company on my weapon, not just the best in the platoon, and that was a pretty good feeling. I'm not saying this made me unique. The recognition simply gave me confidence. I knew now that I had skill, that I could be an effective soldier. But I think everyone around me felt the same way. Each of us had a job, and we were getting better by the day.

What struck me, though, was the seriousness with which the Army addressed this type of training. There was absolutely no messing around.

Most of us were young and hyperactive, and eager for a fight. But the Army was careful to harness that energy in a way that was productive, not merely to help us become better soldiers, but to protect us from our own impulsiveness. And I'll say this: When you shoot a live round past one of your friends, or allow him to shoot past you, or enter a shoot house with your buddies, it fosters a degree of trust and respect not normally found in the everyday world. By the time we returned from that second month of training in Germany, I was ready to go to war with these guys. Not only had we slept in mud-filled holes together, but we had placed our lives in each other's hands. It was in Germany that I felt for the first time that we were becoming a band of brothers, to the point that I was utterly confident in our ability to fight.

What we really knew of war, of combat, was nothing. And little was shared by the men who had just returned from Iraq or Afghanistan. Some of them had seen multiple deployments, but rarely would they offer specific advice or expertise about what we could expect to see when our turn came up. There's an interesting dynamic that occurs among soldiers: Men who have seen combat tend to share their stories only with others who have been through it themselves. It wasn't like someone would come up to me and say, "Giunta, wait until you get out there; you won't believe it." More common, and acceptable, was the practice of combat vets telling tales, sometimes matter-of-factly, sometimes with a bit more gusto, while those of us who were new to the game would eavesdrop and absorb. That was our role—to sit quietly and listen, and to pick up as much knowledge as possible. It was unacceptable for us to interrupt their stories, or even to comment or ask a question. I can tell you that I learned a lot in this manner, and that some of what I learned was every bit as valuable as anything I was taught in formal training. The truth is, when a young, inexperienced soldier hears a war story from someone who has been in the thick of the shit for the past year, he tends to listen. You have to consider the source, and in this case, the source was basically unimpeachable.

There are as many different types of war stories as there are soldiers to tell them; they all come out different, spilling forth with anger, resentment, bravado, humor. Some are told with a tone of one-upmanship. "You guys had it easy! Fuckin' Fallujah—now that place was a shithole." Others, though, are much more somber—recollections of the ugliness and brutality of war, the death and destruction and sadness. In my experience, most combat vets, especially those who might be facing another deployment, do their best to avoid the appearance of softness. Sometimes, though, in the telling of tales, they reveal more than they'd like to reveal, and a listener will hear the entire gamut of emotions. While the stories are punctuated with jokes—"Wow, that one was so close I almost shit my pants!"—there's often a different tone just beneath the surface. And it's much more serious and heartfelt.

And yet, I don't deny that the primary effect of these stories, at least on me, was motivational. Several months down the road, when we received notice of our first deployment, I had never been more enthusiastic about anything in my life. Not even Christmas morning when I was a little kid, or the greatest vacation ever, could compare to the sense of anticipation and pure, unadulterated excitement. I could not wait. So while the stories did provoke a sense of respect for the men who told them, and for what they had seen and endured, they did not dissuade me in the least. Far from it, actually. They got me stoked.

Of course, I had no idea of the cost that came with war. You have to be there, and you have to see it for yourself, to fully understand.

———

By mid-January, Jen had left for Spain to resume her education. She still had to pick up a semester abroad in order to complete the degree requirements for a minor in Spanish. Meanwhile, the 173rd was in heavy training mode. No more trips to Germany, no more sleeping in mud-filled holes. Just endless hours of PT and range practice and familiarization with equipment and tactics. Our training was now geared specifically to the type of conditions we'd be facing in Afghanistan. Iraq had been a close-quarters conflict—knocking down doors in urban settings. Afghanistan would be much different, and by now we knew with virtual certainty that this was our destination. We were simply waiting for someone to call us together and give us a departure date. We hoped they'd give us at least a month's notice, but there was no requirement for them to do so. All information in the Army is dispensed on a need-to-know basis. When the 173rd first dropped into Iraq, they did so with only a few days' warning. We could expect no greater consideration. Our job was to be prepared. When the Army told us to leave, we would leave. And that was that. In the meantime, we trained. And our squad trained hardest of all, thanks to Staff Sergeant Dave Barberet.

My introduction to Sergeant Barberet, shortly after I arrived in Italy, was a memorable one. I'd been assigned to First Platoon, First Squad, and told to report to my squad leader. I was clueless at the time—tired, disoriented, confused, jet-lagged. In this state I rushed to company headquarters, looking for Sergeant Barberet. I found him standing in the entranceway, just outside the front door, smoking a cigarette. This immediately struck me as strange, as the Army does not permit smoking within a fifty-foot radius of any building. But I didn't say anything. I simply walked up to Sergeant Barberet and told him I was reporting for duty.

He looked me up and down, shrugged his shoulders, took another drag on his cigarette.

"You smoke?"

"No, Sergeant."

"Well, you're probably going to want to start that. You drink coffee?"

"Uh, sometimes Sergeant."

"Yeah, well, you're going to want to drink some more of that."

He paused, looked out over the company area. Sergeant Barberet was not a big man. Maybe five-foot-seven, 140 pounds. But he was cut to the bone, all sharp angles and muscle. He reminded me of some of the wrestlers I'd seen back in Iowa, guys with about 2 percent body fat. He also looked very young, and I soon found out he was only about three years older than me.

"Okay, Giunta, here's the deal," he said. "What do you do well?"

"Sergeant?"

"What are you good at? You fast?"

"Pretty fast, I guess."

He shook his head in disgust. "That's not good enough. We'll have to work on it."

By this time my head was spinning. I'd answered every question incorrectly, and my new squad leader seemed to think I was basically worthless. Sergeant Barberet took a seat on a bench and proceeded to remove one of his boots.

"See these socks?" he said. "Don't wear these. They're not allowed."

"Yes, Sergeant."

Then he pointed at his own midsection.

"See this belt?"

"Yes, Sergeant."

"Don't wear this, either. Not allowed."

"Yes, Sergeant."

He grabbed one of his boots, held it up for me to see.

"Your boots had better be shinier than this, Private."

I couldn't tell if Sergeant Barberet was playing with me or giving me honest advice. And it really didn't matter. Crazy or not, he was my new boss.

As it turned out, Sergeant Barberet was one of the toughest guys I would meet in the Army. He came from Massachusetts and spoke with an accent I'd heard only on television, thick with *chowdah* and *cahs* and *bahs*, and peppered with colorful obscenities. Sergeant Barberet was my squad leader throughout the whole first year in Italy, and through the first year of my initial deployment. He was a tireless little guy whose motor seemed to be fueled almost exclusively by cigarettes and coffee. He didn't appear to need much in the way of sleep or food, and he was fast as lightning. Despite being one of the smallest guys in the squad, he could carry as much weight as anyone else, and hump better and faster. And not once, no matter how shitty the conditions, no matter how challenging the obstacles, did I hear Sergeant Barberet complain about anything.

The guy was like a miniature version of the Terminator, and he expected the men who reported to him to exhibit a similar degree of durability.

"We're going to work harder than everyone else," Barberet explained to the squad shortly after we all arrived. "We're going to run farther and stay out longer. I will hold you to a higher standard than everyone else."

He paused.

"And if you don't like it, fuck you."

That was Barberet's promise, and he made good on it. In the beginning, I didn't know what to make of him, didn't think I could possibly live up to his expectations. But I did. We all did (most of us, anyway), and eventually we came to view it as a badge of honor that we were in Barberet's squad.

"Hey, we're going to the gym for PT this morning," I remember another soldier from a different squad saying one morning. "What are you guys doing?"

"Uh, well, I'm pretty sure we're going to go out and run ten miles, come back, and then go to the gym for PT. And we'll probably be done with PT just in time to change into our uniforms and start the workday."

On countless occasions, that's precisely how the day began. It was crazy. But that was Barberet. He didn't care what anyone else thought. And he'd be with us every step of that way—or several steps in front. We'd be sucking wind, and this guy wouldn't even be breathing hard. Then we'd get back, and the whole squad would be shaking, Starvin' Marvin, couldn't even think straight until we got to the mess hall, and Barberet would be hanging out, smoking a cigarette, drinking a cup of coffee, calling us pussies.

That was the routine, day after day, month after month, until finally, one day in early March of 2005, when Sergeant Barberet called the squad together and gave us the news. Our deployment orders had come down. We'd be leaving for Afghanistan within the month. There was virtually no emotion in his voice, which struck me as odd. Why wasn't he excited? In retrospect I realize that Barberet's experience in both Iraq and Afghanistan, where he had deployed previously, had no doubt changed the way he viewed his job. Combat has that effect on a person. Inexperience and ignorance leads to zealousness. But once you've been there and done that, you don't ever look at war in quite the same way.

Barberet looked around the room.

"This is going to be harder than anything you've ever done," he said flatly. "I hope you're ready."

I couldn't understand why he was the slightest bit concerned. I'd never been more prepared for anything in my life.

Or so I thought.

PART TWO

First Deployment

CHAPTER 5

My Son, Sal—

It's been too long. I am sorry for the time that's passed without handshake, hug & a kiss. I don't know how I turned into the stubborn bear that I am, because it doesn't seem that long ago that I was you.

Even though you took the path less travelled, you made it!! Praise God. You have become a good man and you are able to see the world. Wow! I am proud of you. I am excited for the places you have seen, the tasks you have completed and the challenges you have met.

There is honor in service. You are in an honorable place, doing an honorable thing, and that makes you an honorable person. I am proud of you, son.

Sal, have as much fun as you can. Keep God in your life. Moderation is the key. I look forward to the next time I see you. I will be the one with open arms.

Love,
Dad

The Army, God bless its big, bureaucratic heart, has a way of taking the fun and excitement out of almost anything.

Now, first of all, you have to understand that deployment in the modern era is not at all what it was like for past generations of soldiers. The massive, emotional patriotic sendoffs associated with World War II are a dim memory. Even troops fighting in the Vietnam War would leave en masse from American shores and find themselves deposited shortly thereafter on the battlefield. It's different and in some ways more disorienting for the modern soldier, who usually finds himself leaving one foreign country to go to another foreign country, to fight on behalf of a country he hasn't seen for the better part of a year or two.

There was a buzz in the air on the day we deployed from Vicenza in May of 2005. No question about that. But it was a weird sort of buzz, our departure witnessed and applauded nervously by a handful of wives and girlfriends and children. Most of us, though, had left family and friends far behind. Jen was in Spain, and we had allowed ourselves no big teary good-bye before she left. It never occurred to me that I might not come back, and if Jen was scared, she didn't let on.

As for my parents back home in Iowa, well . . . I'm not sure what was going through their minds, but I think it's fair to assume they were worried. That might explain the letter from my dad. It had arrived totally out of the blue, a few months before our deployment. Given the fact that we had not shared a single conversation in the previous three years that wasn't hostile or confrontational, and that we hadn't spoken at all since I'd come to Italy, the letter caught me completely off guard. At the time I viewed it as an olive branch, and a welcome one at that. But I probably didn't realize the full measure of its weight until some time later. I can see now what that letter actually represents: a father's way of reaching out to his estranged son on the eve of war, because he knows (better than I did, perhaps) what might happen, and he can't bear the thought of his son dying with so many things left unspoken.

So he wrote a letter, and I wrote one in return. Neither letter could erase completely the countless episodes of incivility and disrespect and anger that had accrued over the years, but at least we were corresponding. That was a start.

I felt pretty good about my life and my work when I got on the bus at Caserma Ederle. Our journey would take us from Italy to Kazakhstan to Afghanistan, and I couldn't wait to get going. The same impulse that had compelled me to join in the first place—the same simple logic—fueled my excitement now. Some people grow up and they feel like they're going to be in the Army from a young age and that's what they do. I never intended that. That wasn't the life I wanted. I truly believe that at nineteen years of age, I wanted in the worst way to go off and fight for my country, and to kill as many bad guys as possible, and then come home and get on with my life while I was still young enough to do whatever I might want to do. That I might not come home at all, or that I might come home permanently disfigured or disabled, hadn't really occurred to me—at least not in any tangible way. For all my training and preparation and skill, combat remained an abstract concept.

Sitting on that bus, though, I felt exactly as I had when I enlisted: proud of what I was doing, and eager to get started. I would defend my country, attack for my country, give blood, sweat, and tears for my country. No one had to twist my arm to convince me. I wanted to be there. And then . . .

Out came the needles.

Oh, man . . .

It made sense, of course. When you visit a third-world country, whether you're a tourist, a diplomat, or a soldier, you have to be properly immunized in advance. Still, it put a damper on the proceedings. Here we were, heading off to war, facing the reality that we might be shot or blown up, and they were protecting us against malaria? It was hard to take that threat seriously.

I'm not one to get all freaked-out about needles (some guys do, even the toughest ones), but it still bothered me to get stuck three times before we pulled out of the parking lot. I was trying to get pumped about going off to war, and suddenly I was rolling up my sleeve for vaccinations, just like a kindergartner getting ready for his first day of school. What a buzzkill.

———

It's important to make a distinction between combat and war. While each is terrible in its own way, one is far more tolerable than the other. As terrifying and deadly as it might be, I never looked at combat as something to fear or dread. Quite the contrary. Like most of the guys in the 173rd, I wanted to fight. I lived for it. And I'll be brutally honest here: Sometimes I miss it. Even now, as a father and husband who has moved on to other things in his life, there are days (and nights) when I want nothing more than to be back in Afghanistan, if only for a few short hours, sitting alongside my buddies, squeezing the trigger of my SAW and hearing the crack of gunfire all around us.

There is nothing more exhilarating, nothing that makes you feel more alive, than being so close to death. It's sweet and sick, and so very simple.

There is a level of intensity that you reach in combat that is attainable only when your options are success or death. I think in combat it comes down to that: It's us or them. This isn't paintball. This isn't a dispute with an office coworker. This is my entire future on the line. I'm betting the whole farm on black, and they're betting on red. Spin the wheel! Let's do this. The difference is that roulette is about chance and probability. While there is luck involved in combat, there is also skill. I know going in that I am better trained than the guy shooting at me from across the valley. I'm more experienced. I'm more confident. I have better weapons and I come from the best country in the damn world. You want to spit at me? That's fine. But understand that my response will be swift and terminal; it won't be a fair fight.

I look at combat as a calculated risk, one that requires every ounce of ability and focus I can muster, with a potentially fatal outcome, but an outcome over which I have some control. One of the things I tried recently, that I really enjoyed, is downhill mountain biking. Why? Because it comes as close as anything possibly could to giving me that same rush of adrenaline. Downhill mountain biking is intense and dangerous; it demands extraordinary levels of fitness and skill and focus. It's not about making one or two quick decisions and then settling in for a comfortable ride. Every decision matters and affects dramatically the one to follow. Can you execute a hairpin turn at thirty miles an hour? And if you do, what happens on the next turn? There is no margin for error, no opportunity to relax.

Until it's over.

There is no jumping off; there is no time-out. It's just this continuous accumulation of energy and excitement and worry, until eventually you sort of get in a groove, and then it's almost like you're outside your own body, watching events unfold.

I remember being disappointed the first time I went skydiving and discovered that it wasn't nearly as much of a rush as I thought it would be. I mean, it was fun and interesting and there was a moment when I first jumped out of the plane that I felt my heart practically pop out of my chest. But it passed in an instant. And then it became more of a ride than anything else. Skydiving, to me, is like a roller coaster: a fail-safe system. If you're looking to up the ante a bit, maybe you throw the pack out of the plane first, then jump and grab it on the way down, but that's something else entirely; that's an unnecessary risk. It's like getting all boozed up and then jumping behind the wheel in the car, driving down the highway at a hundred miles an hour, and seeing if you can stay alive. That's just stupid, unnecessarily risky behavior. It doesn't benefit anyone. In combat (theoretically, anyway), there is a higher purpose—you get to bet the farm on something that matters more than yourself. But if you win, you don't get the other guy's farm; you just get a chance to bet the farm again.

Combat is the confirmation of your practice. In school, you have to sit for hours and study and then you take a test, which measures your level of proficiency and in some way determines your worth, and that worth is continually updated and assessed as you move through the system. In combat the results are instantaneous: Some people who were alive moments earlier are suddenly no longer on this planet. And that is the most dramatic, visceral sort of validation you can ever hope to receive.

There is nothing quite like it.

I don't know how else to explain it, and I don't expect anyone who hasn't been through it to understand it. But there are times now, as I sleepwalk through the world in civilian clothes, that I wish I could find some way to get back in the game. I'd like to step into my closet and be teleported to the mountains of Afghanistan, where bullets are whistling and people are screaming, and all that matters is whether I have the ability to shoot my weapon accurately and lethally. I wish I could do that—join the fight for a little while, then teleport back and wake in my own bed, next to my wife, and then walk down the hall and hold my baby girl in my arms.

Just a quick fix of combat, and I'd be good for the next few weeks or months. And I wouldn't have to put up with all the other random, oppressive bullshit: the endless MREs, the lack of communication with the outside world, the bugs and the dirt and the dysentery.

And, worst of all, the crushing boredom.

Perverse as it might sound, the fighting was awesome. The fighting I truly miss. But as I was about to discover, modern war isn't mainly about fighting.

It's about downtime.

For the first two months our platoon was a designated Quick Reaction Force (QRF). Upon briefing, the job sounded pretty good. We'd be based in Kandahar, prepared on a moment's notice to assist troops located anywhere in southern Afghanistan. In theory, it was a soldier's dream. A firefight would erupt in some remote province: we'd rush out to the airfield, jump on a waiting helicopter, and get there as quickly as we could. Then we'd return to the comparative comfort of Kandahar. Having spent the better part of three years in Afghanistan, I can say with some assurance that the two safest places in the entire country, for an American serviceman, anyway, are Kandahar and Bagram. In Kandahar we'd have clean, running water and hot food. We'd have television, Internet, and showers. It was a sprawling military base, probably three or four times the size of Caserma Ederle, with all the requisite amenities.

Kandahar had very little in common with the Afghanistan that I came to know and, eventually, despise. The fight was not in Kandahar or any other city. The fight was in the mountains and small villages, in the most remote areas of a country that is notoriously remote and inaccessible; a country that had proven itself unconquerable throughout history. We'd be walking in the exact same places the Russians had walked three decades earlier. The war in Afghanistan had broken the Soviet Army, which was just about as well trained and well equipped as any fighting force on the planet at the time, and had contributed to the collapse of the Soviet empire.

Would it be different for us? Well, yes, I thought so, and for a number of reasons. First of all, I had complete faith in the power and might and skill of the U.S. Army. Equally important, though, was the fact that our mission was fundamentally different. We weren't trying to conquer anyone; we weren't trying to *beat* anyone. Our objective, and it did seem noble, was to engage the populace—to help improve their lives—while simultaneously rooting out the Taliban and reducing the threat of terrorism worldwide. I guess history will determine whether we succeeded in either of these goals. I'd like to think so, as a lot of good men and women have given their lives in the cause.

Certainly it seemed worthwhile in 2005, when we arrived in Kandahar. Beyond simply listening to the experiences of guys like Sergeant Barberet, I did a fair amount of homework on my own—scouring the Internet for anything I could find. As much as I relished the thought of a good fight, I liked the notion that we weren't really at war with the Afghan people, that we were instead trying to loosen the grip of the Taliban. To attempt anything beyond that seemed like an almost impossible task.

We're talking about a country that is uniquely oblivious to the outside world. I came to believe that there were places in Afghanistan so remote that 99 percent of the population had no idea what was happening beyond their own province; nor did they care. I'm talking about villages in which not a single resident had ventured more than ten kilometers from home. They didn't read. They didn't write. Their information—their knowledge and their reasoning—came from someone else who couldn't read or write, and who also hadn't spent a single second outside his province. I don't think most people in the Western world, in this age of instant information, can comprehend that degree of seclusion, but we faced it daily.

———

Forget for a moment the indomitable will of the Afghan people, sharpened by centuries of conflict, cultural isolation, and economic hardship—and aside from terrorism, the most viable export was opium—the mere fact of Afghanistan's rugged topography made combat a difficult proposition at best. This was something I expected, given what I'd heard and read. But there's nothing quite like firsthand experience to drive a point home. You go for a twelve-mile road march at Fort Benning or Vicenza, and you're tired afterward. You want to hike twelve miles in Afghanistan? It'll take you two days and leave you utterly exhausted. I don't think you can comprehend walking over a mountain range until you actually walk over a mountain range. And at some point during that walk, you come to the stark realization that someone might be out there watching you, just sitting on the high ground, waiting for you and your tired ass to get close enough to be fired upon.

When that happens, you're going to get smoked. And it absolutely will happen. The only question is . . . *when?*

Not that this was a concern to the vast majority of the soldiers stationed at Kandahar, most of whom did not have any skin in the fight. These were support troops, not infantry; they didn't join because they wanted to shoot a gun. They joined for other, perfectly valid reasons and somehow found themselves half a world away, too close to the fight for comfort, but not really in the fight. They could deploy for an entire year and never hear a bullet rush by, or feel the concussive power of an IED. Chances are, they'd never see a dead American unless they worked in the morgue on the base. That was their war.

Ours was a different war.

A couple of restless weeks passed before the first call came in. A Special Forces unit had drawn fire in a remote area, some forty-five minutes away. Within a matter of minutes we had scrambled aboard a pair of Chinooks, with fifteen men on each, and were flying toward our first firefight. My heart raced. It was the strangest combination of excitement and anxiety—knowing that soon we'd be facing combat for the first time, without having gone out on a single patrol. But that was the job of the QRF—to jump into any situation and handle it professionally and with overwhelming force.

So this was it . . . finally. The big show.

Except it wasn't.

By the time we landed, everything was calm. I jumped out of the Chinook and saw three or four dudes from Special Forces—just hanging out, chillin' like they were back home, like everything was under control; not one of them was even wearing a helmet at the time. I knew right away we'd missed the action, and instantly I felt a mix of disappointment and envy.

The SF guys, in my view, had it best. These were the toughest guys, the soldiers whose sole purpose was to fight. They'd go in, fire their weapons, do their job, and return to base. Then they'd do it all over again. They didn't have to put up with the drudgery and monotony of patrolling and waiting. I have several buddies now who are in Special Forces, and they've confirmed that the image and job description are basically accurate. Soldiers in the Special Forces represent the epitome of the professional fighter. When they go on assignment, they're not interested in diplomatic conversations with the village elders; they're not building roads or schools. They're going to shoot insurgents, and then they're going to come back to their well-equipped base, take a shower, maybe drink a beer, send an email to their wives or girlfriends, then hang out and lift weights until there's someone else who needs to be shot in the face. Call it what you will, but to a serious soldier, that's cool-guy stuff. And a lot of my friends who decided to stay in the military opted to go down that path precisely because of the simplicity of the job (which is not to say that it was easy; just narrowly defined).

Sergeant Barberet talked for a while with one of the SF guys, a man they referred to only as "Bear." I don't know what was said between them, and since I was brand-new to this whole business, I didn't ask. For the next two days, though, we walked through the mountains, trying to make contact with the enemy. Nothing happened, but for those of us who had never experienced altitude, the hike was incredibly difficult and debilitating. We had trained in the Dolomites, a formidable mountain range in northern Italy, but we did so slowly, acclimatizing over a period of several days until eventually topping out at maybe nine thousand feet. Now we were starting out at nine thousand feet, and climbing higher still, wearing fifty pounds of body armor and ammunition, and another twenty-five pounds of gear in our backpacks. Not everyone carries that much weight, but the SAW gunner does. Bullets are his priority, and bullets are heavy.

On this particular hike they were unnecessary, as it turned out. For two days we walked through mountain passes, looking for people or spent ammunition shells—anything that might have indicated we'd stumbled across a fighting position. But there was nothing. Finally, after the altitude had finished kicking our asses, the Chinooks returned, picked us up, and brought us back to the base at Kandahar, where we began watching the clock all over again.

Frankly, I found the entire experience disappointing. Maybe Afghanistan wasn't quite the hell-hole I'd been led to believe it was. Maybe combat wasn't as dramatic as I'd expected.

A week later, though, word filtered down that Bear had been fatally shot in the head in the course of a subsequent mission. I didn't hear the details, don't know exactly what happened, but the news was sobering, to say the least. Bear was the first person I'd ever met who later died in combat. I wasn't alive during the Vietnam War, and everyone I'd met in the military since then was still alive. Until that day, war remained abstract, without consequences; now I realized that wasn't the case. Here was a man at the top of his game—a member of the Special Forces. I didn't know him well, of course, but he had seemed cool and confident those two days that we hiked through the mountains, chatting amiably with Sergeant Barberet at the front of the line.

Now he was dead, and that very fact got my attention. But there was something else I recalled from the day we landed, something about Bear and the other SF guys, something that had seemed more confident than foolish.

They weren't wearing helmets.

I don't have any way of knowing whether this might have made a difference, whether a helmet might have saved his life, but it made an impact on me nevertheless. There is so much time during war when the bullets aren't flying, so much time spent waiting and wondering and walking. Some guys invariably made the mistake of removing their helmets, if only for a short time. We all did it once in a while. The truth is, sometimes it's more of a priority to get to a gun than it is to grab your helmet. That may sound crazy, but think of it this way: The helmet is your protection; the gun is everyone's protection.

Other times, though, you'd just be too lazy to grab your helmet, or you'd think you were safe within the confines of a particular area. Even on my second deployment, in the far more dangerous Korengal Valley, we'd often walk around our base at Outpost Vegas without our helmets on, despite the fact that we were taking fire practically every day. As long as you were within the compound, or very close by, it wasn't unusual to walk around without a helmet. Then, one day, our platoon sergeant was shot roughly one hundred feet from our home. Basically, he died standing right next to our latrine, which was nothing more than a hole in the ground with a couple of branches spanning the gap. You'd sit on the branches and do your business. Every so often, if gas was available, we'd burn the contents of the latrine to kill the smell and the swarms of flies that called it home. I'd use the latrine once a day, typically, and rarely wore my helmet on the trip. I mean, you'd think you were safe taking a shit in your backyard, right? Well, you weren't. You never knew when hell might break loose, and the long periods of inactivity that we endured, especially on my first deployment, only contributed to a false sense of security.

———

A few weeks later First Platoon was called in again as a QRF, backing up Second Platoon. Another forty-minute helicopter ride into the mountains, only to discover once again that we were late to the party. We spent the next four days hiking, until we arrived at a small village. The Afghan police in this area had been repeatedly overrun by insurgents, so the Army determined that a show of force was appropriate and necessary. Our plan was to leave a squad behind at that location while everyone else returned to Kandahar. The squad members would live with the villagers for a period of time, working and supporting local law enforcement officers, trying to stay out of sight. Day after day, week after week, until the enemy showed up and started shooting. Then, and only then, would we be permitted to return fire. But we would do so with the considerable might of a U.S. Army infantry squad. That, we figured, would teach them a lesson.

Second Squad, led by Staff Sergeant Jerry Plantis, was assigned this task. I was in First Squad, and immediately felt discouraged that we wouldn't be part of this maneuver. As luck would have it, though, the next person in the platoon who was up for leave happened to be a Second Squad SAW gunner, which meant they needed a replacement. So we swapped positions—he trekked out with First Squad and went on leave, while I stayed behind with Second Squad. *Finally*, I thought, *I'll see some action.*

Hours passed. Then days . . . weeks. Nothing but silence. Our assignment was open-ended. We were to stay in this village until . . . well, until something happened. In the meantime we subsisted on rice and beans, depending largely on the generosity of the Afghans. They cooked for us; they brought us water. Eight of us—the entire squad— lived together in a room that could not have been more than three hundred square feet. We did not patrol. In fact, we rarely ventured outside, as the entire point of the mission was to surprise the Taliban whenever they showed up.

But here's the part where it gets murky: They might already have been there.

As I think back on it now, I believe many of the very same people who offered us shelter and food were probably working with the Taliban. And I am one hundred percent convinced that every member of the police department was either himself a terrorist or supplying the terrorists with weapons. I don't believe for a moment that they were overrun by the Taliban; more likely, they were taking their own guns and selling them to the Taliban, or giving them away, and then asking us for more.

How do you cope with a situation like that? How do you fight the enemy when the enemy is so ill-defined?

You don't . . . and you can't. Not with any degree of efficiency. Basically, it's like fighting a war in a hall of mirrors.

After five weeks I was more confused than I'd been on the day we arrived. We ran an inventory of the police equipment, and of course much of it either was missing or hadn't been logged in the first place.

"You have to keep track of this stuff," we'd tell them. "The U.S. Army is paying for these weapons, and we need to know that we're getting our money's worth. We need to know it's a good investment. Understand?"

They responded mostly with shrugs or blank stares. The apathy and incompetence were stunning. But then, this was a group of supposed law enforcement officers accustomed to hanging out all day and smoking weed and opium. There was no discipline, no professionalism, no appreciation for American military involvement. After minimal training, they'd been given guns and power and left to their own devices; the results were predictably catastrophic. I came to believe very quickly that the only way to gain control in Afghanistan was to exert force. Diplomacy did not work. It's a primitive culture, one in which strength rules and weakness is trampled. The man with a gun has the power . . . until someone else gets a bigger gun.

One day, after maybe five or six weeks, the inevitable happened, and an argument erupted between Sergeant Plantis and one of the Afghan police officers. I honestly don't know how the dispute began, but it quickly escalated into a potentially deadly showdown, with the Afghan waving his gun at Plantis, shouting and spitting. Sergeant Plantis pulled his gun in response, and within seconds he was surrounded by more than two dozen Afghan officers, all with guns trained on him.

Our guns. American guns.

I'd never been involved in anything nearly this intense. The rest of us stood nearby, following Plantis's lead. He was our boss, and we would do whatever he wanted, but it was quite apparent that the slightest misstep would result in a pile of dead bodies. If just one of these stoned rent-a-cops squeezed the trigger, we'd light up the whole village, and probably get killed in the process. Somehow Sergeant Plantis kept his cool, just stood there as calm as could be (or as calm as you can appear with your gun drawn).

"Jimi . . . Corey," he said, calling out two members of the squad. (Jimi's real name, incidentally, was Seth Hendrix. But there was no way that anyone with the last name Hendrix was going to get away with being called Seth; we all referred to him as Jimi.) "Get up on the roof."

The face-off occurred outdoors, in the center of a compound that served as a police station, so Plantis wanted to make sure he had support from above, and on the perimeter. To my surprise, the Afghans did not object to our leaving. I'm sure they were scared shitless, and the fact that they spoke little or no English, and we had just one translator to handle conversation between eight of us and all of the Afghans, contributed to the general chaos of the entire situation. I tried to imagine how this could possibly turn out well.

"Giunta, go outside and get the Dishka," Plantis said, still as cool as if we were back at Fort Benning going through a mere training exercise.

I walked slowly away from the compound and did as I was told and shooed away a handful of Afghan officers hanging around the Dishka, a tripod-mounted antiaircraft gun that was capable of laying waste to most of the compound. The gun, logically, was facing out, away from the walls. Chioke (who had also been switched temporarily to Second Squad) got on the radio. I wheeled the Dishka around so that it faced the compound. I could squeeze off fifty shots and bring down the entire wall if necessary. That was the plan: At the first sound of gunfire, just let her rip, because in all likelihood the victim of that first gunshot would be Sergeant Plantis; once that happened, we would not stop firing until every one of the Afghan officers was dead and the compound had been obliterated.

Complete and utter devastation.

I'm not sure how long this went on. Five minutes . . . maybe ten. Crouched at the Dishka, staring at the walls of the compound, anticipating the worst, thinking I wanted a taste of combat, but maybe not quite this big a bite. I was isolated, couldn't hear Chioke on the radio, couldn't see Corey and Jimi on the roof, although I knew they were up there, watching with a bird's-eye view, poised as I was to respond instantly to the crackle of gunfire.

But there was only silence.

Finally my walkie-talkie came to life. It was Corey on the other end.

"Yo, Sal, come on in here. Everything's cool."

And that was that. I slowly backed away from the Dishka, took a deep breath, let my pulse come back to a normal resting rate. Then I walked into the compound, where Sergeant Plantis and the Afghans, through the translator, were carrying on a far less animated conversation. Some of them were even smiling. All guns had been holstered or lowered.

What the hell?

Talk about being in the Twilight Zone—five minutes earlier we had been on the verge of a catastrophic encounter. Now it was like the whole thing had never happened. Back to business as usual.

That was the first of many "light bulb" moments I experienced in Afghanistan, a realization that no matter how normal and safe things might seem at any given time, we were never more than a moment away from a life-threatening situation. Most alarming of all was a sudden awareness that it wasn't just the bad guys we had to worry about. We had to worry about anyone and everyone. This was a deadly standoff not between the U.S. military and the Taliban, but between the U.S. military and Afghan police officers, a law enforcement unit we had helped train, arm, and support.

Up was down . . . down was up.

My understanding of the conflict in Afghanistan, and our role within that conflict, was severely challenged that day. What I knew to be right and true was not necessarily right and true, and I found that to be sobering and disorienting. It was crazy—the idea that the good guys might be the bad guys; that, in fact, there were no good guys, other than those wearing the uniform of the U.S. Army. We went into Afghanistan expecting one thing and then found out it was something else entirely, that the very same people to whom we gave paychecks—the same people with whom we sometimes ate and slept and provided protection—were capable of drawing down on us.

But I wouldn't say that I was filled with hatred or fear, or that I had any strongly formed opinion about the Afghan people or the nature of our mission. That would come later. I simply felt a heightened sense of awareness, which isn't a bad thing for a soldier in combat. Mainly, I was relieved that a crisis had been averted. That I understood neither the genesis of that crisis, nor the resolution, was irrelevant. It was over and everyone was safe.

For the time being.

CHAPTER 6

Hey, Babe —

*Today is July 11, 2005. Time is moving right along, I got your
letter about our anniversary. So June 21. Cool. I forgot the first day
of summer and I don't have a calendar so I was thinking the 22nd.
For some reason. A lot has happened since I came to Baylough. For
the most part I have been up for the past three days. Good news—
I got promoted to Specialist five months early, so that's an extra
$150 a month. I'm pretty happy about that.*

*I have been trying to think about how I am going to tell you
what has happened in the past 24 hours, and the best way I can
think is just to come out and say it. First, I will start by saying that
I am 100% okay. Now, with that being said, I got an award or will
be getting an award that should give me some good benefits later in
life. OK, once again, I am OK.*

So we got into a bit of a firefight yesterday . . .

Zabul Province, Afghanistan

We never did make it back to Kandahar. Shortly after our standoff with
the Afghan police officers, our QRF assignment ended and we were
airlifted to Forward Operating Base (FOB) Lagman, which served as

battalion headquarters and was staffed by roughly five hundred soldiers at any given time. We were given a few days to rest and clean up, and then we joined the rest of First Platoon at FOB Baylough, an isolated base some sixty kilometers away, in the foothills of the Hindu Kush mountain range. I say "foothills," but that doesn't do the place justice. The Hindu Kush is a vast and rugged range that stretches from central Afghanistan to northern Pakistan, with peaks as high as twenty-five thousand feet; the median height of the Hindu Kush is nearly fifteen thousand feet. So, to an American (from Iowa, no less), Baylough, at seventy-five hundred feet above sea level, might as well have been a Himalayan peak.

We called it the Baylough Bowl, because the base had been constructed in a valley dotted with lush green apricot and almond orchards (and by the way—who knew almonds grew on trees? I didn't, until I got to Afghanistan), and with mountains rising all around it. I suppose if you were to see photos of the region, or stand there for just a few brief moments, it would be impossible not to be struck by the awesome physical beauty of the place. But there were practical matters that made daily life for a soldier stationed at Baylough something less than ideal, and they intruded upon his ability to commune with nature.

Simply put, the place sucked. Or so it seemed. I had no idea then how much worse it could actually be, as you ventured into the mountains, to places more remote, and more firmly controlled by the Taliban. For the thirty-five to forty American men (there were no females) stationed at Baylough, life was a daily grind of shitting in holes, swatting scorpions and spiders and other bugs, and fending off attacks from insurgents, who seemed at times determined to use Baylough for target practice.

The first time I saw Baylough, in early July of 2005, I couldn't believe how small it was—basically just a mud hut of a fortress, with guys sleeping eight to a room. We were supposed to be there for approximately one month, but Baylough ended up being home for the remainder of our deployment. I rejoined First Squad at Baylough; the other guys had been there for a few weeks by the time I arrived, so I got the shittiest of the shitty spots in our little room, on an upper plywood bunk in the corner. I didn't care. I was so happy to be back with my boys from First Squad that I would have slept on the floor without complaint.

Berg and another of my buddies, Greg Card, were the first to greet me. We hugged, made a few jokes about the accommodations, and caught up on old news. It's interesting how you become so close to guys when you're in the Army, and how quickly the friendships develop. Before my QRF assignment, I never went more than a day without talking with Berg and Card, and I didn't realize until this moment how much I missed them. Card was twenty-four years old, a comparative adult with grown-up experiences under his belt. While I'd been working at Subway, waiting for something better to come along, Card had been using his considerable mechanical skills doing auto body work. Card was a smart guy, really friendly, but he had a sharp sense of humor and could be a dick if he felt like you were being stupid about something, which happened on a regular basis. When the generator broke down, Card would just walk over, grab a toolbox, and fix it. Me? I'd bang on it with a hammer, maybe give it a kick, and swear at it for a while. That was the extent of my knowledge when it came to repairing just about anything. Card thought that was kind of funny and would take great pleasure in pointing out my complete lack of mechanical aptitude. Card had survival skills. Not in a wilderness sort of way, but in a more practical sense. Because of the experiences he had accumulated before joining the Army, he was in some ways better equipped than most of us to deal with life during deployment. In short, he was a great guy to have around, a good friend and soldier, and a terrific facilitator.

Throughout that first deployment, Card, Berg, and I were pretty much inseparable. I mean, we were all on the same team, we slept in the same room. On patrol or standing guard, we were always within earshot of each other, whispering and telling stories. Unless you've been through something like that, I don't think it's possible to understand the depth and complexity of the bond that is formed.

When I first arrived, though, I had some catching up to do. You see, while I was out with QRF, dealing with a bunch of crazy Afghan police officers, Card and Berg and the rest of First Platoon had been busy in a different sort of way.

It had happened about a week earlier; we'd listened over a shortwave radio as the entire incident unfolded. First Platoon was down nearly a full squad at the time, so there were approximately twenty-five soldiers at Baylough, and one day they found themselves surrounded by insurgents. I don't know exactly what "surrounded" means, and neither did anyone else. They simply reported to battalion headquarters at Lagman that the compound was under heavy fire from close range, all around the perimeter—360 degrees. No one at Baylough asked for help; there was no panic in their voices. They simply wanted to relay the situation. I can still remember the way I felt hearing that exchange, knowing my boys were involved in their first firefight, and I wasn't there with them.

I was worried.

And envious.

At the time, the commander of Battle Company was Captain Michael Kloepper, and I will never forget his words as they crackled through the radio:

"Soldier, you are a United States Army paratrooper. It is in your nature to be outnumbered and surrounded. Now go out there and fucking do something."

All I could think was *Holy shit . . . our guys are in deep trouble, and the captain isn't even worried.* I didn't know whether that was a good thing or a bad thing. Kloepper was an intense and experienced leader. Still, it's easy to talk like that when you're not standing in the shit yourself. The truth is, he didn't know any more about what was happening on the ground than we did. I wondered at the time whether he was being too cavalier or insensitive, but I know now that what he said was exactly the right thing. Everyone in First Platoon had trained for precisely this type of scenario. This is the reason why we do push-ups. This is why they tell us the history of the 173rd—so that we understand the trials and tribulations, and we can expect to face them ourselves. This unit is only great because it's been put in such shady situations that it made itself great. If you are the best unit in the world but you're never tested, then you have no stories. If you are the best unit in the world and you are put to the test every single day, against seemingly overwhelming odds . . . well, that's what makes you great.

"Do something."

Basically, that's code for "Stop being a pussy." And it was all First Platoon needed to hear.

There were two armored Humvees at Baylough. Sergeant Barberet commandeered one of them, with Berg and Card as passengers. The three of them drove the truck outside the walls and began laying waste to everything. The truck took heavy fire, but somehow not one of the men was hit. And after a few minutes of withering fire at close range from the Humvee, and support fire from the rest of the platoon, the enemy began to scatter. First Platoon, in its first live combat encounter, had responded admirably, even heroically. I was proud as hell.

Not surprisingly, when I showed up at Baylough, having experienced nothing more traumatic than a showdown with thirty batshit crazy Afghan cops, the rest of the guys let me know what I had missed.

"Hey, cherry, welcome to the real war!"

They were kidding, of course, and I fully expected and deserved their derision, halfhearted as it was. But there was a whiff of truth to it as well, and I have to admit that it stung a little. I'd been out in the hinterlands for six weeks, and it sucked in every way imaginable. Now I had to listen to my buddies talk trash about how I hadn't earned my place in the unit, since I was still unproven in combat. It sounds silly, I know, but to a professional soldier—and that's what we were, in the purest sense of the term—that stuff really matters; it's important. There is a divide between soldiers who have experienced combat and those who have not, and there is only one way to cross the chasm: You pick up your gun and fire it at the enemy, and he fires right back at you. You can't really call yourself a soldier—not in the 173rd, anyway—unless you've been tested in combat, unless you've been put in harm's way. A soldier wants that experience; he needs it. And once he's survived it, he's a member of a very different fraternity. In a way it's like the simple Afghan philosophy of life, and the pecking order that naturally occurs. If you're older, you must be smarter, simply because you've lived longer. Similarly, if you've been in combat and survived, you must be tougher and braver than someone who hasn't been in combat.

I fell into the lesser category. I hadn't been tested.

———

Movement to contact . . .

That's what we called it. It was a military term for going out on patrol and actively seeking out the enemy, trying to engage the enemy, and generally just acting like prey when you're really a predator. Basically, our job was to leave Baylough and walk through the mountains, or into villages, and try to tempt or otherwise piss off the Taliban to such an extent that they couldn't resist shooting at us. That way, we could shoot back while still adhering to acceptable rules of engagement. It's worth noting that by the time I returned to Afghanistan for my second deployment, things had gotten considerably hotter and more intense, and the rules of engagement were less stringent. By that time, the definition of danger had evolved to the point where common sense was an acceptable battle-field strategy. For example, if you were an Afghan male who was carrying an AK-47, and you were in the vicinity of an active firefight, you were presumed to be an insurgent, and thus a fair target. Whether you had actually discharged the weapon was irrelevant. That's your predicament. Wrong place, wrong time.

For now, though, the handcuffs were on. Our orders were to "return fire," not "initiate fire," and I can honestly say that everyone in Battle Company took those orders quite seriously. We didn't necessarily agree with them or like them, but we did as we were told. The orders were not open to interpretation; they came down from Big Military, and as such were carved in stone.

On the morning of July 10, as we did most mornings, we went out on patrol, with the uncomplicated goal of stirring things up. We walked probably seven or eight kilometers, and while it didn't involve a lot of climbing, it was a fairly hard walk nonetheless. The terrain in Afghanistan is so rocky and uneven that any hike is challenging. It's high desert, very hot (ninety-plus degrees) and dry in the summertime. Every step would displace a pile of rubble and produce a little puff of smoke—like moon dust. Four or five hours into the hike, as we passed through a valley, the afternoon sun was sitting high in the sky, giving us a good bake. We were tired and bored. Ahead, maybe a kilometer or so in the distance, was a little village.

Any village presented the possibility of insurgent activity, and it was always wise to approach a population center from high ground, so as to avoid being an easy target. Yes, it's true that we were in effect deliberately offering ourselves up as targets, but that didn't mean we wanted to get shot; we wanted them to shoot and miss! To reach the village in the safest manner, though, would have meant hiking up one side of the mountain and down the other—a trek that would have added at least four or five more hours to our patrol. We weren't about to do that willingly in the heat of a summer day. As a compromise, we decided to climb halfway up the mountain and approach the village from what appeared to be a relatively safe vantage point.

There were roughly a dozen men in our group. Three of them, from the gun team, hung back with our team leader, who was suffering from dehydration. It seemed a reasonably good plan. They'd watch over us with a 240 Bravo while we walked the last kilometer. The 240 Bravo is a serious weapon that sits on a tripod and basically shoots a rope of bullets at up to nine hundred rounds per minute, allowing the gunner to fan the horizon and basically hit a target at one thousand meters, simply by spraying his ammo.

It was a sound strategy.

Until the shooting began.

They opened up on us from above, two guys with machine guns

maybe three hundred meters away—virtually straight up. At almost the same time, the gun team began taking fire from another position overhead. So, in a matter of seconds, and without warning (there is almost never any warning), everything had turned sideways. The gun team couldn't support us because they were pinned down and involved in their own fight, and we couldn't turn our backs to the fire and support the gun team. Moments earlier, everything had been exactly the way it was supposed to be—tactically flawless. And now? Chaos. Our group effectively had been split in half, greatly reducing the efficiency of either unit, and we were under ambush from a position that could not be attacked; we'd have to climb straight up (not possible) or zigzag up the mountain, taking fire the entire time, and risking exhaustion along the way. Neither option was appealing. So we did what we had to do: We hunkered down and returned fire.

There is no way to predict how anyone will react the first time they encounter a live combat scenario. The toughest badass in the world might cower in fear; and the quietest, scrawniest guy might turn out to be an absolutely ferocious fighter. You just never know. The loss of control that comes with combat, coupled with the natural inclination for self-preservation, can do strange things to a person. When the flight-or-fight response kicks in, well . . . either you flee or you fight.

I was relieved to discover that I was a fighter. I don't mean to toss that out frivolously or boastfully. The same can be said of most everyone in the 173rd, and certainly in Battle Company. But you want to know that you belong, that when the moment of truth comes, you will respond appropriately, nobly. What I discovered, though, is that it's possible to be killed in battle before you even realize the fight has begun.

Despite all my training, what I knew of war had come mostly from the movies. No one had ever shot at me before. Live rounds used in training had always been fired from behind, at a safe distance, under strict protocol. Now, though, the bullets were coming at us. We were the targets, and I was so disoriented at first by the sound of the bullets—a sound I'd never heard before—that I wasn't sure exactly what was happening. I could hear the guns discharging from above us—*pop! pop! pop!*—and it sounded fairly benign; almost fake. If I could liken it to anything, I'd have to say that it reminded me of when we were in early training, getting accustomed to the experience of gunfire, and we'd use something known as a blank firing adaptor to simulate what we would encounter in combat. This reminded me of that experience, and it didn't register immediately as something lethal.

So for a few moments, as the guns popped around us, I just stood there like an idiot, taking it all in.

"Incoming!" someone shouted. "They're shooting! Get the fuck down!"

I did as instructed. Within seconds we are all on the ground, crouching behind whatever meager cover we could find, and returning fire with a vengeance. I'm not sure exactly how long it went on—one of the strangest things about combat is that time becomes distorted, almost to the point of irrelevance. The clock slows down; every movement, every squeeze of the trigger, is illuminated and amplified. A battle that lasted a mere five minutes might seem in retrospect like it went on for hours; conversely, a longer battle might pass in what seems like a heartbeat. Regardless, in this case the shooting ended fairly quickly, with no casualties on our side, and we presumed that we had either killed or chased away the enemy. But we had to be certain, so the next step was to climb the mountainside and inspect the ridge from which the attack had originated. We hoped to find a couple of bodies, maybe some handwritten notes or radios, anything that might prove useful in terms of intelligence. Truthfully, the bodies we neither wanted nor needed. While it wasn't unusual for the Taliban to try to desecrate human remains, we had no interest in such barbarism. If there were bodies up on the ridge, their friends could retrieve them at a later date. We simply wanted information about their mission, if there even was a mission. So we started making our way up the hill, tired nearly to the point of exhaustion.

The entire area seemed secure, all shooting from both positions having stopped. By this time we were almost out of water, and dehydration was a legitimate concern for everyone in the squad. I'd started the day with about a gallon of water in my pack. Now it was gone. So while my load had been lightened by more than eight pounds, I was desperately in need of a refill. Not a good tradeoff. Fortunately, there was a stream further below us, where we could get a drink and replenish. It was always somewhat risky to drink from local water sources, which could be contaminated by everything from human sewage to animal carcasses, but we often did it anyway. In this case, at least, the water would come from a moving stream, which was far preferable to, and safer than, a pond or lake, where stagnancy promoted the likelihood of contamination. The water, though, would be a reward following the inspection of the attack site and a subsequent trek into the village.

We climbed slowly, trying to conserve energy. In theory, a reasonable thing to do. In practice, though, it was hazardous. Training had taught us always to move with a purpose, to never appear weak or complacent. But we were all very tired. In our minds, the battle had ended and the danger had passed. In reality, the battle had barely begun. Approximately halfway up the mountainside, shots rang out from a peak on the opposite side of the range, maybe eight hundred meters away. There were many more bullets this time. It appeared that they had established at least half a dozen positions, and the shots were coming much closer.

As the bullets strafed the ground, the realization set in: We had been set up. Beautifully, too. They had baited us perfectly with the first ambush, drawing us in, compelling us to return fire, and making us think we had emerged victorious, when in fact that first encounter had been nothing more than a tease. And now we were halfway up the mountainside, out in the open, exhausted, taking even heavier fire from a far more dangerous vantage point. They had the higher ground, and they were looking right at us.

"*Fuckers!*"

It was Sergeant Barberet. Like a firecracker, he just went off. Turned around 180 degrees and began sprinting back down the mountain. We'd been zigzagging upward because it was too steep to climb straight up, but on the descent Barberet showed no regard for caution or danger. As one of the SAW gunners, my job was to return fire as quickly as possible, so that the rest of the squad could move. And that's what I did. Our other SAW gunner, Kyle Harden, did the same. The two of us got down, nearly prone, and began firing our weapons at the opposite ridge, spraying the top, in the general vicinity of their muzzle flashes, with as many rounds as possible in an attempt to force the enemy to keep their heads down, and open a safe path for the five remaining members of our squad, with Barberet leading the charge.

Before we could move, though, I heard a thump, and then a whistling sound. Again, it wasn't anything I'd heard before. I looked up and saw something coming at us, weaving and whirring, displacing air all around it. A rocket-propelled grenade (RPG), I thought. But it was bigger, slower, almost like a huge, black baseball (we later found out it was an eighty-millimeter round shot from a recoil-less rifle). Bad news, whatever it was.

"Incoming!"

I remember getting down, lowering my head, and waiting for the explosion, hoping it wouldn't be close. Waiting, waiting, waiting. Finally, I looked.

Holy shit! It's still coming!

And so it was. Corkscrewing like a paper airplane, dipping and diving as it flew lazily over the valley. I lowered my head again as it flew off into the distance and crashed harmlessly into the hillside, half a mile away.

Closest to me at the time was our radio operator, Christopher "Toph" Miller. We didn't always have a radio man with us when we went out on patrol, but Toph joined the squad for this operation because we planned to be out for a while, maybe push further than usual into the backcountry, and didn't want to be too isolated from command back at Baylough and Lagman. Toph was a good guy, knew his shit, and since he'd been at Baylough one week earlier, when the base came under fire, he had more combat experience than I had. But he was still a relative newcomer to this combat business, and as a radio operator his primary function was to simply stay alive and be prepared to call for help.

"Dude!" I shouted. "Just run—I've got you covered."

The only creatures capable of sprinting down an incline of this sort are mountain goats and Sergeant Barberet; no one else would willingly do it. But there was no choice now, so there was Toph, careening madly down the mountainside, each step kicking up a spray of rubble, bullets giving chase, bouncing in the dirt all around him. Again, it seemed almost fake, like it wasn't really happening. But I just kept shooting and screaming, urging Miller to run, which he did, faster than I thought possible. Somehow he stayed on his feet.

Then it was Kyle's turn. The plan—well, it was more of a reaction, informed by months of training, than it was a plan—was for him to pick up his SAW and begin running down the mountain as well, trailing the others. I'd cover him with gunfire until he found a safe place to lie low and begin returning fire. Once he was set and I could hear his gun, I'd start running. And so on, until we all reached the bottom and then began ascending the other ridge: We'd find the assholes who were shooting at us and we'd extinguish them. It was as simple as that.

Only it wasn't simple at all, not when they had the higher ground, an advantageous position from which to fire, and we had only automatic weapons (since our gun team was still pinned down further back). We also had no idea how many insurgents were out there, but judging by the amount of firepower they exhibited, it wasn't a small group. We were better soldiers—better trained and better equipped—but this was unquestionably a dangerous situation, which is why we repeatedly called for air support. But none was forthcoming. I don't even know what happened—whether there was no one on the station or no helicopters in the vicinity—but we were on our own. Air support would have helped a great deal in this case, since there was room to use it safely and effectively. In some cases—when the enemy is within a distance of roughly one hundred meters—air support is ineffective or so potentially hazardous for all combatants that the risks outweigh the benefits. That wasn't the case on this day. An Apache or two would have helped. Mortars would have helped; artillery would have helped.

There was nothing.

It was combat, and as I was quickly discovering, shit happens. Crazy, inexplicable, unpredictable shit. You do the best you can.

I ran—wildly and with no regard for consequence, stopping only when I saw Miller, crouched behind a rock, bullets ricocheting all around. The two of us were pressed together, trying to shield ourselves from the onslaught. The rock wasn't really big enough to protect two grown men, but it was preferable to having one person behind the rock and the other standing out there alone in a hailstorm of bullets. Toph was the first to reach the bottom. Despite our cover, he had to dodge a spray of gunfire all the way down, and there were several times when I was sure he'd been hit. Then it was my turn to move out from behind the rock. With bullets bouncing everywhere, I took off, sprinting as fast as I could; apparently it wasn't fast enough. Within the first half dozen strides I felt something hit me in the calf. My legs became entangled and I fell to the ground. It was a stinging pain, sharp and precise, but not incapacitating. Of greater concern than whatever it was that had caused the pain was the fact that I was now tumbling head over heels down the side of the mountain. In full pack, with a loose rifle, I was basically a rolling bomb. I'd get up, try to regain my balance for a step or two, and then stumble and roll again. Somehow I didn't crack my head open or shoot myself along the way, and eventually I reached the bottom.

Moments later Kyle arrived. We were at the rear, the last to get down, and as I was on the ground, I reached around to my calf, which was still throbbing, and said, "Dude, I think I just got shot."

Now, Kyle is a white guy, but like a lot of Caucasians in the Army he had a little gangster to him, talked like a rapper, liked to give shit.

"No way, bro! Where?"

I fumbled around with my pants leg, which was tucked tightly into my boot, and tried to squeeze my calf through the fabric. It hurt, but there was no blood, no obvious sign of trauma.

"Never mind, man. I just tripped."

Kyle gave me a funny look. I started to think of the ramifications.

Ah, crap. He heard me say I got shot when all I did was fall down. I'm never going to hear the end of this.

"No worries, dude," Kyle said with a shrug. "Let's keep going."

By now all firing had ceased and a B-2 bomber had arrived on the scene. The B-2 is a huge beast of a bird, but since we were in pursuit, we'd closed the gap to such an extent that now we were too close for the B-2 to safely drop anything on the ridge.

We climbed again, ultimately reaching the ridge and finding it vacated. And there the mission became even more complicated thanks to the sudden resignation of our interpreter, a young Afghan named Star. We got to the top and the guy just quit on the spot. I guess he'd had enough for one day, which took us all by surprise. The interpreter had worked for another unit previously; he supposedly had loved the job and they were satisfied with his work. He could speak English fluently, which was essential, of course, but apparently he'd never been tested in a combat situation. Understandably, he didn't much like it.

Sergeant Barberet was pissed, of course. The two of them stood on the ridge, arguing for several minutes, until Barberet just threw up his hands.

"Star, give me your fucking gun!" he yelled.

Star backed away and shook his head.

"No, no, no. This is my gun."

"The fuck it is," Barberet shouted. "That's an American gun. And if you're no longer with the Americans, you are not entitled to it. Now hand it over."

There was a look of utter horror on Star's face. An unarmed Afghan who was known to be supportive of the American military effort, left alone in the countryside, in a region literally crawling with Taliban, would be in very deep shit indeed.

"You can't just leave me here," Star said.

"The hell we can't," Barberet said. "It's your choice. You want to keep the gun, stay with us."

He paused, gave the interpreter a hard look.

"You can quit when we get back."

Star shook his head and muttered something under his breath. But he had the good sense not to walk away.

——

By the time we began descending the mountain, we'd been out on patrol for nearly fifteen hours. We were completely exhausted and dehydrated. We'd been shot at and we'd returned fire, but without any noticeable sign of victory. We were hungry, pissed, eager to simply stop walking and rest. Under such conditions, in the dark, it's easy to become separated, which is precisely what happened. When I reached the bottom, I couldn't see anyone. I realized I was completely alone, in a valley, in Afghanistan, which was not a good thing for an American soldier.

In reality, the rest of my squad was no more than fifty meters away, right around a little bend, but I didn't know it at the time. I was disoriented, perplexed. Finally Toph caught up with me and we gave each other a big hug, drank from a stream, and continued, eventually rendezvousing with Barberet, Card and Berg, and the rest of the squad.

Together we hiked another three kilometers, but we were toast; we had nothing left, none of us. Fortunately, a small contingency force from Baylough had been sent out when they heard about our encounter with the enemy, and we ran into them about halfway back and camped for the night. They brought us food and water, and pulled security while we slept for a few hours; the next morning we all walked back to Baylough together.

Interesting thing: When you return from a firefight, you'll see guys stripping off clothes, checking their bodies, making sure everything is in place. The adrenaline that feeds you during a battle can serve as an anes-thetic, temporarily masking the pain that comes with getting wounded. So I reached down and gave my calf a good rub, noticed it was still sore and somewhat sticky.

Huh . . . that's weird.

I rolled up my pants. There, about halfway up my calf, was a small hole with blood encrusted around the edges. I touched the hole. Some-thing hard was just beneath the surface of the skin, but too deeply embedded for me to easily pluck it out. While it was kind of gross, the wound didn't seem serious and I was reluctant to even consult the medic about it. I already felt like a pussy for having cried out "I got shot!" in front of Harden. The last thing I wanted to do was make a big deal out of something that seemed so minor. I figured I'd probably just been poked by a branch or sharp rock while running. But it's always better to be safe than sorry, and we'd been told often enough to beware of seem-ingly minor wounds. Any time the skin is broken, infection is possible. No sense in taking a chance.

Our medic at the time was big guy named Doc Lemon, probably six-foot-four, about 250 pounds of pure muscle. Most of the guys in our platoon were small and lean—hard to be anything else when you're out hiking all day in the mountains. Doc Lemon spent more of his time at Lagman, where they had better food and a well-stocked gym, so he was always working out. We all loved Lemon, but the very fact of his size made you hesitate to show any pain or discomfort in his presence. You just didn't want him thinking you were weak.

"Feel that?" Lemon said, pinching the wound between two fingers.

"Uhhh . . . yeah," I said, trying not to wince.

"You've got something in there."

"What do we do?"

Lemon laughed. "Take it out."

And so he did, using only his fingers. Doc rooted around for a minute or so, squeezing and manipulating, like he was trying to pop a pimple, until finally a small, bloody piece of metal emerged from the wound.

Doc smiled and held it up for me to see.

"You know what that is?" he said.

"Shrapnel?"

He shook his head. "Nope. That's a Purple Heart."

I laughed incredulously.

"You're telling me I'm going to get a Purple Heart? For that?"

It didn't seem possible. I mean, it was sore. But Purple Hearts, in my mind, were reserved for soldiers who had been seriously wounded in battle. Turns out that is not the case. The Purple Heart is presented to any soldier who is wounded in combat; the severity of the wound is not much of a factor. I had indeed been shot. That sting I felt while running down the mountain had been a bullet fragment ripping into my calf—in all likelihood the bullet had been shattered while hitting the ground and a piece of it had hit me on the rebound. Whether I wanted it or not, I qualified for a Purple Heart. In fact, I was the first person (though not the last) in the platoon to receive one.

"Come over here!" Doc Lemon yelled to anyone within earshot. "Look what Giunta brought back."

They sent me to Lagman for five or six days, so that I could recover and just sort of chill out. That was fine with me. The food was better and I was tired as hell. Then they sent me back to Baylough with a pat on the back and a slip of paper commemorating the award. A couple of weeks later, though, a strange thing happened. I noticed a boil festering on my hip, approximately at the spot where the waistband of my pants met my skin. While in the privacy of the latrine one morning, I gave it a squeeze, which hurt like hell, and out popped a tiny piece of metal about the size and shape of a snowflake.

Well, I'll be damned.

I squeezed again. More metal. And again. More . . .

After five or ten minutes I had a little pile of shrapnel in my palm. Apparently I'd been hit more than once that day on the mountainside and didn't even know it. I looked at the shrapnel for a moment, then dumped it into the latrine. No need for anyone else to know.

CHAPTER 7

August 21, 2005

Baylough was a pedestrian operation.

By that I mean we walked everywhere. Even though the base was equipped with a pair of Humvees, protocol dictated that they be left idle the vast majority of the time. The terrain was so rigorous that patrolling by foot was the only sensible option. Roads were few and far between, and even those available typically were nothing more than dried creek beds or stone paths. Traversing in this manner was both laborious and dangerous, and not merely because you might lose control of the truck and fall off a cliff. Since there were only two possible roadways approaching Baylough, the likelihood of encountering an improvised explosive device was significant.

While it's true that IEDs at that time were far more common in Iraq than in Afghanistan, it's also true that there were many more travel options available to the military in Iraq; if one road was known to be hot with insurgent activity, you could find another route; at the very least, since many of the roads were modern enough to have been designed with high-speed traffic in mind, you could buzz right along in an attempt to minimize the effect of any potential blast. Afghanistan was different. Even in metropolitan areas it was a country with a distinctly ancient feel. In the remote provinces, where most of the fighting took place, it seemed sometimes as though we had been transported back to the fourteenth century. Trucks traveling around Baylough could barely muster a speed of twenty-five miles per hour; anything more than that was prohibitively dangerous. And a vehicle traveling at such a slow pace, along a rutty dirt highway, was an easy target.

Frankly, we didn't like the odds.

So we generally used the Humvees only on rare occasions. For example, when helicopters from Lagman or Kandahar delivered supplies, a few of us would jump in one of the Humvees (at least one gunner always made the trip), drive up a hill to the Helicopter Landing Zone (HLZ), then load everything into the truck and get back to Baylough as quickly as possible.

The only time I can recall anyone at Baylough using the trucks for any other purpose was the incident that had occurred the week before my arrival, when the compound was surrounded and Berg and Card used it to defend themselves against the enemy. But that was a desperate situation that called for desperate measures. Practically speaking, our trucks never went outside the wire.

Just about everyone who fought in Afghanistan understood the danger and impracticality of vehicular travel, but sometimes there was no other option. In late summer Third Platoon was assigned the task of making a significant delivery to Baylough. They would come out in a convoy of trucks carrying HESCOs and other gear. HESCO is actually the name of a company that manufactures a product that was indispensible in Afghanistan: collapsible wire mesh containers, lined with heavy duty fabric, that could be used as a barrier against enemy fire or explosive devices. Each container was approximately eight feet long, eight feet wide, and eight feet high. We'd set them up around the base and then begin digging. The dirt and rubble unearthed would be deposited into the HESCO, ultimately producing a sturdy fortification. Even when empty these bad boys were heavy; filled with dirt, they were immovable. You'd look at a HESCO and wonder whether it could get the job done—until you saw it basically smother an incoming RPG. These things were impressively designed and constructed, and we depended on them in a big way.

In the first couple of months at Baylough we were largely unprotected. All we had, really, was a small house surrounded by concertina wire adorned with whatever type of little jingly noisemakers we could find. Sounds simplistic, I know, but that's what we did. That way, if the Taliban attacked during the night and tried to breach the perimeter, we'd hear them coming. The concertina wire, we hoped, would slow them down enough for us to get into position and return fire, but it offered no legitimate defense or protection. To a great extent, we were naked out there. Since the fight was evolving on an almost daily basis, and our needs evolving along with it, we had to adapt on the fly.

Sometimes it was frustrating, but I came to accept the fact that the military is an extraordinarily vast and chaotic organization. That it works as well as it does is remarkable, a testament primarily to the men and women who serve, at all levels. It took time for me to realize that the chaos was controlled. From day one, in basic training, when they threw all our bags into a pile and gave us five seconds to retrieve the right one, the military tried to instill a sense of grace under pressure. Obviously there's no way fifty soldiers are going to find the rights bags in a matter of seconds, but they expect you to try, and to grow accustomed to such tests, and to be desensitized to the screaming and other outside interference you experience in the process. You fail, you get down and do push-ups, then you try again. The point is this: You're never going to get it exactly right; things will never be easy and smooth and predictable, so you might as well get used to it. Learn to deal with the madness. Find a way to achieve some peace amid the chaos, and then move on, because the next thing is going to be just as chaotic. Life in the Army is chaotic.

And war is almost incomprehensibly chaotic.

If you're okay with that notion, you have a much better chance of surviving, of doing your job well. When we got to Baylough and discovered that it was a more dangerous place than we'd first anticipated, and that concertina wire was insufficient, we didn't panic or freak out. We adapted. The HESCOs were part of that adaptation.

Third Platoon left in the morning in a convoy of heavily armed Humvees. They traveled all day, hauling a boxcar filled with HESCOs, generators, cleaning supplies, and other stuff we needed. It was a tremendously helpful delivery on their part, and we appreciated it enormously. By the time Third Platoon arrived, the sun had set. These guys were tired and naturally didn't want to make the return trip in the dark, so they decided to spend the night with us. Well, not really the whole night—their plan was to get up well before the break of dawn and be nearly home before the sweltering midday heat set in.

By two o'clock in the morning they had packed and departed. A couple of hours later, around four o'clock, we heard an explosion far off in the distance. It woke everyone on the base. At first we didn't know what to think of it. Sure, it was strange, especially at that hour of the morning, but it was so far away that we weren't terribly concerned—until a call came in from Third Platoon, informing us that they had been the target of the explosion. The lead truck in their convoy had been hit by an IED.

Sergeant Barberet quickly gathered everyone together and assigned several of us to drive out to the site of the attack and offer help. I jumped on one truck, along with Barberet, Berg, Card, and Harden. A second truck, filled with guys from Second Squad, was right behind us. There was very little conversation on the way. We had two Humvees and roughly a dozen soldiers prepared to do heavy battle. We had no idea yet what sort of casualties, if any, Third Platoon had suffered, but we expected the worst.

The attack had occurred maybe five kilometers from Baylough, but it took us more than an hour to get there, driving slowly, in the dark, on narrow dirt trails. By the time we arrived on the scene, all of Third Platoon was there, the remainder of their unit having come to help as soon as they found out about the explosion. There was no fight; this had been a simple and brutally effective IED attack, and no insurgents remained in the area. All that was left was the cleanup.

That, of course, was the worst part of the job. I'd seen dead bodies before, but I'd not encountered any American bodies. We all felt over-whelming grief and anger, but we couldn't show it. Not then, not under those circumstances. Third Platoon had already done a commendable job of securing the area and cleaning up much of the debris. The attack had been devastating. The lead Humvee had been carrying some sig-nificant firepower, including a pile of forty-millimeter grenades, so there wasn't just one explosion; there were multiple explosions, the net effect being that a truck had been ripped apart, and then melted into a heap of unrecognizable metal.

There's no way to prepare for something like that—no way to adequately explain the horror of seeing five people dismembered and disfigured, some burned beyond recognition. Especially when you know them personally. And we did—every one of them. If I wasn't as close to these men as I was to Berg and Card, to Chioke and Harden, I neverthe-less felt a kinship with each of them. It was my friend Michael Mason's platoon. We were all members of the 173rd, and we were all in Battle Company. We were on the front line of this strange and moving target that we called the war on terrorism.

We were brothers.

So how do you put into words the feeling of walking around a scene like that, picking up pieces of American soldiers, people you have known by name? Men with wives and girlfriends; sons and daughters; mothers and fathers; people who care about them and love them, and now will never see them again.

We did the job silently, stoically, swallowing back the revulsion and anger and nausea. This part of the job was ours, and it required quiet dignity and professionalism. It's common practice in combat for mem-bers of one platoon to help another with cleanup following an attack. Better for all concerned if the people closest to the deceased are not asked to deal with the remains. You shouldn't have to pick up the pieces of your buddies.

Five soldiers were riding in that Humvee; four were killed instantly. A fifth, the vehicle's gunner, somehow managed to survive, despite getting both his legs blown off and absorbing so much shrapnel that it looked as though he'd faced a firing squad. That's one of the things people may not realize about the conflicts in Iraq and Afghanistan: tens of thousands of American lives have been affected. It isn't just the men who have served and died in combat, and the families they've left behind; it's the men who have served every bit as honorably, and who suffered catastrophic injuries in the process.

I can't begin to imagine how many of the soldiers wounded in Iraq and Afghanistan would have died if not for advances in modern medicine. So many of these injuries—traumatic amputations and the like—resulted in fatalities when suffered in previous wars. If you stepped on a landmine in Vietnam and ruptured your femoral artery, the likelihood was great that you'd bleed out right there on the jungle floor. Our ability to cope with the most devastating injuries has improved dramatically. Soldiers are treated expertly on the battlefield and removed by Medevac so quickly that they have a chance to return home and get on with their lives. But those lives are not what they might have been. These men and women are survivors of something known as "technical dismounted complex blast injury"—a fancy way of saying they have been blown to bits but somehow continue to draw breath. They have lost arms and legs. Some have lost their genitals and sections of their digestive tracts. They are living with unspeakable pain and hardship.

But they are living. And so are the people who love and care for them. By the spring of 2012, the war in Afghanistan was producing an average of twenty amputees a month among American servicemen, and they deserve to be remembered and honored every bit as much as the men who gave their lives.

I couldn't think about any of that, obviously, while I was cleaning up the bomb site. I'd heard about IEDs and other weapons that produce mass casualties, but I had no firsthand experience with any of it. I'd been in combat; I'd fired my gun, and I'd been shot at. This was different. This was truly horrifying. I think we all recognized the possibility that we could be killed in combat. But this wasn't just being killed; this was desecration. If I was going to lose my life in combat, I wanted to lose it while looking at my enemy. I'd rather be shot in the head, point-blank, than get blown up by a roadside IED. It just seemed wrong. It seemed unfair. As I walked around the site, grimly completing the job of cleanup, a part of me couldn't help but think that these men had been denied the most fundamental part of a soldier's experience: the chance to fight back.

They'd been cheated.

It didn't make their deaths any less honorable or important. It just made them seem less . . . sensible.

There was very little discussion as night gave way to morning. We took turns pulling security, maintaining an air of professionalism and respect, in spite of the anger that simmered inside us. We surrounded the site and scanned the perimeter, looking constantly for any sign of movement in the hills. As much as we might have wanted to grieve or talk about what had happened, we couldn't. There was no guarantee that the fight was over, no way of being certain that only one IED had been placed in the vicinity. There aren't any rules governing guerilla warfare, no terrorist handbook to consult (not that I know of, anyway). So we sat there, silently stewing in rage.

A couple of days passed before we said much of anything about the entire incident, and by that time Third Platoon had left. Months would pass before we'd see any of those guys again, despite the fact that we were separated by a distance of only a few miles; that was life in the sand. Even when the subject was finally broached, it was done without emotion or reflection, but with pragmatism: *That's why we don't fuckin' drive out here.*

It wasn't that we didn't care, of course; we cared deeply. But there was nothing to be gained by reminiscing about the men we'd lost, or by complaining about what had happened and the generally fucked-up nature of this entire conflict. We had a job to do, and as long as we were out there, the job required our total concentration and commitment. If nothing else, the IED attack had confirmed what we knew in our hearts, but sometimes overlooked during the long stretches of boredom and inactivity: Any one of us could be killed at any given moment.

But there was something else, something we didn't want to address or admit, and that was the responsibility we felt for what had happened. The guilt. It wasn't our fault that the Taliban had planted a roadside IED; nor was it our fault that a vehicle from Third Platoon had been hit by the bomb. Those were the risks inherent in war. We had all signed up for this willingly. No one twisted our arms.

And yet . . .

There was no escaping the fact that these four men had been killed while completing an assignment that brought them to Baylough. They'd come out to deliver supplies and defense matériel for us. So while we weren't there when the attack occurred—while there was nothing we could have done to prevent it—we knew the chain of events that precipitated the attack:

1. If First Platoon hadn't been at Baylough, we wouldn't have needed HESCOs.
2. If we hadn't needed HESCOs, Third Platoon would not have been asked to drive out to Baylough.
3. If Third Platoon hadn't come to Baylough, no one would have been killed.

This is the way life works. It's easy to pick things apart and to find an apparent cause for every effect. You can drive yourself nuts tracing things backward, looking for the proverbial butterfly flapping its wings in the Amazon and causing thunderstorms a world away. But in war, it's actually pretty easy to connect the dots, because you can always recount a person's position and the circumstances that led to his being in that position.

A leads to B, B leads to C . . . and C leads to a soldier getting killed.

———

Not more than a few days later we were running around Baylough, preparing for an assault on a High Value Target (HVT). This wasn't merely a colloquial term. An HVT was a person or resource designated by military brass—sometimes as high as the upper levels of the Department of Defense—as being of extraordinary importance. The pursuit of HVTs often involved troops from Special Forces. Sometimes the objective was to capture the target so that he could be interrogated and valuable information might be extracted. If capture was not possible, though, it was acceptable to simply eliminate the target by any means necessary. This practice had been widely implemented during the Iraq War, with the Department of Defense actually not only authorizing HVTs, but rating them on the basis of importance, and assigning playing cards to depict that pecking order. Saddam Hussein, rather infamously, was the Ace of Spades.

The practice continued in Afghanistan, though we never found ourselves in pursuit of High Value Targets that rose to such an important level. There were no Kings or Aces in our region, just a bunch of really bad actors creating havoc, promoting terrorism, and killing American soldiers. On this occasion, though, we had been informed that particularly valuable HVTs had been traced to our sector; they were important enough, and familiar enough, that we actually knew them by name. Did we know exactly why they were considered High Value Targets? No. And frankly we didn't care. That wasn't our concern. Just as it wasn't our job to weigh the political ramifications of U.S. involvement in Afghanistan, neither was it our job to seek information about the guilt or innocence of HVTs. If the military wanted them captured or killed, then we would capture them or kill them. Simple as that.

Well, it wasn't really simple at all. A rather intense briefing preceded each one of the missions—and there were several during my two deployments—during which photographs of the targets were distributed and the assignment was laid out in great detail, using whatever materials were available. Typically, since we were in Afghanistan, this involved the construction of a fairly large and detailed sand table. Exactly as it sounds, the sand table is a depiction of the battle plan using sand and rocks. We'd set it up right on the floor—mounds of sand serving as houses, barns, fortifications, and so on. The effort that went into these sand tables was enormous, the detail impressive. Then we'd stand over the table and literally walk through the mission:

"Okay, here's house number one. That's yours. Over here is house number two. That's yours. There's a little hut over here, a barn or something. I need you two to take care of the barn."

And so on . . .

This particular mission was assigned to Second Squad, simply because we did everything on the basis of rotation, and First Squad had already been out on a long and difficult patrol the previous day. Generally speaking, we patrolled every day, but we tried to alternate hard and easy days—"easy" being a highly relative term, of course—and it was Second Squad's turn to take a hard one. And this assignment, as it turned out, was particularly hard.

The importance of the mission could be measured by the presence of several higher-ranking officers from Battle Company, including Captain Kloepper, the company commander, and Lieutenant Derek Hines, the fire support officer (FSO), and an additional medic. The fire support officer's job is to oversee the medics and the forward observer (who is responsible for calling in support from artillery in the event that things really heat up). The FSO typically sticks close to the company commander, who ultimately makes the decisions on when and where to strike.

I don't know exactly what went down that day, but there was significant resistance when Second Squad reached the target, and in the firefight that ensued, Lieutenant Hines was shot and killed. The HVTs were eliminated, so I guess you could call the mission a success, but it came with a steep price, and that weighed heavily on all of us. After not experiencing a single casualty during the first four months of our deployment, Battle Company had now lost five men in a span of roughly one

Family photo, 1993.

Fishing on the Iowa River, 1996.

Hanging out with my cousin
Will in Clinton, Iowa, 1999.

Berg, Chioke, and I as new privates, spring of 2004.

As M249 SAW gunner, Afghanistan deployment, fall of 2005.

Getting promoted to specialist, the hard way. FOB Baylough, Afghanistan, August 2005.

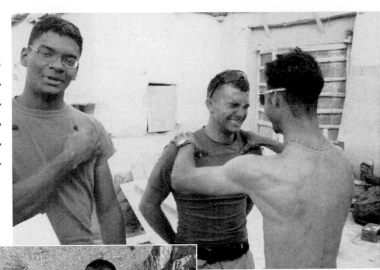

An interpreter and I humping up to an observation post in the Saygez Valley, 2005.

My wife, Jen, and I enjoying a weekend in Rome, summer of 2004. I was nineteen years old. Man, I love Europe's drinking laws.

Saygez Valley, Afghanistan, summer of 2005.

Korengal Valley at OP Rock, winter of 2007.

Battle Company, First Platoon, in Italy, winter of 2004.

Firebase Vegas, summer of 2008. *Left to right*: Me, Hunter, and Gallardo.

Mason and I celebrating after a month-long training exercise in Germany.

800 feet AGL in Aviano, Italy, taking a picture to show my folks what being Airborne really means.

Battle Company, First Platoon, First Squad, Alpha team, at Firebase Vegas. *Left to right*: Casey, Clary, Griego, and me.

Jen and I after our first Century Ride (100 miles) during RAGBRAI 2010.

Mendoza, Brennan, and I waiting to go on patrol in front of Firebase Vegas, July 2007.

Walking with President Barack Obama and First Lady Michelle Obama into the
East Room of the White House for the Medal of Honor ceremony.

Walking out of the East Room at the White House after the Medal of Honor ceremony.

Picture of some of the folks at the Pentagon after the Hall of Heroes ceremony. *Left to right*: Casey, Gallardo, Griego, Clary, Gangwer, me, Jen, Izzell, Eckrode, Velez, Perry, and Zaski.

week. And they all had died essentially at our doorstep—within five kilometers of Baylough.

I began looking at the war differently after that, began seeing it not as an adventure or a game, or even a job with clear and attainable goals, but rather as a complex and extraordinarily dangerous situation, one in which my skill and training might ultimately prove insufficient. When that sort of shit starts creeping into a soldier's head it can really have a negative effect on his performance, and on morale as well. It wasn't like I wanted to quit or anything like that. It wasn't like I started to question our mission or our purpose. I just starting thinking a bit more philosophically about the whole matter, and that led to a much more realistic, even fatalistic outlook.

Wow . . . things are going downhill fast. I may spend my last days on earth right here, in this compound.

For a twenty-year-old kid, that was a pretty heavy dose of reality, and I'll admit now that I had some difficulty coping with it. I was fortunate, though, to have a terrific and supportive new team leader in Sergeant Nicholas Post. Nick was six years older than me, a veteran of both Afghanistan and Iraq. One day, not long after Lieutenant Hines was killed, Sergeant Post and I sat down together and began talking. I don't know exactly why or how the conversation began. Maybe he passed by and saw me sitting there, moping a bit, and felt like I needed to get something out of my system. Whatever the reason, he reached out to me.

"You all right?" he asked.

I shrugged. "Not sure, Sergeant."

There were countless opportunities for intimate conversation on deployment. I mean, what else did we have to occupy our time? It wasn't like we had cable television or video games. Basically, when you weren't out on patrol or in a fight, you'd pass the time by playing cards or writing letters or bullshitting with your buddies. Much of the time these conversations were limited to brutal and vulgar ball-busting, but sometimes you'd let your guard down and actually talk about the things that mattered: wives and girlfriends, family, children, life back home. And as time went on, the war itself became fodder for debate and discussion. "What are you thinking?" Sergeant Post asked.

"I guess I thought it would be different. The war, I mean."

Post nodded, smiled.

"Yeah, well, don't feel bad. Everyone is like that at first. But this is exactly what it is. You're going to win some days and you're going to lose some days, and no matter what you think you did, chances are they're going to take more from you than you feel like you owed them."

That was it, wasn't it? That was it in a nutshell. There was no winning and losing. There was just a job to do, day after day after day. We were soldiers, and it wasn't our role to question the validity of the war, or a particular mission, or the way a particular scenario played out. Our job was to go out there and do what we were told to do; what very few people were willing or able to do. It didn't matter whether people back home knew or cared about how difficult and deadly the job was; it didn't matter whether the objective often seemed too nebulous and ill-defined.

"Just do your job to the best of your ability," he said. "Whatever happens . . . happens. You can't control it."

If I want to be completely honest with myself, I have to acknowledge a bit of arrogance in the beginning. I'd come to Afghanistan thinking, *I'm a rock star; a member of the 173rd. I'll be fine.* Now, though, doubt had seeped in. While I still had faith in my training and in my fellow soldiers, and in my own ability, I wondered whether any of that mattered. What Sergeant Post seemed to be saying was "It might not be enough. And you just have accept that."

He was right. There was no point in dwelling on the obvious. Fixating on the fact that some of our buddies had been killed, and more would likely be killed in the future, wasn't going to change a damn thing.

What made this conversation so memorable to me was not just the simple wisdom of Sergeant Post's message, but the fact that he had breached conventional military protocol to share it. See, in the Army it's understood that you remain in your peer group. A senior will talk to a subordinate, but not in a buddy-buddy sort of way. That would be considered fraternization, and it's generally frowned upon. On deployment, though, the rules are different. We lived in such close quarters at Baylough, spent so much time together, and under such difficult circumstances, that by the time we left the country, virtually all lines had been crossed. Not blatantly, not openly, but they had been crossed nonetheless.

"Call me Nick," Sergeant Post had said when we started talking. And I did, from that point forward—as long as there were only two of us in the room. I never referred to him as "Nick" in front of the other guys, but when we were alone, just shooting the breeze? Yeah, all the time. And he called me Sal. It was a way of acknowledging that while he was higher in rank, and we were thus unequal in the eyes of the Army, we were brothers nonetheless, and we were equals out here in the mountains of Afghanistan; we were both human beings, dependent on each other, protective of each other.

Nick and I developed a close friendship that transcended our combat experience and endures today, well beyond the conclusion of our military careers. We live only about forty-five minutes away from each other in Colorado, and we hang out together all the time. He's an amazing dude, served his country in exemplary and courageous fashion for almost a decade before getting out. And he carries the scars of his service, though you'd never know it by looking at him. Nick developed some sort of weird immune system problem while he was in Afghanistan. The way he explained it to me, his body became allergic to itself. If he breaks out in a sweat, his immune system goes into hyperdrive, which can cause all sorts of complications. But Nick is not one to complain. He carries an EpiPen with him at all times, in the event that he suffers anaphylaxis. And he goes on with the business of life.

And what a life! Because of his disability, Nick qualified for the Army's vocational rehab program, which pays 100 percent of your education, with no stipulation on when the education must be completed. As long as you are working toward a degree that will help you qualify for a specific job, the Army picks up the tab. Nick earned that benefit, and he's made the most of it. He's been going to school for five years now, studying vinology and other aspects of wine culture and history. I don't know shit about wine, but I know that Nick is considered something of an expert in that world. He's not just a sommelier—he's one of the guys who teaches sommeliers. He writes books about wine; he consults for restaurants and hotels. He also works for a wine institute.

I have to admit, it's strange to see Nick in a suit and tie, and hear him talk about such sophisticated stuff, but I'm stoked for him. As he likes to say, "Inside, Sal . . . I'm still the same guy."

I remember the day he left Afghanistan, when it had become apparent that his condition would no longer permit service in a combat setting. He gave me a big hug, jumped on a bird, and waved from the open doorway.

"See you on the other side!" he yelled.

I could only hope he was right. But there was no point in dwelling on it, in obsessing over things that could not be controlled. The best soldiers—and there were many good ones in the 173rd—were those who did not obsess about the big picture, things like the philosophical merit of the war, or even a particular mission, but rather lived each day while looking through a rather narrow prism. They fought to the best of their ability. They didn't fight for God or country, although maybe those things provided some inspiration, but they fought for the men with whom they patrolled each day. They fought for their buddies. That simple yet profound motivation could keep you alive, for the success or failure of an operation depended on nothing so much as the ability of each man to perform in the manner that was most likely to produce a positive outcome for the entire unit.

There is a tendency to think that combat is nothing more than madness. To a degree, that's true. But the infantryman is trained to handle the madness, to not panic even though his life is at risk and all around him is violence and chaos. But even in the craziest of scenarios, there is a protocol for the optimal response. You return fire in an ambush; you cover each other. You respond as a team, not as a collection of individual targets; not as rogue warriors. Part of this (maybe much of it) is accomplished through endless hours of drilling and training, and then of course through actual combat experience.

But part of it is simply innate. I truly believe that some people are just made for combat. It's who they are, and they are drawn to the infantry, and to units like the 173rd. One guy like that was a Southern Californian named Peter Roberts. The first time I met him was in Italy, shortly after we arrived at Caserma Ederle. Pete was a soft-spoken guy, about six feet tall, lean and wiry. He kept to himself a lot in those early days, preferring to hang out in his room at night, while the rest of us would get together and knock back a few beers. One night we were trying to get a party going in the barracks, and Pete was nowhere to be found. Well, his room was next door to mine, so I decided to stop by and see if he wanted to join us. This was around nine o'clock at night, pretty early even by Army standards, and really early by the standards of most twenty-year-old guys.

I knocked at the door and waited for several minutes for Roberts to answer. I was about to walk away when the door finally opened. And there stood Pete Roberts, a massive set of earmuffs on his head and a neck gaiter pulled up over the lower half of his face. He looked like a POW.

"Uh . . . dude," I stammered. "What the fuck are you doing?"

Pete shrugged. "Trying to get some sleep."

"Okay, well, we're having some beers if you want to join us."

He didn't. Pete rarely joined us, in fact, and when he did, he usually just kind of sat there alone, quietly holding up a chair in the corner of the room. He was one of the most laid-back guys I have ever known. But Pete had trouble sleeping sometimes, so he would wear the big sound-dampening headsets used in artillery training when he went to bed at night. The gaiter would be pulled up over his eyes.

Here's the ironic thing: Roberts was an absolute gun nut, which is why he quickly received the nickname "Pistol Pete." He could look at a bullet and tell you the exact make and model, the number of grains within the shell, the degree of accuracy. Some guys join the Army at least partly because they like the idea of being able to shoot guns legally and endlessly. I guess that's no great secret. Hell, I fell into that category. But Pistol Pete was different. This dude was a connoisseur of weapons. And not just guns. I'd see him sitting around, perusing catalogues devoted entirely to ammunition. Just bullets! Now, I understand the value of being well schooled on the subject of weaponry—it's important for a soldier to know his equipment and the equipment of the enemy. But I have never met anyone in my entire life quite like Pistol Pete. He could walk into any gun shop in the world and hold his own in a conversation with the owner. I've seen him do it. They'd start talking, and within a minute or two it was obvious that the owner, who devoted his life to the marketing of weapons, had less knowledge than Pistol Pete.

Guns were in his blood.

Pistol Pete confirmed my opinion that true gun aficionados, like most serious hobbyists, are highly meticulous people, and in ways that spill over into other aspects of their lives. The first time I actually walked into Pete's room I noted that he had three separate water purifiers.

"What's all this?" I asked.

"Water is bad here, man," he explained. Then he pointed to the first purifier. "I put it through this one . . ." He pointed to the second. "Then this one . . . and then this one."

"You triple purify your water? Man, I just drink it right out of the sink using my hands."

Pete shrugged.

"Probably shouldn't do that."

Pistol Pete was the kind of guy who, when we went out on patrol, would always pack an extra tube of toothpaste, just in case he ran out. Nothing was left to chance. And if some of his quirks and eccentricities seemed odd around the base, well, I suppose they might have helped make him a better soldier in the field.

Despite his love of guns, Pistol Pete was primarily a radio man when we went out on patrol. One of the first times I saw him in this setting was just a few months after we arrived in Afghanistan. We were on a five-day mission in support of a small number of soldiers from the Afghan National Army (ANA). And when I say "support," I mean exactly that. There were maybe a dozen members of the ANA who had decided they were going to make contact with the Taliban and try to fight for themselves. Our job was to hang back in a little compound and help them in the event they were overrun, maybe call in support from Baylough if necessary. Basically, though, we were just setting up security and watching the ANA take on the fight themselves, which thus far they had demonstrated little ability or inclination to do.

Well, the ANA hadn't gone more than about four klicks from our compound before they got lit up by the Taliban. To me it was a clear demonstration of just how unprepared these soldiers were to fight on their own. They came back a few hours later, all ragtag and shot to pieces, having lost roughly half their unit. Not only that, but they left the bodies of their fellow soldiers behind. Well, that was something the Americans never did, and since we were in a mentoring position with the ANA, we weren't about to let them do it, either. We were trying to help them take control of their own country, fight for their own freedom and governance. If these men had been willing to take up arms and die for that cause, then the least that could be done in their honor would be to retrieve their bodies.

So out we went.

They were scared shitless, of course, and really wanted no part of another mission. But that was part of our responsibility on the first deployment: to work with the ANA and teach them about authority and responsibility. The truth is, abuse of authority is common wherever power is gained almost exclusively through strength and brute force. We were trying to teach basic steps of leadership in a country that did not have a traditional leadership hierarchy. That can be daunting, but it started with a fundamental respect for human life. And for those who give their lives in the name of a supposedly greater cause. A few of us stayed back at the compound to pull security that night; another ten of us went out with the remaining ANA soldiers to retrieve the bodies.

As we drew near, the Taliban opened fire again, spraying what appeared to be fifty-caliber rounds across a hillside. They must have been using a Dishka, or some other mounted weapon, but we couldn't really tell. All I knew was that they were spraying our position with huge rounds. Even though their blanket approach to shooting at us made it seem apparent that they weren't exactly sure where to fire, it was a dangerous situation. The strategy, under the circumstances, was to seek cover and ride out the onslaught until there was a break and we could move and return fire. If we revealed our precise position at that moment, the Taliban were far more likely to start firing accurately and putting those fifty-caliber rounds right on us.

In Afghanistan, seeking cover usually meant ducking behind the nearest rock. Not usually a problem, since it was basically an entire country of rocks. Sometimes, though, you could get caught naked and find yourself running about, trying to squelch the panic while looking for shelter. I was crouched behind a small rock, barely big enough to hide a single person, watching the rounds splatter across the hillside, when Pistol Pete came bounding up beside me.

"Pete, man, what the fuck?" I said, moving over a few inches, so that my extremities were now unshielded. "This is my rock."

"Sorry, dude," he said. "They're blasting all over the place out there. This was the closest one."

By this point I'd been in a few fights. But because he was the radio man, Pistol Pete's primary job was to hang back with the lieutenants and relay information to company headquarters; he'd never been involved in anything quite like this.

I looked at him. He seemed completely calm, but it was clear that he was somewhat disoriented. I knew how he felt; I'd been there myself. I've often thought about how I'd like to have a do-over on that first firefight, when I got shot in the leg. There is, after all, no substitute for experience.

"Okay, man," I said. "It's our rock."

Pete nodded.

Here's the thing about soldiers in combat: They don't talk about fear. They don't admit to being scared. Nervous? Yes. Anxious? Sure.

Excited, pumped, worried?

Absolutely.

But not scared. That doesn't mean fear never entered into the equation; it simply means we didn't talk about it. For me, each situation was different, and the amount of trepidation or unease I experienced depended largely on the degree to which I felt we had control over a situation. In every firefight, my heart would race and my breathing would become labored, almost like I was hyperventilating. But I learned to control that, which was essential, because you can't function if you're not clearheaded and breathing normally. A couple of choruses of "Hey Jude" and I'd be ready to go. Battlefield meditation. It's a strange combination of focus and intensity—almost like tranquility—that comes over you, allowing you to access memory and training and gut instinct, all at the same time. I don't even think of it as "courage." It's much more analytical than that. You find yourself doing quick calculations about a given situation, trying to figure out what is required for the most positive outcome. And it all happens almost instantaneously.

Training and experience keep fear at bay. You learn to access, analyze, and attack, in that order, and in a tightly compressed window of time. Sometimes you attack by moving forward; sometimes you attack by finding cover. It doesn't really matter. The point is, training informs your response, to the point that whatever fear you might feel is channeled appropriately. I've heard that some combat veterans have acknowledged feeling less anxiety in the middle of a firefight than they do on a commercial airline flight. Crazy as it might seem to a civilian, I don't have any trouble believing that. When you get on a plane, you're just a pea in the pod. From the moment they close the door and taxi away from the gate, you have absolutely no control over anything that transpires. Intellectually, I know that going into combat is exponentially more dangerous than flying on a commercial plane. And yet, I completely sympathize with the soldier who might prefer combat to giving up the controls in any potentially dangerous aspect of his life.

Let's put it this way: If you are a crazy driver, I don't want to be in the passenger seat while you're behind the wheel. That would legitimately scare me. But even if I'm a crazier, more aggressive driver than you are, I have no problem taking the wheel myself; and then you'll be scared shitless. As long as I'm in control of the situation—or at least feel like I am in control of the situation—I won't be scared at all. I dictate the movements of the car, no matter what those movements might be, and that provides a sense of security . . . a sense of control. That's an extraordinarily powerful psychological security blanket. And it applies to just about every aspect of life. Think about it: Any time you walk into a situation—whether it's in your work life or your personal life—you instantly assess the degree of control you have over what is about to transpire. The less control you have, the more anxiety you experience.

I could imagine what was going through Pistol Pete's mind as he crouched beside me on that hillside, the shells exploding all around us. A radio man in his first firefight. Whatever he felt, though, he kept it to himself. He did his job, on that night and countless others, through two deployments stretching across twenty-seven months. Got out alive, went back home, then moved to Arizona, where the gun laws aren't as strict as they are in California.

He's still the same soft-spoken, easygoing guy he was when I first met him, the kind of guy you'd pass on the street and barely even notice. Whippet-thin and nondescript. The kind of guy who looks like he wouldn't push back if you gave him any trouble. But that would be a mistake, for I'm sure Pistol Pete has a permit to carry a concealed weapon, and he's probably packing as much as you're legally allowed to carry in the state of Arizona. You'd never know that by looking at him; you'd never know some of the remarkable things he's done.

And he'd never tell you.

CHAPTER 8

November 2005

I'm sitting in an airport, waiting glumly for the first of three flights that will eventually take me back to Kandahar. I've been on leave for the past couple weeks, enjoying time with my family and friends, reconnecting with Jen, but now it's time to get back to work. There is nothing quite as disorienting as coming home in the middle of deployment; nothing, that is, except going back when the vacation is over. But this is my job and I signed up for it, and though the last few months have been sobering and at times terrifying, I still believe in the fight and the work that we're doing. And there is comfort in knowing that the vast majority of people back home support the troops, even if they may disagree politically with our involvement.

I can see that on the faces of civilians as they pass by. Sometimes they smile and nod. Sometimes they offer a quiet thank-you. That means a lot, especially when you're on your way back to a combat situation.

There are other times, though, when I wonder what people are thinking, times when it becomes apparent that we aren't really a nation at war. A nation at war is invested fully, from the top of the government right down to the very last private citizen. We all pitch in; we all do our part, in some small way. But this war is different. There is no draft; this is a war being fought by an all-volunteer military, half a world away, by professional soldiers making tremendous sacrifices, while the rest of their countrymen sit quietly on the sidelines. They go about their lives, occasionally griping about the rising cost of oil, or the annoyance of waiting in long security lines at the airport. Beyond that, there is little personal accountability on the part of the average American. If you don't have a dog in the fight (or a sibling, or a son or daughter, or a husband or wife), you don't really feel it. So guilt and appreciation are all you have to offer.

Most of the time, that's enough. I'm a big fan of the all-volunteer Army. I think it fosters pride and professionalism, and prevents the military from being infiltrated by reluctant warriors, people who would rather be almost anywhere else. I've been in combat, and if I have to go back—which I do—I'd rather be there with men who have willingly accepted the assignment.

All I ask—all any of us ask—is for some sense of awareness about the nature of our job, and appreciation for what it involves. We've earned that much.

So I don't quite know how to react when the woman approaches me, a smile on her face, and a warm, almost motherly air about her. She's in her sixties, I would guess, and she's clearly interested in chatting. She takes a seat next to me in the gate area. I'm wearing the Desert Combat Uniform, as we usually do while traveling, so it's not like there's any doubt about my line of work. The woman turns to me and begins speaking.

"Excuse me, young man," she says. "Are you on your way back to Iraq?"

A fairly common question, actually. I'm used to it.

"No, ma'am. I'm going to Afghanistan."

She nods, smiles. Then she reaches over and puts a hand on my knee. She pats it warmly.

"Good for you, honey," she says. "I'm glad you're going to be safe."

It had been a terrific break, starting with my return to Iowa, and a re-union with my family. I can't really describe how strange and wonderful it was, to be home again after being away for so long. Literally, I'd been gone for nearly two years; metaphorically, I'd been away a lot longer than that, detached from my roots, estranged from my father. But now here they all were—Mom and Dad, my brother and sister—greeting me at the airport, welcoming me home as if everything was fine; as if there never had been a problem between us. What a blessing that was; what a gift.

As he'd promised in the letter he'd sent many months earlier, my father was there with open arms. We embraced, didn't say much. No need to, I guess. Instead we all just went home and enjoyed each other's company for the next week or so. Dad and I never did sit down and have a heart-to-heart talk about all the things that had happened over the years, all the stupid fights and hurt feelings. I know how he feels, and he knows how I feel. I fully acknowledge my wrongdoing, and I see now that he only wanted the best for me, and that he was genuinely con-cerned about how my life might turn out. I don't put an ounce of blame on my dad. Yeah, he could be difficult and demanding, and he certainly lost patience with me while I was growing up. But you know what? It takes two to tango. You can't negotiate with unreasonable people, and I was being unreasonable one hundred percent of the time.

Before I left that week, I sat down with Dad and briefly shared with him my feelings, acknowledged my flaws and faults, and told him how sorry I was. He forgave me, said he was sorry, too, and that was that. I don't think either of us felt any great need or desire to dissect five years' worth of conflict and pain. Here's what I know: Our time on this planet is short, and our time together as a family is even shorter. How much time do you really have with your father? How many years to be best buddies? To fish and play ball and hang out? You get childhood, and that's about it. I regret enormously that my father and I forfeited much of that time. I take the blame for it. But you can't change what's happened, you can't undo what's done. All you can do is move forward and try to make the best of the time you have left. That's what my father and I have done, and it started that week, when I came home on mid-deployment leave, no longer a hardheaded, self-indulgent kid, but a young man who had seen suffering and death, and who realized there was nothing more important in life than family and friends.

It's funny how the simplest of things can take on added weight—like eating a meal with real utensils. (Hell, how about just eating real food, as opposed to MREs?) Like taking a hot shower every day. Sleeping on a real mattress. These are things most people take for granted, but they are unimaginable luxuries to a soldier on deployment. By the time my two-week leave ended, I suppose I'd gotten a bit soft, but that was the point of going on leave. After a week in Iowa, Jen and I took off for Mexico, spent a few days at a resort, did some scuba diving and lots of relaxing. We chose Mexico not merely for the sun and sand, but because I wanted to at least feel like a grown-up. Seemed odd and unfair that I was a combat veteran with a Purple Heart, and yet I couldn't buy a beer legally in the United States (I was still only twenty years old). Well, dammit, I wanted a beer. I mean, who knew whether it would be the last one I'd ever get to drink? I don't mean to be melodramatic, but you think about shit like that once you've spent time in combat.

Anyway, Jen and I stopped off in the Dallas–Fort Worth area on the way back from Mexico, spent a couple of days at Six Flags, and then came home. Before I knew it, I was getting out of a car at the airport, saying good-bye to everyone, watching them wipe away tears, telling them not to worry, that I'd be fine. Whether I believed it or not was beside the point. What else are you going to say?

And then came that disturbing encounter with the well-meaning woman at the gate.

I'm glad you're going to be safe.

How do you respond to something like that? I am not by nature a confrontational or self-righteous person, and I'm sure as hell not the type of person who would get in the face of a sixty-year-old woman and tell her she's clueless. But that was most definitely the case. I was lost in thought at the time, saddened by the realization that it would be six more months before I'd see Jen, and that every minute of it would be difficult and dangerous, maybe deadly. Afghanistan sucked. Simple as that. But here was this lady, I suppose just trying to be encouraging and thoughtful, telling me how lucky I was, simply because I wasn't traveling to Iraq.

Now, I'll be the first to admit that I didn't really know what was going on in Iraq in 2005, but I had firsthand knowledge of what life was like for an American soldier in Afghanistan, and it was neither comfortable nor safe. But very few people understood what was happening in the war against terrorism; if they were vaguely aware of the United States having troops overseas, they were mostly unconcerned with the boring or bloody minutiae of life in the trenches. By that time, I think, war fatigue had already set in, even as the focus had begun to shift subtly from one hot spot to another. Mainly, though, it was a function of numbers. There were roughly 120,000 American troops in Iraq in the middle portion of the decade, and a fair number of them, unfortunately, were getting blown up in spectacular fashion on a regular basis. Media coverage of the Iraq War frequently focused on the dangers and challenges of urban warfare in Iraq, punctuated by graphic depiction of U.S. troops being killed or maimed.

Look, I get it; I understand human nature. When you're sitting at home, watching television, and you see the aftermath of an IED blast, with charred trucks smoking in the background and body bags everywhere, there is an immediate and visceral response. For a while that sort of thing seemed to be happening every day in Iraq. Meanwhile, fewer than fifty thousand troops were stationed in Afghanistan, doing work that was no less risky or meaningful, but with far less attention being paid by the media. Part of that was due to the fact that so much of the conflict in Afghanistan took place in areas of remote wilderness, against an enemy that *seemed* less defined than the one in Iraq—Saddam Hussein could be thanked for that—but it also had something to do with the nature of warfare, and the fact that so much of the conflict in Afghanistan was being waged the old-fashioned way: with simple guns and grenades. The occasional IED attack notwithstanding, most wounds suffered by American soldiers stationed in Afghanistan in the mid-2000s could be attributed to gunfire. Bullets kill, of course, but they're not nearly as messy as bombs.

And the media are naturally drawn to mess. We all are.

Still, how could that not hurt, to have someone suggest that my life was somehow easier than that of the soldier serving in Iraq; that one of us was slacking, while the other put his life on the line for his country? I sat there and let her do it, let her pat me on the leg and tell me how "lucky" I was. And I seethed. She might as well have slapped me in the face.

Lady, I don't have any idea what's going on in Iraq, but I do know that two months ago I got shot in Afghanistan, and now I'm going back there, because the war is still going on. I'm in a safe spot? My life and the lives of my buddies are in jeopardy every single day.

That's what I wanted to say, but I couldn't bring myself to do it. In the entire time that I served in the United States Army, that was the single most disappointing thing that anyone said to me, revealing as it did such a complete and utter disregard not only for my feelings, and what I had experienced, but for the truth.

I know—she did not intend to be mean; her intent was to be thoughtful, compassionate, encouraging. She was merely ignorant, and she can accept only so much responsibility for that. There was, after all, more action in Iraq at the time, and therefore more media coverage. Unless you're actually in the war, on the ground, you know only what the reporters and cameras tell you. Nevertheless, this was not what I needed to hear on my way back to Afghanistan, for it had the disheartening effect of invalidating nearly everything the 173rd had done in the previous year.

—

By the time I got back out to Baylough, it was nearly December and winter had descended upon the region, which meant it was time to hunker down. For the American soldier, you see, there were two distinct seasons in Afghanistan: fighting season . . . and winter. The former lasted from roughly early March until the end of November, peaking in the dry, hot months of summer, when daylight stretched out over sixteen hours. The fighting season was long and intense, with contact several times a week. The winter seemed nearly as long, though far less intense. By the very nature of its topography, Afghanistan does not lend itself to winter combat, nor much of anything else, for that matter.

In some ways life at Baylough had improved by the time I returned. Yes, it was relentlessly cold and dark, but at least we had a reliable generator, which meant we had electricity, an ability to cook rudimentary meals—the Army actually assigned a cook to our base—and even Internet access. This was a good thing, for Baylough in the winter months was one of the most remote and monotonous places on earth. Everything came to a virtual standstill. Fighting stopped. Movement stopped. People stopped. Like the Afghans—both civilians and insurgents—we were mostly in survival mode. Practically speaking, you couldn't go out on a five-kilometer patrol when there was three feet of freshly fallen snow on the ground and a subzero windchill factor. It was impractical, if not downright unfeasible. Simply walking to the nearest village was an arduous and unnecessarily dangerous journey.

There were days when we'd just sit around, taking turns on guard duty, peeking out through heavy gear at the windswept, snowcapped mountains. Staring at nothing, listening to silence. I grew up in the Great Plains so I never quite got used to the idea that weather could come from below as well as above, but that's the way it works when you're seven thousand or eight thousand feet above sea level. You get those clouds that roll in almost sideways, and you can't really tell where they're coming from. The storms were eerie and unpredictable, but at least they offered some reassurance, for we knew that in the aftermath of a storm, the odds of being attacked were at best remote.

When the weather permitted, we'd go out on patrol; more often than not, however, those treks provoked no interest on the part of the Taliban, who presumably were sequestered in their own bunkers or mud huts, waiting for the snow to melt. Once a week or so we'd get in a little skirmish, though rarely anything of great consequence—maybe ten to fifteen minutes of annoying fire. It usually started with us cresting a hill while out on patrol and hearing shots off in the distance. If they came close enough we'd return fire, forcing them to drop back, and then we'd give pursuit, chasing them to the point from which the shot had emanated. They'd be gone, of course, so we'd mark their coordinates in the hope that maybe they'd be stupid enough to return to precisely the same position at a later date, which would allow us to shell them with mortar fire from a relatively safe distance, and then we'd return to Baylough.

That was a day's work. It was frustrating, tedious, unfulfilling. I can honestly say that there were many days during the winter months when we actually craved a good fight.

Please, God . . . let one of them take a shot at me today.

Time crept by in the winter months. Daylight was scarce, but the days incredibly long and drawn-out. To pass the time we built a rudimentary gym in the middle of the compound—basically just a couple of benches and some heavy rocks and dumbbells. It was like a prison weight room, only without the cages. We'd sling a tent over the top of it and pull the flaps down so we could work out at night. For heating, we used these pot-metal stoves that ran off five-gallon tanks of mogas—similar to what you'd use in a backyard grill for barbecuing steaks. It was extremely primitive and generated heat to a radius of not more than a few feet, but if several men gathered together, the combination of their body heat and the warmth radiating from the stove was sufficient.

Our needs were minimal, and folks back home did their best to help alleviate the discomfort. People were always sending us stuff, or getting their employers to pitch in and send us stuff. One day we got a shipment that included a hundred boxes of Dunkin' Donuts coffee. Another time, not long after someone mentioned that his toothbrush had fallen apart, we received five hundred toothbrushes in the mail. Another day brought a giant box of deodorant, which came in handy during the winter months. (We rarely used deodorant in the fighting season, as the scent could carry for great distances and actually prove dangerous.) Stuff like that happened all the time, and while it was funny, it also did wonders for morale: Just knowing that people wanted to help, or that they appreciated what we were going through, made the job more tolerable.

Eventually, and perhaps inevitably, given the shitty conditions and the lack of contact with the enemy, thoughts of going home began to creep into our heads. Although we had been give no specific date, we knew that our deployment was expected to last approximately one year, so we figured that sometime in May we'd be returning to Vicenza, where we'd be warm and well fed. It's a dangerous thing for a soldier to spend too much time fantasizing about when he's going home. During those long winter months, we had ample time to daydream, but we had to remain focused, for we knew that as soon as the weather broke, life would become a whole lot more dangerous.

And that is precisely what happened.

———

One morning in mid-April of 2006, I jumped out of my upper bunk to take guard duty and landed on a boot that had been left on the floor. My ankle rolled badly to the outside and then snapped back quickly. I knew instantly that I'd suffered a fairly severe sprain. It was the kind of injury you might get playing basketball, when you take a shot or jump for a rebound and come down on someone else's foot. I could almost hear the ligaments pop as the ankle rolled.

Ahhh . . . shit!

I fell to the ground, tried to stand back up, and hobbled around. Within a few minutes the ankle had swollen to the size of a baseball, and

I knew that I was fucked for the foreseeable future. This was both frustrating and embarrassing. It's one thing to miss work or patrol because you've been wounded in combat. It's quite another to be housebound because you sprained your ankle getting out of bed. Regardless, when First Squad went out on an extended patrol two days later, I was left behind. I felt pissed and guilty, but what I could do? These guys were going out for five days, and I could barely walk. I would have been nothing more than a liability. Under the circumstances, I was told to stay back; my spot in the squad was taken by Toph. We didn't say much to each other before they left. He gave me some good-natured shit about doing my job for me, and I told him not to have too much fun. I also told him to be careful.

While First Squad was out on that mission, they encountered an ambush and took fire from two separate mountain ranges. At some point Toph took a round to the chest. He began bleeding badly from both lungs. I followed what was happening from Baylough, anxiously listening to radio communication. There's nothing quite like that—knowing that the fight is intense and hot, and that one or more of your buddies has been hit, and you can't do anything to help. The frustration and sadness is overwhelming. I could hear Berg and Card yelling; I could hear the staccato rhythm of gunfire. And in the middle of it all, I could hear Toph dying.

Toph . . . who was only out there because I had sprained my ankle jumping out of my bunk.

There wasn't much time. Toph was bleeding from both lungs and needed to be airlifted out of the battle zone by Medevac and brought to a hospital as quickly as possible. His wounds were far beyond anything that a combat medic could handle in the field. As often happens, though, the area was deemed too hot for a helicopter to safely land. Until the shooting subsided, there would be no Medevac. And the shooting, from the sound of things, was not going to subside any time soon. It was a worst-case scenario: a squad pinned down, engaged in combat, with a wounded soldier whose life depended on immediate care.

Somehow, though, Toph got out, thanks in no small part to the heroic efforts of a pilot who had spent more years in the military than I'd spent walking on this earth. I don't know his name, nor did I ever have a chance to meet him, but I do know how he was described by the guys in First Squad who saw him in action that day. He was a crusty old guy, deep into his fifties (seriously "old" by our standards). A noncommissioned warrant officer, this guy had been flying choppers and executing dangerous rescue missions since the Vietnam War, so I can presume that there wasn't much that fazed him. How else do you explain what he did that day, disregarding warnings—I don't know whether he disobeyed actual orders—and dropping into a hot zone in order to help a fellow soldier. Toph was taken to Lagman, where surgeons cracked his chest and saved his life.

You'd hear stories about guys like this sometimes—older, battle-hardened veterans who kept coming back for more. Usually they were in their late thirties, maybe forties, having served in Desert Storm. Every once in a while, though, you'd hear about a real old-timer, a Vietnam vet who never left the Army or a doctor or nurse who re-enlisted—or, even more remarkably, enlisted for the first time—so he could serve as a medic. I'd heard these stories, never saw much of it myself in Afghanistan, simply because the terrain was so severe, and the patrolling and fighting so arduous that it really was a young man's war. I mean, that's true of most wars, of course, but it seemed particularly true of Afghanistan. A couple of deployments in the mountains could wreck the back and legs of even a healthy twenty-two-year-old. Frankly, I couldn't imagine how someone in his late thirties or forties would hold up.

There are, however, exceptions to every rule, and sometimes you come across soldiers who defy all convention and stereotypes. It's important to recognize these men and women, for their service says so much about this country, and what some people are willing to do in order to preserve the freedoms and principles on which it was founded.

A few years later, right before I left the Army, while I was working at a desk in Vicenza, I came across a kid named Ellison. He was a private, only eighteen years old, smart as hell, and full of piss and vinegar, couldn't wait for his first deployment. I spent a few weeks helping him and some of the other guys in the company get ready to leave, so we got to know each other a little bit. He was one of those kids who seemed almost too sharp to be in the infantry (I can say that without it sounding offensive, because I was in the infantry myself); not only that, but he had just recently been switched to Battle Company, for reasons I could not quite figure out. New guys do not get switched indiscriminately. But this kid had landed here rather suddenly, and without explanation.

"How did you end up in the 173rd?" I asked him one day.

He seemed a little uncomfortable with the question.

"My dad used to be here."

"Really?" I said. "How so? Can you tell me his name."

Ellison sort of kicked at the dirt.

"I'd rather not, Sergeant."

I tried not to laugh.

"I didn't mean to phrase that as a question, Ellison. Who is your father?"

Ellison took a deep breath.

"Sergeant, he was a brigade surgeon here. So I got pinpoint orders to come to the 173rd, and my dad made sure I was in Battle Company. I guess he really respects you guys."

We talked for a while longer, and eventually it came out that Private Ellison's father was the same surgeon who had operated on Toph. That realization, coupled with the fact that the man had thought highly enough of Battle Company to make sure that his son was placed with us, raised goose bumps on the back of my neck.

"Dude," I said, dropping the military protocol, "that's the most awesome thing I've ever heard."

He smiled.

"Thank you, Sergeant."

Understand that the sons and daughters of surgeons do not ordinarily enlist in the military. They might go to West Point or Annapolis; they might take the ROTC route while in college. But this kid had enlisted right out of high school. He had chosen the infantry. He had spat out the silver spoon and elected to join the 173rd Airborne Brigade, which guaranteed that he would find himself in Afghanistan. He would jump out of planes, shoot guns, and kill bad guys.

Just like the rest of us.

How could you not admire a kid like that? He had options, and this was the choice he had made.

And he wasn't alone.

Right around that same time I saw a kid show up in Vicenza, a young lieutenant assigned to the 173rd. He walked by me one day and I noticed his name tag:

Petraeus.

"Wow," I said, just trying to make conversation. "Bet that name haunts you, huh?"

My assumption, of course, was that this was just a coincidence. By no means did I think that this kid could possibly be related to General David Petraeus, who had been in charge of the multinational peacekeeping force in Iraq, and more recently had been named commander of the United States Central Command. In short, Petraeus was just about the most powerful and well-known officer in the U.S. military. Why on earth would his kid be assigned to the infantry? Couldn't happen, right?

"Yeah, it can be difficult at times," the young lieutenant said with a shrug. He paused, looked at my badge. "But I'm sure yours is hard, too."

I laughed.

"Yeah."

What the hell is this guy talking about?

It wasn't until later that afternoon, while bullshitting with some of my buddies, that I learned the embarrassing truth. Someone mentioned the name "Petraeus," and how he was in the 173rd.

"Yeah, I met that kid," I said. "Seemed a little weird. I made a joke about his name and he didn't even laugh."

The other guys all stared at me.

"Sal . . . you do know that's Petraeus's son, right?"

I was practically speechless.

"You're kidding."

They all laughed.

"Oh, man . . . he must think I'm a real asshole."

I still get a wave of embarrassment just thinking about it. But you know what? I also feel flushed with pride. Let's be honest: When your father is a four-star general, you don't have to spend a day in the infantry. Hell, you don't have to spend a day in the military. You don't have to fight. You don't have to struggle. General Petraeus had the power and the authority to place his son anywhere in the Army. (There were far safer and more direct routes to the Pentagon, that's for sure.) But apparently he chose instead to sit back and let the kid take care of himself.

Or maybe not.

There is one other possibility: General Petraeus used his influence to ensure that his son would be in the fight; that he would be here, with us, preparing to go to Afghanistan, which was just about the shittiest place on the planet; the place where he could very easily be shot or killed or blown to pieces; a place where he would be asked to fight and to lead other men into combat.

And if that's what happened . . . well, it sure says a lot about the 173rd.

CHAPTER 9

In theory, coming home from war should be the greatest thing in the world. And it is, in some ways. There's nothing quite like hugging the people you love—your wife or girlfriend, your children or your parents—after not touching them or seeing them for months on end. But after the initial reunion and the flood of emotion that comes with it, there is a period of settling in, of readjustment. And that can be difficult and disorienting. The fact is, when you've been living the Spartan life—a warrior in the wilderness, surrounded only by other young men, with few creature comforts—the civilized world can seem like a strange and unwelcome place, oddly hostile to the habits a soldier naturally accrues on deployment.

I can recall vividly one day early in the summer of 2006 when Jen and I took a trip to the gym together. I was working out hard in those days, trying to keep the lean, muscular physique I'd acquired in Afghanistan. That's a challenging task when you're hanging out on the base between deployments, drinking too much beer and wine in the evenings, visiting nice Italian restaurants, and generally getting soft. So I'd made a commitment to hit the gym every afternoon, following morning sessions of PT with First Squad. On this particular day Jen and I were working out together, moving from one machine to another, and during a break between sets, while chatting, I absentmindedly cleared my throat and spat.

Jen looked on in horror as a thick puddle of saliva and mucous landed with a splat on the gym floor.

"Sal . . ." she began, her voice filled with astonishment.

Realizing what I'd done, and suddenly overwhelmed with embarrassment, I kicked at the mess with my foot, tried to rub it into the rubber mats that covered the floor. The gym was busy and loud, so I'm not sure how many people saw it, but that wasn't really the point. Jen had seen it, and she was appropriately disgusted. Where was the guy she knew? The young soldier who had been so polite and attentive? The man who held doors and spoke softly and wrote love letters? Well, he was still here, just buried beneath a harder shell.

"Wow . . . I'm sorry, babe," I said, rushing to grab a towel, so that I could finish cleaning up. "I don't know what I was thinking."

Actually, I knew exactly what I was thinking. I was tired, sweating, and I had a mouthful of crap that needed expectorating. At Baylough, when that situation arose, you simply spat, without giving it the slightest consideration.

I tried to explain:

"Where I came from, the floors were made out of dirt. We always spit on the ground." I paused, shrugged, and smiled sheepishly. "What can I say? I'm not used to being inside a real building."

Jen gave me a funny look, like she didn't quite recognize me or understand what I was trying to say.

"You know what, Sal? That's pretty weird."

She was right . . . and wrong. When you spend more than a year living like an animal—trying to kill people, getting shot at, pissing in the bushes, shitting in a hole, cleaning yourself with baby wipes or, at best, taking a cold shower every few days—you forget how to live like a normal human being. The simple constraints of everyday life in modern society simply do not apply. In the mountains of Afghanistan I'd constantly find my sinuses clogged with dirt and dust, so I'd walk around spitting and firing one-handed snot rockets without giving it a thought. We all did. That was common. Adjusting to an environment where that sort of behavior wasn't considered normal or acceptable required time and vigilance. And patience on the part of others. A sense of humor came in handy as well. I was lucky. I had Jen, and she was willing to accept the fact that for a little while, at least, she'd be sharing her life with a twelve-year-old boy.

———

There's a video floating around somewhere that was made by Toph shortly after we returned to Italy. It's nothing more than a few minutes of footage taken late one night (or early in the morning) in front of the barracks. A bunch of the guys had been hanging out for a few hours, tossing a football around, drinking beers, telling stories about Afghanistan. Basically, this is what we did a lot of the time on deployment (without the beer, of course)—hang out together and shoot the shit. We were accustomed to being outside, or virtually outside, one hundred percent of the time; we also were accustomed to hanging out together 24/7, in spaces so tight you couldn't fart without everyone knowing it (not that anyone cared or tried to hide their flatulence). So when we got back to Italy, we naturally did the same thing. And in this one video, as Toph pans the crowd and conducts some impromptu, drunken interviews, Berg continually passes through the scene, wandering back and forth, asking the same question over and over.

"Anybody seen Card or Sal?"

I don't know where Card was, but I was with Jen. We were both perfectly fine, but Berg, in the video, seems anxious and worried. I remember giving him some good-natured shit about that when I saw the video.

"You miss me, Berg? Hell, we've only been back a few days."

"Fuck you, Giunta! I just didn't know where you were."

The truth is, his concern was understandable, when you consider that for an entire year, we were all virtually inseparable. If you had asked me at any given time during the deployment, "Where's Berg?" I'd have been able to give you an answer. If he wasn't in his room, then he was probably out taking a shit or messing around with one of the laptop computers. And he would have had the exact same information on me. There was no privacy; there were no secrets. Berg, Card, and I were like the Three Muske-teers, always keeping an eye on each other, aware of what the others were doing, and what information needed to be shared. That wasn't unique to us; it was the way things operated on deployment. Large groups became smaller groups, and friendships and working arrangements were tight and intense. If time passed without seeing one of your buddies, you nat-urally assumed something bad had happened; no one just wandered off or disappeared without letting someone else know where he was going.

You don't break those habits easily when you return to a quiet, safer existence, any more than you can suddenly stop spitting on the ground. So there is Berg in the video, a few thousand miles from combat, drunk-enly wandering around, fretting about friends who were perfectly safe.

Readjustment took its toll in ways large and small. Spitting on the floor is one thing; figuring out how to channel the aggression and hos-tility that fuels the soldier on deployment is quite another. One of our mortarmen died after overdosing on pills and alcohol shortly after we returned from Afghanistan. He wasn't alone at the time, either. He'd been partying with another soldier, who also overdosed, but managed to survive; that soldier was dishonorably discharged. I have some fairly strong feelings about how that situation was handled. In my opinion, while the Army does a terrific job of training men to fight and go off to war, it does not necessarily do a great job of helping those men adapt to their new surroundings when they return from combat. With a shrink-ing military and expanding demands throughout the world, multiple deployments have become commonplace. The strain is apparent in all kinds of ways, and I could see it even in men who hadn't yet left the Army, and were simply going about the day-to-day existence of life on a foreign military base.

Part of the problem is learning to define your terms. Is it a "problem" when you're taking four painkillers a day? If so, then a lot of soldiers had a problem while on deployment, because that's what we did. Injuries were common; pain was with you every day. Like I said, you can't hike eight hours a day, or more, with twenty-five pounds on your back (and hauling another seventy-five pounds in weapon and ammo), and not develop chronic pain. Vicodin or hydrocodone work wonders in that setting. I don't look at the use of those drugs, in a deployment scenario, as particularly abusive or dangerous. I consider it necessary for getting the job done. Maybe we all had a problem, but I don't think so.

Now, if you're talking about taking four painkillers a day and washing them down with alcohol, then you definitely have a problem on your hands. Unfortunately, that's the way things developed for a fair number of guys after they returned. Whether their pain persisted, or they had developed a physical or emotional dependence on the drugs, they continued to take hydro or Vicodin when they got back, and suddenly alcohol was added to an already volatile situation: young men returning from war and looking to fill a gaping hole in their lives. Like I said, combat, for all its brutality and horror, is also exciting and aggressive and weirdly beautiful in its simplicity. What do you do with all that energy and anger when you come home? How do you channel it in positive, productive ways? Well, sometimes you don't. You'd see guys come back from Iraq or Afghanistan, and they'd be wandering around the base, sort of lost and agitated. Evening would come, and people would start talking.

"What are you doing tonight?"

"I don't know. I figured I'd go hit the bars and drink."

"All right, I'll come with you—I've got nothing else to do."

So maybe they have a few beers in the barracks, then head into town and drink some more, stare at the pretty Italian girls, listen to everyone talk in a language they don't understand, and they drink some more, and they take some pills . . . and before you know it there's some sort of ruckus and a lot of people get in trouble. We were young and wild and no longer had anyone shooting at us. And we kind of missed it. I'm not saying it's right—I'm just saying you can't expect young men to put away all of that testosterone and act like civilian gentlemen just because the bullets are no longer flying. It doesn't work that way.

In those first ninety days back from Afghanistan, our standards became fairly lax, simply because everyone was tired and happy to be home, and we were trying to act like normal people again. The only thing that separated work from play was drinking. I mean, in all honesty, work wasn't hard at that time. There were physical tests, drug tests, interviews with psychiatrists. I got a kick out of that—everyone sitting in a long line, waiting for their turn to meet the shrink. It wasn't an option, either. You were absolutely required to walk through those doors and speak with a therapist. What you said in that room was completely up to you. You could say, "I don't believe in this and I think your profession is a hoax," or you could go in there and pour your heart out. No one had to know anything, and there was no stigma attached to the visit, simply because it was a hard requirement for each and every one of us. Despite my view of the psychiatric profession, I think it's a positive thing that the Army provides every soldier with this opportunity, and an accompanying layer of privacy. Whatever works for each individual is fine with me. God knows the transition is not an easy one.

I certainly wasn't immune to the challenges. Following both of my deployments (the second, in particular), I found it hard to adjust to a world in which physical aggression was not just unnecessary, but unwise. And like most of my buddies I self-medicated with alcohol. Most of the time it wasn't a problem.

Sometimes it was.

Like the night of July 21, 2006.

Jen and I went out to dinner with some friends that night. We were still becoming reacquainted, having spent so much time apart in the previous year. Jen had returned to Italy after graduating from the University of Iowa, and we had moved into an apartment off base. The Army wouldn't pay for the apartment because we weren't married. But I was due for a promotion soon, and that would allow me to move off base and the Army would foot the bill, and life would be sweet. Jen and I figured we could pay out of pocket for a few months. We were just happy to be back together.

There was nothing special about the evening—just four friends hanging out at a nice little Italian restaurant, splitting a bottle of wine and eating some great food. Afterward we jumped into my car, a crappy little Saab 900 with a ton of miles on it. This car was just a miserable money pit, but it got us from point A to point B well enough, and when it wasn't in the shop, it was kind of fun to drive. Well, my buddy, who was riding in the backseat, started making fun of my ride, and before too long we were arguing over who had the less shitty set of wheels.

"Dude, this thing's turbocharged," I said. "Blow you right off the road."

"I doubt it," he said.

"Yeah? Watch."

I hit the gas, shifted into turbo mode, and the car leaped forward. We cruised through a fifty-kilometer speed zone at roughly 120 kilometers per hour (translation: We were going 60 mph in a 30 mph zone). We were all laughing when we passed an officer from the local *policia*, standing on the side of the road, furiously waving his multicolored lollipop of a flag. That's the way speeders are typically corralled in Italy: You pass through a zone that is being monitored by radar, and further down the road or highway another officer waves you to the side of the road.

"Shit!" I muttered. "This is going to be bad."

My concern was only about what this was going to cost me. Speeding is a serious offense in Italy, and American drivers often receive the steepest fines. I knew I was going very fast and figured it would be a gruesome ticket, and I didn't have a lot of extra cash in my savings account. Still, that was about the worst I anticipated. It never occurred to me that I might be guilty of a more serious infraction—like driving under the influence. The threshold for DUI is extremely low in Italy: A blood alcohol count of .05 is sufficient—as opposed to .08 or .10 in most of the United States. Still, I wasn't terribly worried. I weighed about 180 pounds at the time, and four of us had split a single bottle of wine over the course of an hour or two. And I *felt* thoroughly sober, in part because I had a ridiculously high tolerance for alcohol, having averaged about a twelve-pack per day since getting back from Afghanistan.

A Breathalyzer test is virtually assured if you're pulled over while driving at such an excessive rate of speed. I got out of the car pissed about how much this was going to cost me, but brimming with confidence about taking a Breathalyzer. I inhaled deeply, as instructed, then blew into the machine. Then I stepped back and watched the meter rise. It's almost like playing roulette—*No red! No red! No red!*—as you helplessly wait for the game to run its course. I could see exactly how high I wanted it to rise, knew precisely where the limit was. And it just kept on going, flew right past the magic number, before settling at what I thought was a staggeringly inaccurate .082.

"*Umbriachi!*" the officer shouted, raising a hand in triumph.

Drunk.

I was utterly shocked.

"No, no, that can't be," I pleaded. "Give me another test. I'll do it. I can walk backward. I'll speak in Italian. Come on!"

The officer folded his arms across his chest and watched with amusement as I flailed about. Then he began writing in a little pad. There would be no debate, no pleading of my case. Not here, anyway. Jen took a stab at the Breathalyzer as well, just to confirm the officer's belief that no one in our little party could be entrusted with a set of car keys for the remainder of the evening. Jen is significantly smaller than me, of course, so she failed too. The officer ended up impounding the car and instructing us to find alternative means of transportation.

Here's what I learned that night: While the Italians may have a reputation for appreciating a good bottle of wine, they have little patience for anyone who abuses the privilege. I may have felt sober, but obviously I wasn't, and I paid a serious price for getting behind the wheel of an automobile after drinking a couple of glasses of wine. In addition to receiving a steep fine for speeding, and a significant charge for the towing of my car, my Italian driving privileges were revoked.

For three years!

They don't mess around in Italy. You get a DUI in the United States, and it'll cost you a substantial amount in fines and legal fees, but you won't lose your license. Not on the first offense. In Italy? They throw the book at you. But you know what? While I might have been upset at the time, I look back on it now and realize I didn't have a leg to stand on in terms of defense. I did the crime, and they made certain I did the time. A lot of wonderful things have happened to me in my life, and I proudly take ownership of those things. Whether I want it or not, a lot of attention has come my way in the past couple of years, almost all of it positive and congratulatory. But I am far from a perfect human being; I've made some big mistakes in my life, and this was one of those mistakes.

I've never talked about my DUI publicly before; the truth is, since it happened some time ago, in a foreign country, I might well have been able to keep it a secret. But I see no point in that. If I'm going to take responsibility for the good things in my life, then I have to take responsibility for the bad things as well.

You learn from setbacks, right? You try to evolve and grow, and accept accountability for your actions. Sometimes you do it by choice, and sometimes it's foisted upon you. There was no hiding from this particular transgression, as it provoked punishment not only from Italian authorities, but from the Army also. Long before that evening—before my first deployment, in fact—our company commander had made it clear that we were guests in Vicenza, and that we represented the United States of America. As such we were expected to behave in a manner that would not embarrass our country or the military. That's a lot to expect from a bunch of young men in their late teens or early twenties, but we had been warned. And when we got back from Afghanistan, we were warned again.

"Any of you dickheads goes out and picks up a DUI, we will crush you," the company commander had promised. "No debate, no second chance. We will make an example of you, and you will regret it."

He wasn't kidding.

I was the first member of Battle Company to receive a DUI upon return from deployment, and the Army did indeed hold me up as a poster boy for bad behavior. I was an E-4 at the time, a specialist getting ready to go before the board and receive my next promotion. Next thing I knew, I'd been busted all the way back down to E-1. I was a private again, essentially starting all over, right where I'd been nearly three years earlier, when I first enlisted in the Army. Instead of a pay raise, I received a pay cut; additionally, I was placed on "45 and 45," which means I received forty-five days of additional duty, and forty-five days of being restricted to the base. This, in effect, was like being grounded. I couldn't see Jen at all. Basically, I'd work from six or seven in the morning until eleven o'clock at night. Then I'd go to bed. And I'd do it again the next day.

I don't mean to sound bitter or accusatory. I'm just stating the ramifications of my failure to adhere to the rules. I deserved everything that happened as a result of my decision to get behind the wheel of a car after drinking. I have no one to blame but myself. I sure couldn't blame it on the Army, which did everything in its power to ensure that American military personnel did not take unnecessary risks. Young men like to drink. That's no secret or surprise. And sometimes rational thought diminishes and inhibitions melt away over the course of an evening, and these young men stupidly decide they're perfectly capable of driving a car. The Army knows all of this and does its damnedest to minimize the fallout. Warnings and lectures, promises of demotions and impending doom, are part of the program. But they go only so far. Since abstinence is unlikely, and since bad decisions often arise when people do not abstain, the Army offers a more practical option for its soldiers.

Free rides.

See, every soldier in Battle Company was issued something known as a Save My Ass Card, which he was instructed to carry in his wallet at all times. On the card was a phone number. You could call that number any time of the day or night, and someone at company headquarters would pick up. If you had been out drinking and had no money for a cab, someone would bring the money down to you and pay the cabdriver when he arrived. You'd be required to pay the money back eventually, of course, but the point is this: There was no excuse for driving drunk. Not even an empty wallet was sufficient reason. Taxis and money were always available. So if you chose to drink and drive, the burden of responsibility was entirely on you. You chose not to use the card; you chose not to save your own ass. The Army gave you an option and you failed to exercise it. So you are the dummy.

The fallout was painful on a number of levels. The money hurt, that's for sure. Jen and I were planning a life together, and suddenly I was less capable of holding up my end of the bargain, at least from a financial standpoint. Second, there was the embarrassment factor. Most of my buddies—the guys who had arrived in the 173rd at the same time that I arrived—were now ahead of me in rank. They were specialists and sergeants.

Me? I was, once again, Private Giunta.

Attitude is everything, though. I could feel sorry for myself, or bitch and moan about how unfairly I'd been treated (which wasn't true), or I could accept responsibility for my actions and make the best of the situation. One of the good things about the military is that it is basically a meritocracy. A good soldier is a valued commodity, regardless of rank, and I was still a pretty good soldier. I'd been in the Army for two and a half years, and during that time I'd demonstrated proficiency as a combat veteran. I had a CIB and a Purple Heart. I'd accomplished some things that reflected my value as a soldier, which was no small thing in the 173rd. I had awards for marksmanship and physical training. My behavior on the night of July 21 did nothing to diminish or alter any of those things. Getting a DUI is usually the result of a stupid decision (or a series of stupid decisions), and mine was no different. But one bad choice, made while off duty in a civilian setting, did not have any impact on my ability to serve in the infantry.

My basic skill set hadn't changed one iota. I figured, *Hell, I was a great private two years ago, I can be great at it again. Just tell me what you want me to do, and I'll do it.* There was surprisingly little awkwardness when it came to interacting with my buddies. Most of them understood and were empathetic. Shit happens. People screw up. Sometimes you get caught; sometimes you don't. What happened to me could have happened to any of them. So while there might have been some good-natured ball-busting about it, they didn't treat me any differently simply because of the insignia on my uniform. Technically speaking, we were no longer equals. They held a higher rank than I did. We remained peers, though. We had been through a year of deployment in Afghanistan, and nothing could break the bond that had been formed during that experience.

———

My second term as a private was slightly less arduous and demeaning than the first one had been. For example, when the new guys got smoked for screwing up and were forced to endure hundreds of punitive push-ups, I was usually exempt. Much of the indoctrination that comes with being new to the company did not apply to me. At the same time, I was a private, and with that rank came a lot of lowly, shitty work. Again, I have no complaints. There was a good side to this arrangement as well, for it allowed me to become close to many of the new arrivals while still maintaining friendships with my old buddies. I was in a unique position, and I tried to see the positives associated with that position, rather than dwelling on the negative. I had a lot of friends in the military who were privates, simply because I got to do it twice.

While I regret the incident and certainly learned from it, maybe it wasn't the worst thing that could have happened to me. Shortly after the demotion became public, I was approached by Sergeant Barberet, who was now my platoon sergeant. Barberet wasn't a real softhearted, emotional guy. Like I said—he was tough and fit and one hell of a fighter. But I guess on this particular occasion he figured I could use a little encouragement. And maybe some perspective.

"Hey, I wouldn't worry about this," Barberet said. "Same thing happened to me when I was younger, at Fort Bragg."

"Really?" I was genuinely surprised, not so much that Barberet had ever been demoted, but that he chose to share the information with me.

"Yeah, got kicked back to private." He paused, sort of laughed under his breath a little. "Way I see it, you're not much of a soldier if you've never been demoted."

"I'm not sure I understand, Sergeant."

That was the truth, too. But then, Barberet could be cryptic at times.

"What I mean is this," he said. "The best soldiers I've seen all had one thing in common—they bounced around a little. It makes you stronger. The ones that never got in trouble? They took the easy route. Shit . . . anyone can do that."

"Thanks, Sergeant," I said, and then Barberet walked away, leaving me there all alone, scratching my head. He was wrong, of course, and we both knew it. A lot of very good soldiers never screw up, never get a DUI, never get arrested or demoted.

At the time, though, I have to admit: It was exactly what I needed to hear.

PART THREE

Korengal

CHAPTER 10

Korengal Valley, Afghanistan
May 2007

The moment I stepped out of the Chinook at the Korengal Outpost and saw the men we'd be replacing, I knew things were going to be vastly different than they'd been on our first deployment. The Korengal Outpost, nicknamed the KOP, was the company headquarters in the Korengal Valley, which by definition meant that it was one of the nicer, more well-appointed bases in the region. In much the same way that Baylough had been a far more remote and less comfortable place to live than Lagman, one could anticipate that there would be outposts in the Korengal Valley that would make the KOP look like a Hilton.

That was a sobering thought indeed, for the place was seriously decrepit and unprotected. The KOP had been constructed roughly three miles into the valley, near the grounds of an abandoned lumberyard, halfway up the face of a mountain. This was a counterintuitive decision, as it practically guaranteed that soldiers at the KOP would forever be on the losing side of the terrain in combat. The Taliban would simply climb above you and shoot down. The high ground is advantageous in combat—you never want to shoot up at the enemy. If your base is located halfway up a mountain, the enemy is almost certain to attack from above. But given the history of the Korengal Valley, and the fact that outsiders had never gained a foothold in the region (the Soviets didn't really even try), it was a significant accomplishment for the previous brigade to have gotten this far. The lumberyard no doubt seemed a logical spot for the KOP, simply because it already had been partially built. But it served as a magnet for insurgent activity, perhaps because it was such a glaring example of American intervention, and a reminder to the people of the Korengal of a time when they led a more prosperous existence.

See, a year or two earlier the Afghan government had shut down much of the country's lumber trade, on the premise that revenue from the industry was being used to fund the Taliban insurgency. The sting was felt throughout the country, but especially in the Korengal, where thick forests of breathtaking cedars stretch deep into the sky. Practically overnight, what had been one of the wealthier regions in the country became nearly destitute. Consequently, the people who lived there, not surprisingly, were angry and resentful, and more than a few of them eagerly took up arms against the Americans when we came to the Korengal Valley. I get that, of course. If you want to piss someone off, take away his livelihood. But in the opinion of the Afghan government, and the American military, the money these folks were getting from the lumber trade was not going into crops and it wasn't going into improving infrastructure in the region.

It was going into guns and bullets, and the best way to prevent that from happening was to shut down the flow of money.

Regardless, the KOP looked like a shithole. I'd already spent a year in Afghanistan, living under rigorous conditions, but this was clearly going to be worse—a series of ramshackle huts and tents, with little protection from the elements or enemy fire. There was limited electrical power and no running water. Again—this was the center of operations, not some remote forward operating base.

Looking around, I could only imagine how unpleasant the next fifteen months were going to be.

Even more haggard than the physical plant were the men wandering around the KOP that day, all of them looking like they had been through absolute hell: dirty, hollow cheeks; faces gray with soot and ash, like they hadn't showered in weeks, if not months; oversized pants frayed and torn, like they'd been literally ripped from the bodies of bigger men. That wasn't the case, of course. These guys had simply shriveled to the point where they were nothing but muscle and skin stretched taut over bone, and their uniforms (what was left of them, anyway) no longer fit properly. The overall impression was of a unit so exhausted and battle-weary that they barely resembled American soldiers.

Until I saw the terrain in the Korengal Valley, I had presumed that my second deployment would be much like the first. That was both good and bad. Like I said, as scary and lethal as combat could be, on some level I was attracted to it; we all were. Life in a war zone is almost incomprehensibly simple. Not simple as in "easy," but simple as in . . . *uncomplicated*. For those fifteen months in the Korengal Valley, we would live minute to minute, hour to hour. Nothing outside that tightly confined universe mattered in the least.

Men at war live uncluttered lives, free of all the things that so many of us deem important when we're home. Everything from the truly vital (friends and family) to the materialistic shit we covet and acquire. Combat renders all of that meaningless; it simplifies your life, removing all of those things that cause anxiety and emotional upheaval in the civilian world. The things that make kids slice their wrists or overdose on drugs? Whatever it is that makes them feel inadequate or lonely? Those things are removed in a combat zone. It's a cloistered existence, fraught with danger but oddly comforting nonetheless.

But combat, I knew from experience, would be roughly 2 percent of the deployment experience. The other 98 percent would be the stuff I hated: the miserable conditions, the boredom, the awful food, the spiders and scorpions and fleas, the sleep deprivation, the defecating in holes and subsequent torching of feces, the relentless dysentery that made guys shit themselves on a fairly regular basis, the weeks without showering.

The time away from Jen.

Yeah, that stuff would be awful, just as it was the first time around.

But worse? No, I didn't expect it to be worse. I mean, how much could it change? Was one godforsaken, battle-scarred, mountainous region worse than another?

Well, yes, as it turned out.

We had heard that the Korengal had been the site of some of the most intense fighting in the war, but you learn to take that information with skepticism. War stories are like fishing stories: There tends to be a degree of exaggeration or distortion. Additionally, every brigade or battalion likes to think it's tougher than the previous one.

Oh, sure, it seemed bad to you . . . but I'll bet I've been involved in worse.

I still felt that way when I saw some of the guys from the brigade we replaced; they looked like they were a hundred years old. Weathered and withered. Beaten. And these were not ordinary soldiers. These guys were 10th Mountain Division, a venerable unit in its own right, with a long and proud fighting tradition. They were tough and proud; they were professional soldiers. And it was obvious from looking at them that they had seen some shit. It was clear that there was a battle in this valley. We had been routed through a big American base at Bagram, and there, just a few hours earlier, we had been surrounded by comfortable, well-fed soldiers, most of whom looked like they had never fired a gun at another human being.

Here?

This was different.

And yet, I couldn't help but think our experience would be more successful, that fifteen months down the road, when our deployment ended, we'd look more robust. We'd look like winners.

They're not the 173rd. We're different. We're prepared. We're just better soldiers.

I believed that then, and I believe it now. Still, there's no question that the Korengal Valley was pretty close to hell on earth. It was even known as the "Valley of Death" by soldiers who had been there. It took maybe three weeks to realize there was going to be more fighting than we had been accustomed to, and, consequently, more casualties. In the first two months we lost three soldiers in the valley. And not to RPGs or IEDs, with their lethal and far-reaching spray of shrapnel. These guys got shot. The insurgents were better armed in the Korengal Valley, their numbers were greater, and they were more inclined to engage in combat. It was, in short, a very dangerous place.

There were variants, I discovered, within the Afghanistan conflict— areas in which the fighting and insurgent activity was much more organized and intense, and the terrain infinitely more challenging. This I did not discover until I arrived in the Korengal Valley. By this point I felt like a seasoned veteran. I'd survived one tour of duty and a gunshot wound to the calf. I was scheduled to be released from my military obligation in six more months, at which time I figured I'd come home and resume a normal life with Jen. That was before I was introduced to a little-known military policy known as "stop-loss." In laymen's terms, stop-loss is the involuntary extension of a soldier's active duty service under the enlistment contract.

Here's what it really means: A four-year commitment is actually an eight-year commitment. Under ordinary circumstances, you might serve four years of active duty, and then have four years of inactive duty on your contract. Stop-loss allows the military to arbitrarily extend the active-duty portion of the contract, resulting in multiple tours of combat duty for many soldiers. This, of course, is a consequence of having an all-volunteer military force. Before 2003, stop-loss had never been exercised. No one knew that it would ever be necessary because we hadn't fought a lengthy war since the dissolution of the draft. To most enlisted men, stop-loss is just an initial on the contract—you don't pay any attention to it. But it's actually quite real, and we needed a war to figure that out, and to know how many men we needed.

The reality hit me on the eve of my second deployment. They just said, "Hey, we're going into Afghanistan; we know your time in the military is up halfway through this trip, but we're going to keep you a while longer."

I was like . . . "Ummm . . . can you do that?"

They could, and they did. I was supposed to be discharged on November 13, 2007. I didn't even leave the country of Afghanistan until July 2008.

Stop-loss can be a bit of a morale-killer. You commit to a job, and you think the job is nearly over, and then you discover that the little line on the contract is actually a very real thing. And that can be devastating, especially if that line amounts to another six to nine months in the Korengal Valley. It makes some people sour and sore, and prevents them from living up to their potential. This is a problem moving forward as the United States expands its presence around the globe while continuing to use a volunteer military force. Fortunately, changes are being made. Sensing a public relations backlash and, more important, exhaustion and growing disillusionment among the ranks, the Army essentially got rid of stop-loss in January 2011.

It's a little too early to say how all of this will play out, but I do believe it is in the best interests of all parties to continue an all-volunteer military. I don't think anyone during the Vietnam era would say the draft was a good idea. It put people in uniform to do the bidding of the country, and I suppose that was necessary. But a large percentage of those people didn't sign up for that obligation; it took them from one life and into another that they didn't aspire to. Even at its worst, stop-loss is not like that. It's not a draft.

The only way you create true professionals in the military is by recruiting people who want to be there. I can't speak for the entire Army, of course. I served in only one company, one battalion, one brigade. And the 173rd was a battle brigade, an airborne brigade. The quality of soldier produced by that sort of training, which involves more volunteering at every level, is higher than you'd find in a regular soldier. The 173rd is an amazing unit, with a rich combat history. The more I travel now, and the more units I've come across, the more I appreciate just how special the 173rd is. That said, it is my opinion that the Army today, across the board, is a far more professional and accomplished organization than it was a generation ago, and I think the elimination of the draft has a great deal to do with that.

Admittedly, my opinion now is somewhat different than it was in 2007, when the Korengal Valley was my home, and a fifteen-month deployment felt like a lifetime. There were about 150 of us in the Korengal—which is located in Kunar Province, in the northeastern section of the country, near the Afghanistan-Pakistan border where our mission was centered—but because of the way we trained and lived, I spent most of my time with a group of roughly thirty to thirty-five men, the members of First Platoon. There were times I'd go six months without encountering anyone I hadn't lived with and seen every day, simply because of geographical separation. The Korengal Valley is roughly six miles long. In some places it is only a mile wide; at its broadest point, though, it stretches nearly six miles across. We could look through binoculars and see fellow soldiers we hadn't seen in months, but we rarely made the trek. It was simply too long and didn't meet the needs of our mission.

And what was the mission? Well, just as it was during our first deployment, that was always a bit nebulous. Officially, we were in the Korengal to fight the war on terror (or terrorism, if you prefer). That meant engaging and defending ourselves against the Taliban while also pursuing the more noble (and less obtainable) goal of winning the hearts and minds of the Afghan people—interacting with the populace, letting them know we were there to try to help them; building schools and wells; improving roads so they could get outside the valley; encouraging them to get out and vote, to claim a stake in their own governance. We handed out food and clothing. I can honestly say that we did everything in our power to help them, and in return we were treated with hostility and contempt.

It's hard to explain the complexity of the Afghanistan conflict to Americans. Despite our best efforts, we were always viewed as infidels, even by those we were trying to aid and protect. Whatever appreciation they might have expressed was remarkably short-lived. We'd give them stuff, they'd thank us (some of them, anyway), and in the next day or two they'd be shooting at us, or providing assistance to those who were shooting at us. It's a very primitive, fundamental worldview, one dating back thousands of years. And I realized pretty quickly that we weren't going to change it. In Afghanistan, if you are an outsider, and if you are not a Muslim, then you are an infidel. That's just the way it is. We were never there to "occupy." We were there to help. We would give and give, and they would take and take. They would take with one hand and shoot with the other.

I mean that literally, not metaphorically. I absolutely guarantee that some of the people we helped during the week were the same ones picking up guns on the weekend. The population was too small and widely dispersed for it to be anyone else. There is a perception that Afghanistan is a country of peaceful villagers and farmers, with the Taliban lurking in the background, making threats, holding citizens hostage to their will. But it's much murkier and more complicated than that, with both abject poverty and religious extremism helping to fuel intolerance (if not hatred) toward outside interference, regardless of how well-intentioned that interference might be. The overlap between the civilian population and the insurgent population is far greater than most Americans realize, and that makes a soldier's job extraordinarily challenging. In some ways it's like Vietnam, where soldiers sometimes battled farmers in the fields, because the farmers had guns. The line sometimes became so blurred as to be almost indistinguishable.

As a soldier fighting for my life and the lives of my buddies in the Korengal Valley, I resisted classification. Taliban? Al-Qaeda? Mujahideen? The subtle differences that distinguish one insurgent or extremist group from another are of little concern to an American soldier when mortar shells and grenades are raining down upon him. I didn't know one group of bad guys from another; nor did I particularly care to be enlightened. Similarly, I didn't give a rat's ass whether the person shooting at me was a pathological jihadist or a farmer trying to pick up a few extra bucks on the side by killing Americans.

They were all the same to me, and if that sounds unpleasant, intolerant, or narrow-minded, well, such was life in the Korengal Valley.

War is about two things, really: killing the other guy, and trying not to let him kill you. We were the good guys; they were the bad guys. And among the bad guys, the only difference that mattered was the degree of training they had received. Just as there was a very real and highly skilled military force in Vietnam (the Viet Cong), in addition to the farmers (vict cong) and villagers taking up arms in true guerilla fashion, so, too, is there a well-schooled military presence in Afghanistan. And while both can be lethal, there is a difference. We knew when we were fighting villagers and farmers—the junior varsity team trying to make a buck to save their families—and we knew when we were facing the professional soldiers. It would be wrong to say that the war in Afghanistan is being fought primarily by downtrodden and bedraggled civilians; it is not. There are many competent and professional soldiers, well armed and willing to die for their cause, whatever that might be. And they are supplemented by an ever-changing number of desperate and angry civilians, men young and old who barely know which end of a gun to hold, but are willing to give it a try, nonetheless.

We had to be wary of all of them, couldn't afford to get bogged down in philosophical or moral debates about right and wrong, about taking human life or trying to assess whether the Afghan people had a right to be angry with us. We had a job to do, and that job involved killing people. And we were vigilant. We had been trained to keep our guard up, to trust absolutely no one who wasn't wearing the uniform of the American military. There would be no complacency over the next fifteen months. Not for one moment.

I don't mean to delve too deeply into the political ramifications of the Afghanistan conflict, because they extend far beyond what is happening in the mountains of that country. I am not a politician. I am a soldier. My view is from the ground. I hear a lot of people asking whether we should be in Afghanistan, if we're wasting our time over there. It's a fair question. It depends on how you look at it, and what your goals are. I tried very hard to avoid looking at the big picture. I was there because my country asked me to be there, and that was enough. But if you think we're sending soldiers to Afghanistan and Iraq to help their people, so that one day they'll like us and stop flying planes into our buildings . . . well, you're sadly mistaken. That will never happen.

So how do you define victory? You don't. I didn't go there to win a war; I didn't go there to win hearts or minds. My kill count did not determine whether we were victorious. I wasn't going to measure my worth based on how many wells we dug or how many schools we built. I judged my worth on how well I performed the mission given to me on any given day.

That's all.

And by the time I got to the Korengal Valley, my outlook (if not my attitude or professionalism) was drastically different. I knew the cost of war. I had seen it firsthand. I understood the reality—that the good guys don't always win in war; bad things happen to good people and good things happen to bad people. Combat is life . . . distilled to its very essence.

———

We stayed at the Korengal Outpost for two days, preparing and calibrating our weapons (known as "zeroing" in military jargon), and packing the gear we'd need for the hike out to Firebase Vegas, which would be First Platoon's home for most of the next fifteen months. Each of the platoons in Battle Company had been assigned to a particular area for the duration of the deployment. Second Platoon, for example, was headquartered at Firebase Phoenix, roughly a half mile south of the KOP. We were farther from the KOP, roughly five to six hours to the northeast by foot. Third Platoon was the most distant, at Firebase Michigan, a slightly more hospitable place halfway between the KOP and brigade headquarters at Camp Blessing (although Third Platoon was later moved to the KOP to help fight the relentless insurgent activity in that vicinity).

In addition to the platoon firebases, smaller outposts were scattered throughout the valley, constructed by the platoons to gain a foothold as fighting moved in a particular direction, and to provide greater security for the KOP as the Taliban repeatedly tried to attack from the high ground. Each of the platoons in Battle Company rotated through the KOP with some regularity, to shower and restock supplies, but since Vegas was one of the more remote firebases, First Platoon probably spent the least amount of time at the KOP. This isn't to imply that we were under the heaviest fire or facing the greatest danger; Phoenix, because of its position in close proximity to the KOP, experienced greater fire, so Second Platoon was generally regarded as the "tip of the spear." But the entire Korengal Valley was white-hot, and anyone assigned to the region could expect to face the most intense combat the U.S. military had seen since arriving in Afghanistan.

There is less formality in a theater of war than there is during peacetime, or when a battalion is in garrison, killing time, training up to a deployment. Protocol and tradition take on a heightened importance in garrison. You get smacked around for failing to keep your boots properly shined or your uniformed neatly pressed; you address soldiers of a higher rank only by their title. On deployment, ironically (since you would think that rigidity and adherence to rules might save lives), things are far more casual. The deeper into the valley you'd go, the less likely you were to find men who dressed as soldiers or gave a flying fuck about military formality. Guys would pick up a gun and fight shirtless, or in flip-flops. The use of first names was common. Technically speaking, this was a violation of Army protocol, but as long as the job was accomplished, no one really cared. The best sergeants, and the best officers, were those who understood that combat was different from being in garrison, and they weren't hamstrung by their own insecurities or career aspirations.

In other words, they were fighters.

Captain Dan Kearney, Battle Company commander, was one of those people. I didn't really get to know Kearney until I got to the Korengal Valley. Working out of the KOP, directing each of the platoons under his command, meeting diplomatically with Afghan elders, and answering to senior officers at battalion headquarters at Camp Blessing, Kearney had probably the toughest job of anyone in the valley. And he did it remarkably well.

Kearney was a character, and I mean that in the best possible way. A big man, probably six-foot-four, at least two hundred pounds, he was the kind of guy who had a gift for communicating and connecting with people, regardless of their rank. The military was in his blood. His dad was a four-star general, and I doubt there was ever a time that Kearney considered anything other than a career in the Army. He's a major now, stationed at the Pentagon, and I don't doubt that someday he'll follow in his father's footsteps and make it all the way to general—if that's what he wants. But if you saw Kearney in combat, if you watched him swagger around the KOP, dropping F-bombs and chilling with enlisted men, you'd have a hard time picturing him as a political creature of any sort. He was the boss, and there was never any question about that, but Kearney also had the demeanor of a frat boy.

"What's up, Sal?" he'd say to me, using my first name and thus forging a bond between us. Most officers did not act that way, and I'm not sure many could have gotten away with it. Kearney could . . . and did. I'm sure he was everybody's buddy in college. The very first time I met him I thought, *Man, I could imagine just straight-up slamming some beers with this dude.*

If Kearney could be laid-back and approachable, he could also be volatile and intimidating, capable of using his size and physical presence to full advantage. When things were not going as Captain Kearney wanted, whether in a firefight or in a meeting with village elders, or simply when dealing with the daily bullshit that comes with being a company commander, he'd get very intense. His demeanor would shift, and suddenly he'd unleash a torrent of profanity, which put everyone around him on notice. Ultimately, I guess, Kearney was a man who believed in getting things done, and when circumstances interfered with that goal, he responded viscerally. The change could be jarring, but if you wanted someone to put the square peg in the round hole, which was basically what we tried to do every day in Afghanistan, Kearney was the right man for the job. I can't honestly say I know how he behaves when he's in a roomful of brass, but I know that when he was with the boys and with the guys and with the grunts, through the hard times and the crazy times, Kearney was the man. And the reason he was the man was that he was just like everyone else. He was the boss, but in a good way. Kearney seemed to understand instinctively the most important thing about being a strong leader. He knew that we worked for him, but that he also worked for us, and we appreciated the hell out of him for that.

It was Captain Kearney who sent First Platoon off to Firebase Vegas, the easternmost outpost in the Korengal Valley, roughly halfway up the Abas Ghar Ridge. Incidentally, we took fire that very first day, at the KOP, while simply zeroing our weapons. Once again we found ourselves going from sea level to an altitude of some seven thousand feet without any period of acclimatization, so the hike up to Vegas wiped us out. We knew from experience that the Taliban might try to take advantage of our exhaustion by launching an attack on the first day. The Abas Ghar, after all, had proved to be one of the more impenetrable and danger-ous spots in the Korengal. It was here that insurgents had killed three members of a Navy SEAL team in 2005, and subsequently shot down a Chinook helicopter that had been dispatched to rescue the pinned-down SEALs. In what became known as one of the darkest days in the war on terrorism, all sixteen American soldiers aboard the Chinook were killed.

Our loosely defined job at Vegas was to protect American forces in the valley by limiting Taliban penetration from the east. Why was it called Vegas? Beats me. I do know that the U.S. military has a history of naming things in odd and interesting ways. For example, most of our military operations in the Korengal were named after National Hockey League teams: Operation Red Wings, for example. Or Operation Rock Avalanche. On some missions we would identify specific gridlines or phase lines by assigning them the names of American beers: Coors,

Miller, Bud, and so on. It was really nothing more than a psychological ploy, a way to feel more in control of the situation, and maybe a little less homesick.

So this little firebase out on the eastern edge of the Korengal was dubbed Vegas. But aside from the fact that every day there represented a huge gamble, it bore little resemblance to its namesake. In fact, it paled even in comparison to Baylough. Whereas Baylough was a small but functional compound with a courtyard in the middle, Firebase Vegas was basically just a crappy little hillside mud hut, maybe fifty feet long by thirty feet wide. Essentially, it was the size of a three-car garage, and we were going to put thirty men in there—the entire First Platoon. The place was a mess, too, even by the shitty standards of abandoned Afghan mud huts. I attribute this partly to the exhaustion of the 10th Mountain Division. Those guys had been through multiple deployments in Iraq and Afghanistan, and some of them had been summoned back to the Korengal on extended deployments after their time had supposedly been up. I am not trying to pass judgment. There is no question that the Korengal Valley was among the toughest places on earth for an American soldier in 2007. But having been to Afghanistan once, the guys in Battle Company understood that if we were going to live in a place for an extended period of time, we had to improve conditions to the greatest extent possible, because this would have a significant impact on how well we were able to work and fight.

Maybe the boys from 10th Mountain started out with the same lofty intentions, but by the time we arrived, Vegas looked like the home of a unit that no longer cared about its living situation. They were concerned with two things: getting in contact with the enemy . . . and going home. Bundles of hay were strewn about a back room. There were only a few cots, meaning the previous tenants had probably been arguing over sleeping arrangements, with the losers sacking out on bundles of old, wet hay and straw. There were bugs everywhere, and the stench of mold and mildew permeated the air. It smelled like a lakeside cabin with a leaky roof and no basement—the kind of place that eventually just falls in on itself.

Outside, around the perimeter of the base, was a single strand of rusty concertina wire that looked as though someone had simply dragged it outside and left it there.

This was the sum total of the fortification around Firebase Vegas. It wouldn't have stopped a stray dog, let alone an armed insurgent or a rocket-propelled grenade. We were home, and we had work to do.

CHAPTER 11

The first three months in the Korengal Valley were terrible—persistently rougher than anything I had experienced during the entire year of our first deployment. It was harder than anything the Army had ever asked me to do, either in training or in combat. There is no way to prepare for something so arduous; you simply have to live through it and do the best you can. As the days and weeks passed, I could feel my body literally falling apart on me from physical exertion, lack of sleep, and the stress of nearly nonstop fighting. Very quickly we came to understand why the region had such a notorious reputation: It was earned.

The big difference between the first deployment and the second deployment was the frequency and intensity of the fighting. In the Korengal, clearly, there were far more professional soldiers, funded and trained by the Taliban or Al-Qaeda, than there had been in Zabul Province, and they were armed to the teeth and intent on ridding the valley of infidels. Baylough was not a safe place, obviously. But there were times, at least within the walls of compound, that we *felt* relatively safe. Even outside the walls, if you didn't stray too far, you could move with a measure of security, confident that the standoff distance between Baylough and any eager insurgents made it unlikely that you'd be killed in your home.

Here, there was no sense of security whatsoever. We got shot at while inside the house; we got shot at outside the house, behind the house, on either side of the house. We got shot at when we left Vegas, and we got shot at while we were coming back. We faced contact on virtually every patrol. And when we went back to the KOP to restock and get a hot meal, we got shot at there as well. There was, it seemed, no place in the valley where the enemy didn't have some sort of foothold, and that meant every fucking inch of the place was dangerous. You couldn't even take a shit without donning a helmet and full gear, because the twenty-five-meter trek to the latrine was such an unshielded no-man's-land. Twenty-five meters might not seem like much, but it's far enough if someone is out there with a scope, waiting for an opportunity. We all would have preferred to keep the latrine closer to the base, but for sanitary reasons that was unwise: Simply put, you don't shit where you eat. Many days, when the gunfire started, I'd find myself questioning whether I really needed to answer the call of nature.

Is it worth taking a crap today, or should I wait until tonight?

Those are the things you ask yourself in wartime. It's not a normal existence, and if you were to drop a civilian, or even an inexperienced soldier, into the fray, he'd probably think we were all out of our minds.

Each day began with a presunrise "stand-to," a military tactic that dates back to the French and Indian War. The natives were predisposed to attack before first light, when the troops were sleeping; in response, the troops began rising early, under the light of the moon. We did the same thing during those first few months in the Korengal, waking the entire platoon in the predawn hours so that everyone would be prepared to fight. It didn't matter whether you'd pulled guard duty in the middle of the night and thus slept only a couple of hours. Every single man was roused so that we'd have sixty to seventy eyes on the perimeter of Vegas, scanning the horizon for potential contact.

I handled sleep deprivation better on the second deployment, in part because I was prepared for it, but also because I decided to forgo the malaria medication dispensed weekly by the Army. Malaria was a legitimate concern in Afghanistan, and most everyone willingly swallowed the mefloquine distributed each Monday. Deployment was hard enough if you were healthy; it was impossible if you got sick. The long-term ramifications of malaria were serious enough that you'd do almost anything to keep it at bay. Like most medications, though, mefloquine produced side effects, and sometimes they could be fairly unpleasant. For me, personally, it provoked the most vivid and disturbing dreams imaginable. I was so tired on deployment that I hardly ever dreamed, except on the nights that I took mefloquine. I'd wake up several times a night, drenched in sweat, certain that what I'd seen in my head had really occurred. And I know I wasn't unique in this regard. A lot of guys had crazy dreams after taking mefloquine. We all hated it, but figured it wasn't as bad as malaria.

Here's the thing, though: Three or four men in our platoon still contracted the disease, despite taking mefloquine. That's roughly 10 percent, which meant the drug seemed significantly less effective than we'd been led to believe. After that, I had considerable doubts about the merits of mefloquine. Why suffer the disturbing dreams and night sweats if I was going to get sick anyway? There's a saying in the Army, one that applies to just about any cost-benefit scenario: *The juice ain't worth the squeeze.*

That's the way I saw it on the second deployment. I dumped the pills in the garbage. Never did get malaria.

If things were calm in the morning, we'd commence with the normal routine of a day in the Korengal, which typically consisted of either patrolling or guarding the base. At Baylough, we'd patrol at the squad level. In other words, a full squad of ten men would go out each day. At Vegas we operated in larger groups, simply because we knew the likelihood of contact was greater, and we wanted to make sure that we were adequately armed. So an extra gun team would often accompany a squad, meaning we'd patrol in groups of thirteen to fifteen, with roughly an equal number remaining at the base. We also staffed a smaller observation post known as Little Rock, some three hundred to four hundred meters above Vegas, with three to four men pulling security.

The distance we walked varied from day to day, depending on whether we had a specific destination or were merely seeking out contact. But each hike was arduous. Because Vegas was situated on the side of a mountain, and our patrols often took us through the Abas Ghar, it seemed at times as though we were walking uphill in both directions. The altitude was unforgiving, the trails loose and unreliable—one wrong step and you could fall fifty feet to your death. For these reasons, every hike was slow and debilitating. A fifteen-kilometer walk from Baylough might have taken four to six hours. From Vegas, we'd need that same amount of time to cover a distance of five kilometers. In part this was due to the terrain, but it was also because we moved so slowly and cautiously, aware that at every bend in the ground, we might encounter the enemy.

The rules of engagement, fortunately, had been loosened by the time we got to the Korengal Valley. No longer were American soldiers required to wait until they were fired upon before shooting their weapons. Any Afghan carrying a weapon or a radio transmitter was considered to be unfriendly, and thus a fair target; there were times, of course, when women or children could be found in the vicinity of these targets, which obviously made for a serious moral dilemma. The unpleasant truth is that collateral damage is an unavoidable aspect of war. I saw men go to dangerous lengths to minimize the fallout, behavior that I believe reflects the basic humanity of American servicemen, but there is no question that you sacrifice some of that humanity in a war zone. You begin to treat life with a bit less reverence because, frankly, you can't afford to care in the least about the people who are shooting at you.

This, of course, speaks to the heart of the combat experience: death and dying, and it's something very few people truly understand, something you can't even talk about with anyone who hasn't been through it. Not even the people closest to you. For example, I don't believe any parent wants to hear that their son or daughter has killed somebody. The parents of returning servicemen and servicewomen are simply grateful. I think they do their best not to think about the actions of their children—how they might have suffered, the things they might have done in order to return home alive. I don't believe that my own parents are any different in this regard, and I've never talked to them in great detail about what I did in Afghanistan. It's too hard for them to imagine their son pulling the trigger of a gun and obliterating someone four hundred meters away. Like most parents, I'm sure they'd prefer to think that war is cleaner, less painful, that the good guys survive and the bad people simply vanish. But that's not how it is. It's bloody and it's gross and it's gruesome; it's always sick and mean. Regardless of the direction from which they emanate, there is hatred in those bullets. I know. I've felt it, and I don't expect anyone else to understand it. The rage and fear—the instinct for self-preservation that kicks in when someone is shooting at you? That's a hard thing to convey, so it's my burden to carry.

But within the context of my story, and in the interest of full disclosure, I think it's worth discussing. For a lot soldiers returning from war, it's the elephant in the room—the thing people want to know, but are afraid to ask.

Did you kill anyone?

What was it like?

How did you feel?

There are almost as many responses to these questions as there are men fighting. For most men there is a process of desensitization on deployment. Before you see one of your buddies get killed or wounded, I think the probability of your having a problem with shooting someone is higher. Once you have made peace with the concept of war, and the cost that comes with war, and you have a personal investment in it—whether it be one buddy's life or ten buddies' lives—I think your mind begins to work on a different level. For some people it's visceral: They become more aggressive, more hostile, after someone in their unit dies. I wasn't really like that. I functioned best if I maintained the same level of intensity one hundred percent of the time. That's how I chose to do it; I found the yo-yo effect of getting amped up and seeking revenge to be exhausting and counterproductive. I tried to be professional, and part of that professionalism involved being cold and callous, maintaining emotional distance from the people we were fighting.

I'm not trying to validate the way I felt. I came from a good family, with loving, thoughtful parents who did their best to instill compassion and sensitivity in their children. Human beings are programmed to care about other people. I know that. Every soldier knows it. And yet . . . you can't survive multiple deployments, heavy with combat, and not begin to question your core values. We grow up believing in the sanctity of human life—of all life—and we are taught that we should solve our problems through conversation and diplomacy and mutual respect. And then suddenly we are sent off to another country and we learn very quickly that some problems can be solved only with guns and violence. And when the fighting ends we come back to a society that no longer values the things we have been doing, that in fact finds our actions repugnant, even if on some level they understand the basic necessity of having men in combat.

We are taught in our culture to believe that life is precious; that it is priceless. But that's a unique and not universally held point of view. In reality, in many parts of the world, life is not held as something precious but treated as something cheap. And in wartime, life becomes even cheaper. Life is the cost of one bullet. Life is the cost of one roadside bomb. A few bucks, maybe, is all it takes to wipe someone off the planet. In the United States we value life in such a way that it is almost impossible to imagine taking it. But being in the Army teaches us that life is fleeting and easily snuffed out. And that's been proven throughout history, through countless wars and tyrannical regimes and horrific episodes of genocide. You don't have to go back very far, either: Rwanda, the Sudan, Yugoslavia. These are not ancient history. These are recent and brutal examples of millions of lives being taken with very little thought or consequence.

Life is too cheap.

I don't mean that in just a philosophical or moral way. I mean, practically speaking, life is far more disposable and easily extinguished than Western culture would like to acknowledge. I say this as a way to explain—or attempt to explain—how my feelings about killing someone were influenced by what I learned as a soldier and what I saw when I was in other parts of the world.

If I have to kill someone in combat, well, it's not the first time someone has died, and it won't be the last. And my life is worth more to me, and to my family, than the enemy's life. I can pull the trigger or toss a grenade and I can live with the consequences, because worse things would happen if I didn't pull the trigger. The enemy's life, to me, was essentially worthless, and because the enemy was difficult to identify in the Korengal Valley, this made for a blanket dismissal of life.

Is that the right way to think?

Probably not.

But it helped me feel all right about the hard choices I had to make, and the acts of extraordinary violence we all committed in the name of freedom; in the name of survival.

———

At that time I was a member of the gun team, and the gun team always walked in the back, to fend off attacks from the rear. As the last man on the gun team, I was the very last person in the patrol, a position I actually preferred, except for the fact that it involved a great deal of glancing backward, keeping my head on a swivel. Being at the tail end of a fifteen-man patrol can be dangerous in numerous ways, and getting shot was only one of them. With each step, a mountainside goat trail was more likely to break apart, so the tail end of the patrol often found itself tiptoeing over brittle ground that was shaky at best.

If you fell, chances were you would hit something hard. A running joke was that Afghanistan was such a cruel and unforgiving and foreign place that any time you took a spill, you'd land on something hard, sharp, or deadly. That's just the way it was. And it applied to almost everything.

"Hey, what's this bush?"

"Dunno, but it's probably poisonous."

Or . . .

"Man . . . check out this grasshopper. Weird little fucker."

"Uh . . . you ever see a grasshopper with red spots?"

"No . . ."

"Right . . . probably poisonous, dude."

That, to me, was Afghanistan. There was no soft, cuddly, friendly anything. The whole place was angry and hostile and dangerous. From the people to the terrain to the plants and animals. I readily acknowledge that my viewpoint is skewed, shaded for better or worse by the role I played. But it is what it is.

———

They say redheads have a stronger *qi*.

First time I heard that was in high school, when an Asian-American man from a local martial arts academy came to visit my school. He claimed to have multiple black belts and talked quietly but emphatically about the life force that runs through each of us, a flow of energy known as qi (or chi). I'd never heard of it, thought the guy was pretty much full of shit, just spouting Eastern mumbo jumbo to promote his business, whatever that might be. But then he did something weird. He invited people from the audience to come up onstage and do their best to beat the crap out of him. He'd stand there while guys punched him in the chest or kicked him in the balls. And he wouldn't even flinch. I found this patently unbelievable, figured it was probably some kind of trick, like maybe he'd paid off the kids who had volunteered, or he was wearing some type of protective padding that couldn't be easily seen.

I wanted a shot at the guy, so I went back to watch him again when he did another talk later in the day, and this time I volunteered to smack him.

"You gotta pick me," I pleaded.

He stared right through me.

"You're not a believer, are you?"

"No, I am. I just have to see it for myself."

The man smiled, said nothing. But when it came time to call kids out of the audience again, I was summoned. First, he had me stand at the front of the classroom with my eyes closed, facing straight ahead.

"Don't move," he instructed. "Just stand perfectly still."

I could hear the sound of muffled laughter, and I could sense him moving around me, but I felt nothing. He did not touch me, but merely (as I found out later) waved his arms around me. After a minute or two, he told me to open my eyes, and when I did, I was bent over at a forty-five-degree angle, staring straight at the ground.

"What the . . . ?"

As the class giggled its approval, the man told me to stand in front of him. What I did not realize at the time was that the previous exercise had been a test to measure my inner strength . . . my qi. A person with an unusually strong qi cannot be easily directed in this way (or so he explained), so he had to make sure I was compliant before moving on to the next step.

The man planted his feet and tensed his muscles. He thrust his chin forward.

"Go ahead," he said. "Punch me in the throat."

"Seriously?"

He nodded.

"As hard as you can."

"All right, dude. You got it."

I was not a little kid at the time. I was eighteen years old, at least 170 pounds, and I knew how to fight a little. There was no way I was going to let this tiny man (he was maybe five-foot-five, 130 pounds) make a fool out of me in front of my friends. So I reached back and absolutely throttled him, driving my fist into his esophagus with all the power I could muster.

He didn't move.

Not one inch.

Didn't make a sound, either.

"Don't feel bad," he said. "It's not your fault. You have a weak qi."

Oh, well, in that case . . .

He went on to explain that one reason he had agreed to let me take part in the exercise was that I had dark hair, so he suspected I was a safe choice.

"I never take redheads," the man said. "Their qi is too strong. Very dangerous."

Which brings me to Sergeant Thomas Hunter, a redhead in Battle Company, First Platoon. Hunter was a live wire, a quick-witted ball-buster who was one of the funniest guys in the entire company. The very first time I met him, I thought of the little man who had come to my high school. I hadn't known a lot of true redheads in my life, but Hunter was certainly one of them, a fair-skinned guy so ginger-haired that even with his head nearly shaved he seemed almost to be on fire.

His full name, actually, was Thomas Aquinas Hunter IV.

I'd never known a "fourth" before. And I'd sure as hell never met anyone whose middle name was Aquinas. Not that it mattered much to me. I didn't even know at first that Hunter was named after the philosopher Thomas Aquinas, so when Chioke cracked jokes about it, they made little sense to me. I do know this: When your parents give you a name like Thomas Aquinas Hunter IV, their long-range plans for you almost certainly do not include joining the airborne infantry and fighting in Afghanistan. In fact, Hunter did not come from a military background at all, and his decision to enlist seemed as odd to his upper-middle-class family as it did to us. This was a kid who had seemingly endless options, and the one he chose was the Army. This made a big impression on me.

"I used to play a lot of paintball and airsoft with my buddies when I was a kid," he explained to me once. "There was an empty factory nearby and we'd use it as a battlefield. I figured being in the Army was kind of the same thing."

Smart guy that he was, Hunter could say something like that with a wry smile. A lot of guys I met in the Army grew up playing paintball and airsoft. Not many of them were as sharp as Hunter. He was a good if atypical soldier. Although he could be incredibly sarcastic and cynical, he also had the eye and soul of an artist, as evidenced by the thousands of photographs he took during our two deployments. If Hunter didn't have his gun on him, you'd see him wandering around with a camera in his hand. And they weren't just pictures of soldiers at work, or guys hanging out. He'd shoot an empty sandbag bunker in the fading sun, and it would come out in such a way that you could imagine it hanging in a gallery somewhere.

Hunter had been a specialist on the gun team during our first deployment, and had been promoted to sergeant shortly before we arrived in the Korengal. But the elevated status had done little to dull his sense of humor. I rarely got into verbal sparring sessions with Hunter because they'd invariably end with him laughing victoriously and me tossing off a frustrated "Fuck you, dude!" He was one of those guys you come across periodically in the Army, guys who are operating on a different level intellectually. It was best to just let him talk, because he was always entertaining, in an off-the-wall sort of way.

You could count on Hunter to crack a joke during even the most intense times, or to put in perspective how we all felt about a certain situation, but perhaps couldn't find the right words. It was Hunter, after all, who came up with "Damn the Valley," three little words that quickly became Battle Company's unofficial motto.

"Damn the Valley!" someone would shout in the middle of a firefight. "Damn the mother-fucking Valley!"

You'd see it scrawled across walls at the KOP or Vegas or at just about any outpost. You'd see it on helmets and T-shirts and rifles. And, of course, you'd see it on bodies. I'd say more than half the guys in First Platoon eventually acquired some sort of ink that referenced this slogan: either "Damn the Valley" or, like me, a simple "DTV." It summed up perfectly how we all felt about the place, how it sucked in every conceivable way.

And thanks to Hunter, it became our rallying cry.

I said earlier that the primary purpose of the 173rd during this deployment was to limit, if not stop, the flow of terrorist activity into the Korengal Valley. A dangerous and difficult mission, to be sure, but at least it gave us something to focus on, something that spoke precisely to our training and experience. It was not, however, our only purpose in the region. As before, we were expected to assist the Afghan people with such tasks as improving infrastructure and creating jobs. This was known as engaging the populace; that we, as soldiers, often felt we were simultaneously engaging the enemy was beside the point. We did as we were told and tried not to muddy the waters by overthinking. That was left to the officers.

A typical patrol might involve a four-hour walk to a small village, during which we might or might not encounter contact. Once there, we'd set up 360-degree security around the perimeter of the village. Then one of our lieutenants would sit down with the village elders and discuss whatever topic might be on the agenda. This was his job—to be the diplomat. The platoon sergeant, meanwhile, was more concerned with what we referred to as "beans and bullets"—making sure that all of his men were well fed and watered, and sufficiently armed to protect themselves. The platoon sergeant, to be perfectly honest, did not care about engaging the populace, any more than did the private or specialist.

To be involved in the diplomatic discussions, or to be merely in the vicinity when they were taking place, was to be witness to some mind-numbing logic. For example, something as simple as digging a new well. We would hire Afghan workers to dig the well, using American money to create foreign jobs and better the lives of the citizens in Afghanistan. But the people we hired, and paid, were not necessarily people who had proven themselves to be good or even benign. They were simply people who weren't bad at that very moment. There was no guarantee that they wouldn't begin shooting at us the moment the job was complete.

There was simply no way to know.

Similarly, I had trouble understanding how the construction of a new road would make life easier or safer for American troops. A road would help the Korengalis have access to more of the outside world, but it would also give them more freedom of movement, and that sounded like a bad thing to me, given the fact that we were getting shot at almost every day. For me, and for most of my buddies, it was best to just keep a healthy distance from the moral and philosophical minefield. Better to simply focus on the moment and make sure that our people were okay, and that every U.S. soldier would return home alive. That was my hope, my motivation, my reason for being. Unfortunately, it became quickly apparent that we had no hope of accomplishing that task.

I suppose you could argue that one casualty is expected, even tolerable, in war. But it's not. Every person has a first name, a middle name, and a last name. That person has a history. He has a family. He has a mother and a father, maybe a wife and a child. He has friends. Each time an American soldier dies, there is a long and powerful aftershock, rippling across the continents, felt intimately by someone—maybe by many people—half a world away. As far as I was concerned, the only people who really mattered in the Korengal Valley were those who wore the uniform of the United States Army, and we began losing them almost as soon as we arrived.

On June 4, Isaia Vimoto, the command sergeant major of the 173rd, lost his son, a private first class in Second Platoon named Timothy Vimoto, just hours after raising Battle Company's flag above the KOP. By July the fighting had become relentlessly ferocious. Second Platoon's medic, Juan Restrepo, was killed on July 22, and the boys in his platoon immediately went to work constructing an outpost that was named in his honor. Their story, and the hell they endured in the Korengal, became the subject of Sebastian Junger's book *War*, as well as the documentary he produced with photojournalist Tim Hetherington, *Restrepo*. *War* was a tough book for me to read, *Restrepo* even harder to watch, because it hit so close to home. Their story was our story; the story of everyone who served in the Korengal Valley. A story of life and loss, and victories measured in the tiniest increments.

It was hard sometimes to remember why we were there, and to convince ourselves that what we did mattered. But there were other times when it seemed to matter a great deal, and the flush of pride I felt was nearly overwhelming.

The Fourth of July has always been my favorite holiday. I think it's truly important that we remember what we have and that we stop to reflect on our independence, and how it was achieved—the blood and sacrifice that went into it. All these freedoms and pleasures we enjoy as Americans were bestowed upon us, but they came at a great cost. Simply by virtue of being born in the United States, you are entitled to more freedom and more opportunity than anyone born in any other country on the planet. There is luck in being an American, but there is responsibility as well. Being an American means you have the right to freedom of speech, freedom of religion, freedom to gather and assemble, freedom to criticize the government without fear of retribution. There are many countries in the world where acting on those impulses will get you tossed into jail or killed. So exercise those rights, but keep in mind the very simple fact that you have them only because hundreds of thousands of men and women have laid down their lives for you, stretching across parts of three centuries, from the Revolutionary War, through two world wars, and through less popular conflicts in Korea and Vietnam.

And Iraq.

And Afghanistan.

As a kid growing up in Iowa, I didn't really get any of that. I mean, I sort of got it. I understood the connection between Independence Day and the sacrifices that went into gaining and securing that independence. Mostly, though, I was like everyone else. I liked watching fireworks and eating hot dogs off a backyard grill. Still do, in fact, preferably washed down with a few cold ones. But it means much more to me now, and I have two deployments in Afghanistan to thank for that.

There's something poignant about being in a foreign country on the most important of American holidays. On July 4, 2007 (as well as 2005 and 2008), not only were the men of Battle Company not in the United States, but we were in another country, fighting for the United

States. That is an awesome responsibility. It is also a privilege. And I mean that sincerely. But the flood of emotion that comes over you, when you witness fireworks soaring over the battle-scarred Korengal Valley, is a bit hard to describe; to be in Afghanistan at that time, having already lost a few guys to enemy fire, and to understand fully, for maybe the first time, what it really means to be an American. Like so many who had come before us, we were asked to do the hard things, the truly terrifying things, that make this country great. We were asked to put our lives on the line. I don't think there is any way to experience something like that and not feel the power of it in your heart. You know that what you're doing matters; you know it's important. And you aren't burdened by doubt, by the possibility that the people back home do not understand, or do not fully support the war effort. That's almost irrelevant. What matters the most, and what causes you angst, is the possibility that you won't live up to the standards of those who have come before you.

The Fourth of July in a foreign country typically passes unnoticed. It's a uniquely American event, of course, so if you want to observe the holiday, you have to create your own observance. This was true in Vicenza, and it certainly was true in Afghanistan. We did not possess fireworks in the traditional sense of the word; we did, however, have all manner of explosive devices, and these we used to create our own little Independence Day celebration. Fired from a mortar tube at the KOP, a parachute round that floats gently across the Korengal sky, like a Roman candle, can be a surprisingly emotional sight, especially when the parachutes are targeted in such a way that each drops over an area in which an American soldier was killed.

We did this each year, on Independence Day, and both times I was moved beyond words. We all were. We just stood there, watching the sky illuminated, and the parachutes fall, realizing that each one represented one of our brothers, a person who was the best of the best, someone who was supremely fit, active, and sound, and who no longer draws breath; someone who cared so much about his country that he was willing to die for it. That may not have been the thought foremost in his mind while he was fighting, but the very fact that he was here was proof of his patriotism, for he knew the possibility of death existed.

We all did.

To watch that round soaring into the air, burning so bright, and fizzling out as it dropped to the ground was to feel their sacrifice all over again. There were only a handful the first year, eight the next. Each time it was a somber event. Everyone came out of their respective bases, and we all watched and stood quietly, acutely aware that each glowing round represented someone who once walked among us, and fought with us, and who was no longer here. And it wasn't like they were gone because they'd forgotten to look both ways before crossing the street. They had been shot and killed, or they had been blown up. They had died for a purpose. And that purpose—that sacrifice—is what makes America so special.

In some ways, too, the Fourth of July served as a hearty *Fuck You* to the Taliban, for it was a convention of combat to never do anything that would reveal your position. In the nighttime you might fire a "lum round" to illuminate the enemy's position, but you would never deliberately light up your own position. That would be like holding up a sign that read "We're right here—go ahead and take your best shot." In effect, though, that is precisely what we did on the Fourth of July. We put ourselves out there and watched the parachutes fall, casting light over all of us, and projecting shadows on the rocks and the trees and the walls. For just that moment, it didn't matter whether anyone could see us, or whether anyone might try to attack. What better way to honor the men we had lost than by thumbing our nose at the enemy?

Since that time I have spent Independence Day twice in Italy and once in France. I hope this year to be back in the States, watching the celebration with friends and family. I know it will be meaningful to me, because I know now what this day really represents. That it's about more than baseball and beer; more than fireworks and festivals. It's a day of sacrifice, of remembrance, of recognizing the men and women who gave their lives in the name of freedom, or who served and survived. I was fortunate, and I'd like to think, now that I am in that category, that maybe I am one of those people you think of when you watch the fireworks on the Fourth of July. That would make me deeply proud, to know that I did my part; that my daughter was born into a free and open republic, and that I paid some dues on her behalf.

What a gift . . . for both of us.

CHAPTER 12

August 7, 2007

The valley is on fire.

Well, our portion of it, anyway. Gangwer and I are flat on our stomachs, faces pressed against the ground, burrowing our noses into the dirt, trying to get so low that our helmets become shells covering every inch of our precious and delicate little skulls. We are stranded for now, unable to return fire, unable to move, unable to do much of anything except wait it out and hope for the best. We are on the gun team together, positioned on a hilltop above the Korengal Outpost, a place called Nipple Rock. Our job is to man the 240 Bravo that sits nearby. It's an awesome gun with enormous destructive power—a few seconds on the trigger will unleash a torrent of shells on the hillside and give the enemy pause, and maybe open things up for everyone on our side. For now, though, the 240 is impotent, for we can't get to it. All we can do is remain prone, out there in the open, listening to the bullets whistle past, and feel the rubble shaking beneath us.

Thirty seconds is all we need. Hell, we'd take ten seconds. Even five. Just a momentary respite while they reload and let the barrels cool. Give us that much and we'll pop up and grab the 240, and spray the whole fucking valley at a rate of some one thousand rounds per minute. Then they'll back off, and just like that the whole tide of the battle shifts. But we can't get to the gun. It's right there, just out of our reach, and I know that if I can only lift my head three inches off the ground I can squeeze the trigger. There is fear right now, but mainly there is frustration. It's possible we could roll away, take shelter behind a nearby boulder, but we might get shot in the process. Worse, that would mean leaving the 240 behind, abandoning our weapon, when the weapon could save our asses—could save everyone, in fact.

No, you don't leave your gun. You never leave your gun. Even at the risk of getting your head blown off, you stick with your gun.

I turn ever so slightly, just enough to get a glimpse of Gangwer. He is in exactly the same position, body pressed into the soil, trying to create cover where none exists. But somehow it seems worse for him, because he is such a big guy, several inches taller and at least fifty pounds heavier than I am. Gangwer is an immense target, and I can't help but think that if a bullet or mortar finds its way here, he's going to get the worst of it. But he seems not to care. He is with me, as resolute as I am, and I know in this moment that Gangwer is special. Not that he ever needed to prove anything, but I know in this instant, in the minute or so that the withering fire cascades all around us, that Gangwer will never back down. He understands the consequences of his actions, of remaining here out in the open. He knows what is important.

You stay with the gun.

———

Tyler Gangwer was a big, white midwestern boy. Grew up in Cincinnati and was damn proud of it. I spent the better part of five years with Gangwer, and based on our time together I feel like I know everything Cincinnati has to offer. I know it is a city built on seven hills (just like Rome!); I know it is home to Procter & Gamble, and Johnson & Johnson, and the company that makes those damn playing cards with the bicycle on the front.

"Hey," Gangwer would say in the middle of a game of poker. "You know they make these things in my hometown."

"Yeah, Gangwer, we know. Shut the hell up and play."

At six-foot-three and at least 230 pounds, Gangwer looked every inch the Ohio football player he had been. Despite his size, though, Gangwer could hump for days. The guy was a pack mule, tireless and strong—you'd just give him shit to carry, slap him on the ass, and send him on his way. Wherever you were going, he'd probably be the first to arrive. He seemed impervious to pain. I remember the training period leading up to our first deployment, during an airborne exercise, Gangwer actually dented a double-A battery with his ass. I kid you not. He jumped out of the plane, fell to earth, and as you might expect from someone that size, he landed with significant force. (That's the thing no one tells you about skydiving—you don't really float gently to the ground; unless you're really lucky, you tend to hit hard, especially when you're carrying close to a hundred pounds of weaponry and ammo, which was true of anyone on the gun team.) When Gangwer got up, he sort of stretched and rubbed the small of his back for a moment, then reached into his hip pocket and pulled out a battery. He'd been carrying an extra for his night vision goggles. And the battery had gotten the worst of the experience.

"Huh," Gangwer said with bemusement, holding it up for everyone to see. "Look at that."

"Dude," I said, incredulously. "Only time I've ever dented a battery, I used a hammer. You did that with your body? And all you can say is 'Huh'?"

Gangwer shrugged, smiled, tossed the battery over his shoulder.

That was Gangwer: a freak of nature. And not easily riled up. A normal person would have yelped in pain, probably broken a few bones, at least seriously bruised his hip. Not Gangwer. He walked away like nothing had happened.

Gangwer was a year or two older than me. He had joined the Ohio National Guard while still in high school, completed basic training, and ultimately decided he wanted to serve in the infantry, where there would be a much greater chance of serious action. I would describe Gangwer as a proud American, a great friend and soldier, and one of the most unusual people I have ever known.

Like Chioke, Gangwer was extremely smart, but in a different sort of way. While Chioke could solve calculus problems in his head, Gangwer seemed to possess an almost encyclopedic knowledge of arcane shit. He was the kind of guy you'd expect to see cleaning up on *Jeopardy!* But while he could talk intelligently on almost any subject, it was science fiction and fantasy that truly captivated Gangwer. He loved talking about space and wormholes and time warps, and all kinds of stuff I neither understood nor had any interest in exploring. And once he started talking, you couldn't get him to shut up. Gangwer and I once watched part of the *Planet Earth* documentary series together. For my money, *Planet Earth* is one of the most amazing series in the history of television. Well, once Gangwer sensed my interest, he began flooding the room with facts and figures about science and nature, talking so incessantly that I could barely hear the program. Now, because it was Gangwer, and he liked to spout off all the time, I decided afterward to check on his information. You know what? Every single thing he mentioned turned out to be accurate. That was the thing about Gangwer—it only *seemed* like he was making stuff up. In reality, he rarely shared anything that wasn't true or accurate. And he always seemed to stay up on current events, even on deployment, which wasn't true of most of us.

If not for the fact that he was a ferocious fighter, you'd probably call Gangwer a gentle giant. Certainly he was a nerd at heart—a big brute of a man with quick hands and incredible though lumbering endurance, you'd see him lying on his bunk, reading comic books or fantasy novels, and wonder what the hell was going through his mind. I roomed with the guy for quite a while in Vicenza, and I could never quite figure him out. Right before our second deployment, I went on leave, left a few days early so I could attend my buddy Toph's wedding in Las Vegas. Since I left early, I also returned early, which meant I got back a couple of days before Gangwer. I walked into our room and found the lights were still on, even though Gangwer had been gone for almost two weeks. Not only that, but the television was on. And his Game Cube console was spinning. There, on the screen, was Zelda, frozen in time.

Holy shit! Gangwer paused his video game before going on leave.

I tried to imagine his thought process. Had he been in such a rush to get out that he simply forgot to turn everything off? Or had he made a conscious decision to leave the game running so that he could pick up where he had left off?

Two weeks down the road?

I walked into the bathroom and found the sink half-filled with water, the faucet running, flowing freely. The toilet had been used . . . but not flushed.

This was Gangwer's handiwork. How someone could be so intellectual and knowledgeable, and such a competent soldier, and yet be so wasteful and irresponsible in other aspects of his life was utterly beyond comprehension.

"Sal, did you save my game?" Gangwer asked when he returned.

"What? Are you joking?"

Gangwer just sort of stood there, shoulders slumped, looking like a big puppy dog.

"No, I did not save your game," I said. "And by the way . . . you left the lights on and the water running; and you left a deuce in the toilet, thank you very much."

"Sorry, man. I was in a hurry."

So that was Gangwer. I loved the guy; I'd trust him with my life. I did, in fact, on several occasions. But he was a challenging roommate, that's for sure. He was not a "normal" guy. But you know what? Most of us in the 173rd would not fall into the category of "normal." Airborne infantry is not, by any stretch of the imagination, a normal job, and anyone who eagerly seeks it has to be a little different from the average Joe. It's not normal to spend fifteen months in the Korengal Valley, getting shot at every day. It's weird and exhausting and exhilarating and boring and maddening.

Who wants that sort of life?

I did.

Gangwer did.

On some level, we all did.

——

At the opposite end of the spectrum from Gangwer, in all ways except one—maybe the most important one, which was a willingness to fight— was Josh Brennan. Lean and fit, with sandy brown hair, Brennan looked every inch the athlete that he had been while attending high school in Oregon. He had been a hurdler and football player, pursuits that required a lot of skill and endurance and toughness, and you could tell just from watching Josh in training that he was unusually fit, even by infantry standards. He also had a creative side—in downtime, while other guys were engrossed in video games, Brennan would pick up his guitar and just start playing. He was a natural leader: good-looking, smart, could talk to anyone about almost anything, and he had a way of making everyone around him feel comfortable, even though he was an intensely competitive guy.

I got to know Brennan shortly after being assigned to the 173rd. We spent a lot of time hanging around together while training, and during our first deployment. His parents were divorced, but the family had remained close. Josh split time between his mom's home in Oregon and his father's home in Wisconsin. Mike Brennan was a police officer in Madison, and Josh had been considering following in the old man's footsteps, which was one reason he enlisted in the Army: Military experience is generally considered valuable training for a career in law enforcement. Whatever Brennan wanted to do with his life, you just got the sense that he would be successful at it. He was an interesting, thoughtful guy, and always seemed to have something going on. From command's point of view, it's easy to promote a guy who is doing everything right; from a fellow soldier's point of view, it's easy to follow a guy when you know he isn't going to steer you wrong.

Brennan and I spent less time together between deployments, and in the first few months of our second deployment, thanks primarily to my demotion and the fact that I spent much of my free time with Jen. Brennan had been promoted to sergeant by the time we got to the Korengal Valley, and was no longer in Weapons Squad. Still, we were both members of First Platoon and we remained close friends. In the coming months we would be reunited in First Squad. I felt about Josh exactly as I felt about Gangwer: I would trust him with my life.

———

While Gangwer and I were facedown in the dirt, praying for a reprieve from the Taliban assault, Brennan and the rest of First Squad was involved in a fight of its own. At the time, we had no idea what was going on with First Squad. Firefights often developed in this way in the valley, separating units and splintering into multiple smaller, though no less lethal, frays. I didn't like where I was at the time, nor the position I was in, but I was grateful to have Gangwer by my side, the two of us doing everything in our power to remain alive. Although we took fire almost every day in Afghanistan—and sometimes two or three times a day—only occasionally did the bullets come this close without hitting someone. I could actually feel the air displacement of the passing bullets. It was, in fact, something of a miracle that we got off Nipple Rock unharmed.

After a period of perhaps a minute—time becomes nearly impossible to gauge in the midst of a firefight—the onslaught eased. Not completely, and not for long, but for a few brief seconds, just enough time for us to gain a few feet of ground and begin feeding the 240 Bravo. Gangwer, the assistant gunner, fed the belt; I squeezed the trigger. The 240 spat out a ribbon of spent shells as we lit up the valley.

Success in combat is about a lot of things: courage, training, experience, weaponry. But it's also about things you can't control. Things like luck and timing. All guns fire bullets, and at some point you need to either change the magazine or the drum, or you need to link more rounds. Sometimes you have to simply stop and give the weapon a chance to cool, so that you don't melt the barrel. Any of these things can result in a cessation of power; a moment when the firing stops, or at least lessens. Gangwer and I seized that opportunity to jump on the 240 and put the Taliban back on their heels.

And at that point, training takes over. The fact is, the U.S. Army is better trained and better armed than the Taliban. And once their opening is closed, we do our best to make sure it doesn't reopen. While Gangwer and I were firing a thousand rounds, the other fifteen people involved in the fighting could move and reload, and then they could pick up the slack while we linked our rounds. Ideally, we wouldn't give the other side that five-second pause that allows them to get back in the fight . . . that gives them hope.

That moment, that minute or so, with Gangwer is one of my most powerful memories of Afghanistan. There's something about being so close to death, and sharing that closeness with another person, that forges an unbreakable bond. I found myself thinking, *Is this going to be the last face I see on earth—Gangwer's? Not Jen's, not my parents'?*

Tyler Gangwer.

That confirmed to me everything I needed to know about Gangwer: He had my back. And I had his. I felt in my heart that this was true of everyone in First Platoon, and maybe even in Battle Company, but you only get so many opportunities (thank God) to have the point so vividly illustrated.

"That was fucking insane," Gangwer said after we had pumped a few thousand rounds into the valley, and the Taliban's resistance began to wither.

"Yeah," I responded. "But you're good. Right? We're okay?"

Gangwer nodded.

"All good."

There were so many bullets flying all across the Korengal that it was hard to know what was happening. I can speak from experience about the fog of war: It's real. And the degree to which you can cope with the insanity is dependent on a variety of factors, training and innate courage being only two of them. Much of combat is beyond your control. You do the best you can. Sometimes you have no idea what has transpired until well after the shooting has ceased.

It wasn't until Gangwer and I scrambled down the hillside to meet up with First Squad that we got the news: Brennan had been shot. I didn't see him right away, so I didn't know whether he'd been killed, severely wounded, or just nicked, but I immediately began to fear the worst. I don't mean to put more value on one life than another, but a platoon is like any other organization: You're closer to some people than you are to others. Josh and I had come up together and become very good friends. The thought that he might not make it out of the valley scared the shit out of me.

"No, it's okay," someone said. "Clean shot through the calf."

By the time I got to Josh, it was apparent that his injuries were not life-threatening. Painful as all hell, yes. But he'd live to fight another day. In fact, if you were to assess the wound based purely on Brennan's response, you'd never have guessed that the guy had even been hit. He took it like a champ. I mean, that was Brennan—as tough as they come—but still . . . the man did not complain at all. He just swallowed the discomfort while the medic worked on him and we tried to figure out a plan for getting him to a real hospital.

Our platoon sergeant at the time was Sergeant First Class Matt Blaskowski, who had come to Battle Company after a stint in Chosen Company. Blaskowski was a taskmaster, and he was prone to rigidity, but he was a good and experienced leader, one who knew firsthand what it was like to get shot in the leg, as it had happened to him on a previous deployment. Blaskowski immediately took control of the situation, getting everyone ready to move out and making sure that Brennan was stabilized.

"Medevac on the way, Sergeant?" I asked.

There was silence.

Apparently not.

I was pissed, but not really surprised. This, too, was life during wartime in the Korengal Valley. Depending on where you were, you could get shot through the calf and still not merit a helicopter ride to the nearest hospital. I'm not suggesting a lack of empathy or concern for the troops on the ground; it was more a matter of logistics, and a lack of resources. For the most part, we relied on the 101st Airborne Division and random National Guard units for air support. It was the strangest thing: All of a sudden, out of the blue, a helicopter would show up, and I'd look at their uniform patch and think, *Never seen that one before . . .*

"Where you from?" I'd say.

"Texas National Guard."

And then I'd pray that the pilot's two weeks of active duty a year was enough to get us out of there safely.

No knock on the National Guard, of course. Those guys are soldiers as well. But this was serious combat, and almost nothing mattered more than experience. Of course, we weren't in a position to be picky. When it came to air support, we gratefully took what we could get. Unfortunately, on this day, none was forthcoming. We were on our own. Like the rest of us, Brennan would have to hump three hours through the mountains, all the way back to the KOP. The difference, obviously, was that no one else had been shot.

To the extent that you can ever say that someone who has been shot is *lucky*, Brennan was lucky. A bullet typically enters the body scientifically designed to produce catastrophic damage. It comes in fast and hot, ripping through every piece of tissue it hits. If it finds bone, well, the effect is messy and extraordinarily debilitating, with shattered fragments acting like shards of glass. But that's nothing compared to what happens when a bullet pierces a vital organ or major artery. Bleeding is instantaneous and potentially fatal. The bullet that found Brennan chose a third path: straight through solid muscle. It entered one side of his calf and exited the other, traveling with such speed and force and heat that it virtually cauterized the wound. There was almost no blood, and Brennan could actually walk fairly well, although with a pronounced limp.

"Just feels like a really bad cramp," he explained.

Having been hit in the calf myself, I knew what he meant. But my wound had merely been a piece of shrapnel that ricocheted off the ground. Josh had been shot. The bullet had passed right through his body. Clean wound or not, there was a difference. And here's the truly amazing thing: After the firefight, we split into two groups. My group stayed out; a second group, comprising men who were going on leave shortly, along with a pair of noncommissioned officers from the Air Force, returned to the KOP. And Brennan led that patrol! Think about that: This guy got shot in the leg, and then walked everyone back so that he could catch a ride on his own Medevac. On the way back I kept telling Josh that he was due for some serious R & R when all of this was over. After all, I'd gotten a week for a ricochet; Brennan deserved at least two weeks, maybe a month.

"Get some ice cream," I joked. "Have some hot food, relax. You've earned it."

Brennan just laughed. A few hours later he was on a chopper bound for Jalalabad, home to a substantial U.S. Army base—bigger than Camp Blessing—equipped with all the comforts of home: hot running water, decent food, electricity. All the stuff you take for granted in the United States, or even in Vicenza, but which seem like incredible luxuries when you're on deployment in the Korengal Valley. Most guys in Brennan's shoes would have hung out at Jalalabad for as long as possible.

Not Josh.

Five days later he stepped out of a chopper at Vegas, itching to get back to work. I had no idea at the time that he was coming back. When the bird touched down, I just presumed it was carrying the usual assortment of supplies—MREs, bullets, water. All of a sudden, out jumped Brennan.

Are you shitting me?

Brennan had a big smile on his face as he approached. You'd have thought the guy was going home, rather than returning to one of the shittiest places on earth.

"You miss us or something?" I said.

He shook his head.

"Nah, just got tired of eating ice cream. Making me fat and slow."

Again, that was Brennan. I don't know how else to put it. That's the kind of guy he was. He came here to do a job, and he was going to finish that job, even if you couldn't define the endpoint. Jalalabad still represented combat duty, but it wasn't like being out here, in the valley. You don't get shot in Jalalabad; you don't sleep on the ground. Relatively speaking, it's a comfortable place. And Brennan gave it up far earlier than was required so that he could return to his platoon. The very next day—I shit you not—he led the patrol.

Brennan was Alpha Team leader, and therefore almost always at the front of patrol. Walking point is a difficult and dangerous job. Difficult because you're in charge of navigation; dangerous because, well, you're out in front: You're the first person to step on the ground, which in a country that has been heavily mined is a serious thing. So you need to watch the ground. You need to watch in front of you. You need to think about navigation. You need to watch up, you need to watch left, and you need to watch right. You have to make sure everyone else is following safely.

That's what it means to walk point.

And the day after he returned to Vegas, less than a week after getting shot, Josh Brennan walked point. You know how I felt about that? I was pissed—not only because he was being so hardheaded, but because inside it made me feel weak and unworthy. Brennan had been more severely wounded than I had been, and he'd spent even less time recovering. Now he'd always have that on me. We were buddies, and we watched out for each other, but there existed between us a healthy sense of competition as well. Brennan never said anything about it, and I'm not sure he even cared in the least. Brennan was not the type to poke at you or dig seriously at stuff that might be upsetting. He was a natural leader, setting an example for all of us, and challenging everyone in ways unspoken but nonetheless vivid.

Still, on some level this bothered me, the fact that as hard as I worked and as much I tried, I might never be the soldier that Brennan was. And you know how it is: You want respect from the people to whom you're closest. It's like playing pickup basketball against your big brother. You want to beat him more than anyone else.

I did admire Brennan after he returned. More than ever. But right after the admiration came a flush of shame.

Boo to me. Damn! Compared to Brennan, I'm a real pussy.

CHAPTER 13

As summer dragged on, fighting in the valley escalated, becoming more intense and exhausting with each passing week as Battle Company and the Taliban leapfrogged from ridge to ridge, exchanging control of the higher ground. Casualties and reassignments—considerations in any wartime scenario, but especially relevant during the endless deployments of Operation Enduring Freedom—had left First Platoon a bit shorthanded. If we were light on bodies, however, we were heavy with experience. You become a combat veteran by firing your weapon, and there was no place on earth in the summer of 2007 more likely to ensure that you'd get that opportunity than the Korengal Valley.

In late August I was moved from Weapons Squad to First Squad, becoming Bravo Team leader in the process. This might sound like a subtle change, since we were all part of First Platoon, but it actually resulted in some rather significant alterations to my daily routine. I went from living with Gangwer and spending almost every waking moment with him and the other guys in Weapons Squad, to suddenly seeing them only one or two days a week. My life revolved around patrols with First Squad, resulting in my first real experience with Staff Sergeant Erick Gallardo.

Gallardo had grown up in Chula Vista, California, and joined the Army right out of high school. Circumstances had forced maturity on the guy—his then girlfriend (now his wife) was pregnant with their first child. That's not an unusual circumstance for people you meet in the Army, but some of them seem to be running away from the responsibility, rather than embracing it. Not Gallardo. He was as serious and focused as anyone I'd ever met. He wasn't much older than me, but there were times when I felt like we were almost of different generations.

Intense and knowledgeable, Gallardo was a no-nonsense leader who had a unique ability to instill integrity and spirit within the squad. He wouldn't unnecessarily punish you for making mistakes, but he would constantly test and push you, asking more questions than anyone could possibly answer correctly. Everyone knew that if Gallardo was your team leader or squad leader, you were going to get smoked on a regular basis, simply because you were going to be constantly quizzed. But there was a method to his madness: Gallardo would always explain the rationale behind the question, relating it to real-life situations. He wasn't on a power trip. He sincerely believed in what he was doing, and he took the job of protecting his country and leading other men into combat quite seriously. Sometimes his intensity could be misconstrued as meanness, but I don't think that concerned Gallardo in the least.

As a squad leader in First Platoon, Gallardo obviously was above me in the chain of command, so I was well aware of his reputation and his performance as a soldier. But until I was reassigned from Weapons Squad to First Squad, our paths did not often cross. We had different jobs, different schedules. That was fine with me, since I could see that he was unusually hard on his men. Like Sergeant Barberet, Gallardo believed in hard work, and his men often put in more time than was typical. Gallardo considered this to be a badge of honor.

"You're going to say I work you harder than everyone else," he would tell men new to his command. "And that's going to be true."

Unlike Barberet, Gallardo was not lax about his own quirks or foibles. You'd never catch Gallardo wearing the wrong belt or mismatched socks, or making a joke about the fact that what was okay for him wasn't necessarily okay for everyone else. Barberet was a ferocious worker and fighter as well, but he wasn't bound to some of the Army's seemingly trivial rules and regulations. Gallardo was, for the most part, spit and polish, and he expected everyone else to be the same way. He set an almost impossibly high standard in every regard: *You're going to be the best, and there will be no debate about it.*

At first I was somewhat hesitant about reporting to Gallardo, but that soon melted away. I had heard the reassignment was forthcoming, and the first conversation between us established a bar set high, and one that I wanted to clear.

"So, you ready to run with the big dogs?" he asked me one day.

"Sergeant?"

"Time to leave the gun team," Gallardo said. "I'm recruiting you for First Squad. You ready?"

Hell yeah, I'm ready!

Actually, I didn't have a choice, but even if I had, I would have accepted the challenge. Moving to First Squad as Bravo Team leader under Sergeant Gallardo automatically meant that my life was about to become harder. I'd be striving to be the best in a lot of ways that weren't in my control. But the great thing about Gallardo, as I soon discovered, was that he was a natural and gifted teacher, the kind of soldier who, while obsessed with protocol and adherence to detail, understood the value of a hands-on approach.

"Let's put the pen and paper aside," he'd say, "and let me show you how we do this."

He would demonstrate, then ask you to do the same. And then the two of you would work on it together, over and over, until you got it right. He was tireless that way, and utterly unflappable. He was, in short, exactly the kind of leader and mentor I needed: smart, aggressive, demanding.

Here's a story that says a lot about Gallardo. Like many soldiers, he had some tattoos, including one on his neck. Now, the Army is generally lenient on the subject of tattoos, if only because outlawing them would seriously diminish the pool of potential recruits. But there are restrictions when it comes to getting ink in certain prominent places, such as the head, face, or neck. Well, after he joined the Army, Gallardo got one fairly small tattoo on his neck, right behind his jawbone. And one day while we were in Italy I heard him getting reamed out because of it. This alone was alarming, because Gallardo never got yelled at; Gallardo was the one who did the yelling. On this occasion, though, a sergeant major had taken issue with Gallardo's new tattoo. I heard him jumping all over Gallardo, demanding that Gallardo recite rules and regulations regarding neck tattoos in the Army.

Gallardo, unflustered as always, stood erect and spat back, word for word, the regulations regarding tattoos on the neck, including precise verbiage about size and location. As it turned out, there is one spot on the neck, just below the collar, where tattoos are barely visible and thus permissible. And that spot is exactly where Gallardo had gotten his tattoo.

This was long before I ever had a chance to serve under Gallardo, but it told me everything I needed to know about the guy. He knew that getting the tattoo was going to provoke some sort of reaction from his superiors. Maybe that's why he did it. He wanted to push the envelope, see what he could get away with. But he was careful to make sure that his position was defensible. In other words, he wasn't reckless. He wasn't an anarchist. Gallardo believed in order and discipline, but he was also a competitor and a fighter, and as such he wasn't opposed to testing boundaries, especially if it helped facilitate a desired result. In that sense, he was a nearly perfect squad leader.

To understand the way things work in the infantry—particularly in a time of war—you have to realize the delicate balance often struck between blind obedience and personal accountability. The tentacles of authority in the infantry stretch from brigade headquarters to the lowliest private. Really, though, in combat, they begin at the level of lieutenant. The lieutenant is an officer, obviously, and as such responsible for reporting to company headquarters, but he's also generally new and inexperienced, so he works in close proximity to the older and presumably more seasoned platoon sergeant. The platoon sergeant oversees a group of thirty to thirty-five men, including three to four squad leaders. Each squad leader is in charge of eight to ten men, including two team leaders. Each team is composed of three to four soldiers.

In my experience, the squad leader is perhaps the most pivotal person when it comes to carrying out a mission, as each squad leader is given considerable leeway when it comes to running his own men. If a senior officer is by necessity a bureaucrat, juggling the demands of politicians and officers both above and below, the squad leader is more like a sled dog trainer, a handful of ropes in each fist. He controls all the dogs, but mainly he controls the lead dog, and he knows the others will follow like a pack.

The lead dog is almost always the Alpha Team leader. The alpha dog, so to speak, is smart and aggressive. In our case, that dog was Josh Brennan. It was up to Gallardo to hold the reins on Brennan, giving him enough rope to do his job, while also providing direction and assistance. My job, as Bravo Team leader, was similar to Brennan's: to take the fight to the enemy. It's up to the squad leader to orchestrate all of these movements, to pull and assist and direct and maneuver, but at the same time let some slack out . . . allow the dogs to do their work.

Combat is messy business, and it's certainly not for everyone. And it takes a special person to be a squad leader. They are confident and authoritative, but not authoritarian. I look back at guys like Barberet and Gallardo—they never held the reins too tightly. They believed in letting the pack run—and running with the pack, of course. I liked that kind of aggressiveness; I responded to it. I think most men in the infantry feel the same way, because you know that when the shit hits the fan—and it *will* hit the fan, because it always does, eventually—you just follow the squad leader and he will take you to the right path.

He'll bring you home.

It's hard to comprehend that sort of emotional attachment if you've never experienced anything like it. And unless you've been in combat, you probably haven't. It's a willingness to follow someone to the end of the earth, under the harshest of circumstances. That's what we all felt for

Gallardo. If he had said, "Guys, I'm going to Hell this afternoon; anybody want to tag along?" we all would have raised our hands. Because we knew it would be okay; we knew that somehow Gallardo would bring us back safely. That's the way I felt about him—that no matter how terrible the journey or the mission might be, the outcome wasn't in doubt, and the sacrifices made along the way were undoubtedly worthwhile.

I was proud as hell to be in First Squad, to be working under Gallardo, alongside Brennan, and to be in charge of Bravo Team. This was my first time in an actual leadership role, in a combat situation, and I was determined to make the most of the opportunity; to be the kind of leader I admired, like Brennan and Gallardo.

Under my command, on Bravo Team, were Kaleb Casey, Garrett Clary, and Derek Griego. Those were my boys, and what I hoped most of all was that they would someday feel the same way about me that I felt about Gallardo. That was a noble enough goal, for it also included the unspoken goal of getting everyone home alive and in one piece. I wanted to be their version of Gallardo, and they were everything I had tried to be while coming up. Although they were newer in the platoon, I knew them well; thanks to my demotion, we'd all been privates together. Now, though, I was a specialist, and my job was to take care of them. I took that responsibility seriously.

In some respects, Casey and Clary were like twins—roughly the same wiry build, same coloring, same habits and hobbies, and practically inseparable; I had trouble sometimes telling them apart, even though they didn't actually look alike or sound alike. Both were chain-smoking, Skoal-dipping, thrash-metal-loving kids. Casey, our SAW gunner, was a good ol' boy from Florida; Clary, who manned the M203 grenade launcher, had grown up in Spokane, Washington. So you had two guys from opposite sides of the country, and yet they acted as though they had been raised in the same household. Nicotine was a popular drug in Afghanistan—I'd say more guys smoked or dipped than abstained; some did both. But rarely did you find anyone who smoked and dipped at the same time. Casey and Clary each fell into that category. You'd see one of them put a huge dip in his mouth, then grab a cigarette and light up.

"Dude, that's so awful," I'd say. But they were totally cool with it. I suppose when you're twenty years old and people are shooting at you, the prospect of cancer doesn't seem all that bad, or even worth considering.

Casey and Clary were also fond of something we used to call "redipping," for lack of a better term. It's precisely what it sounds like: putting a wad of used tobacco back in the pouch so that it can be used again at a later date. I know this because I fell prey to it once on patrol, when we'd been out for hours and we all were Starvin' Marvin. Unsure of how long we'd be humping, and not wanting to break into my food supply prematurely, I decided to take a little dip. Now, I wasn't a total amateur when it came to chewing tobacco. I'd dipped some in high school, like most of my buddies, but since neither smoking nor chewing was allowed in basic training, I had decided to quit right before I joined the Army. Once I'd kicked the habit, there was no reason to go back. So I was in the minority in First Platoon, in that I had no tobacco habit whatsoever. What I knew from experience, though, was that tobacco in any form could suppress hunger, so I asked Casey for some of his dip.

He held out a pouch and I rooted around a bit, until my fingers came across something solid. A chunk surrounded by all those finely chopped leaves.

"What the hell is this?" I said, holding it up.

"Oh, hey, dude . . . stay away from that," Casey said. "That's my redip."

Slack-jawed, I flicked the chunk back into the pouch. Before I could express my disgust, Clary chirped in.

"No, man, that's not your redip. That's mine!"

I wiped my hand across my chest.

"Are you kidding me? You don't know who this belongs to?"

With that, Casey reached into the pouch, pulled out the used wad of dip, and popped it into his mouth.

"Mine now," he said, spitting on the ground for emphasis.

That was Casey and Clary: Tweedledum and Tweedledee. A couple of funny, vulgar, gifted soldiers. They were great guys who did everything together, whether it was right or wrong. On the battlefield, where it mattered most, they were usually right, sometimes heroically so. But there is no correlation between a soldier's ability to fight and his willingness to live by the conventions of society when he's not in the fight. In fact, sometimes the two things are diametrically opposed. Clary had gotten into a nasty bar brawl in Vicenza, ended up getting tossed down some stairs by a bouncer and suffering a severely broken ankle that required surgery to repair. So he wound up humping around the hills of Afghanistan with a bunch of screws and pins in his leg. Didn't seem to bother him in the least.

Casey and Clary both liked to play video games and drink and party and have fun. They were raw as hell when they got to Afghanistan, and it was interesting to see them grow and develop. As their team leader, I took great satisfaction in watching their progression, seeing how well they reacted to combat, and how they would look out for each other. If Casey had a problem, Clary would help him out; and vice versa. They were a team: "Casey-Clary"—that's what we called them. One word for two men.

And then there was Griego, a rifleman from California who actually came from a military family (his father had served in Ranger Battalion). Griego was one of the smaller guys in the unit, maybe five-foot-eight, 145 pounds. He filled out the team nicely, in that he provided balance to Casey and Clary. He was as quiet and subdued as they were loud and raucous. Griego was an ambitious kid; he talked a lot about following in his dad's footsteps and going to Ranger School. Whether he felt some need to measure himself against what his father had accomplished, I don't really know. But he was a fine soldier in his own right.

My leadership style was modeled after what I had learned from my friend Nicholas Post during our first deployment. I wanted to be approachable and not get too hung up on the differences in our ranks. First of all, as young as these guys were, they were nonetheless experienced

combat vets, having seen more action in the first few months of their initial deployment than I had seen in an entire year on my first deployment. Moreover, a mere two months earlier we had been equal in rank; now I was in a position of leadership. And then there was the fact that when it came to First Squad, I was the new guy.

"Call me Sal," I told the guys. "That's my name, and I like it. I prefer Sal."

I certainly didn't abdicate my authority or responsibilities, but this mode of leadership worked well for me. I worked with the men on my team, and I worked for them. I was open to their input and ideas.

"I'm not right all of the time," I'd say. "In fact, I'm probably not right most of the time, so I want to know what you think. I respect your opinion."

The most interesting and satisfying thing for me was to watch these kids become competent soldiers. The beauty of the Army—and I do think there is a beauty to it, something worth admiring and acknowledging—is that it provides an opportunity for success, in a very large and important way, for people who might otherwise fall through the cracks. As I look back on it now, I can see that we were a collection of people with an assortment of quirks and unusual personality traits, and maybe that's what helped us get through our time in the Korengal Valley—the fact that we weren't quite "normal." In ways large and small, and to varying degrees, we fell out of the mainstream. But we came together in Afghanistan to do the hardest and most dangerous kind of work, the work no one else was willing to do; and for the most part, it was done without complaint.

———

The first time I met Hugo Mendoza was during a training exercise in Germany, while awaiting our second deployment. I'd been sent to a different base for a two-week specialty course; while I was away, Mendoza had joined the platoon as a 68W—a military occupational specialist.

A medic.

I walked into the barracks one day and there he was, a new guy, sprawled across the bare wire springs of a bunk bed. In a room with thirty-five guys, every one of whom I knew intimately, Mendoza stood out not only because he was the only unfamiliar face, but because he clearly was a few years older than most of the guys. You could see that in his face, and you could hear it in his voice. At twenty-nine years of age, Mendoza was a decade older than some of the guys in the room, and while he'd never been in combat before, his voice and demeanor reflected a maturity you simply don't see in kids who are just a year or two removed from high school.

We talked for a while that day, and I could tell right away that I would like Mendoza, and that he'd fit in well with First Platoon. He'd graduated from high school in Phoenix, but still considered himself a Texas boy to the core, having spent most of his childhood and adolescence in El Paso. There was no military lineage to speak of in Mendoza's family. The guy had been working in a sheet metal factory for a while, but wanted to do something more with his life. It wasn't just the guns and excitement that brought Mendoza to Afghanistan (although those might have contributed, as they did for all of us); it was the need to give back, to be part of something larger. Infantrymen, as I've noted, tend to be aggressive, hard-charging types, particularly in the 173rd. A medic surviving in Battle Company had to possess the requisite strength and courage, but he needed something else as well.

Mendoza, like most combat medics I came across, had a generosity of spirit, a willingness to sacrifice for all the other guys around him. We all carried guns, of course, regardless of what our job might have been, but some of us, like Mendoza, had a more complicated specialty. He wanted to be in the fight, but he also wanted to be a first responder. When a fellow soldier went down, his job was no longer to kill the enemy, but to come to the aid of his brother, often at great risk to his own safety. I couldn't possibly have more respect for someone who signs up to be a 68

Whiskey. Those guys are almost always genuine, good-hearted, good-natured, giving people. Mendoza certainly fell into that category. That very first day, as he and I talked, a steady stream of soldiers approached him and asked for aid and advice. The platoon had been on a long march that day, resulting in the usual assortment of lower-extremity ailments: cramps, blood blisters, ingrown toenails. Mendoza calmly inspected the wounds and cheerfully doled out moleskin and Band-Aids and antibiotic ointment. Keep in mind that he had completed the very same march alongside these guys. And now he was taking care of them. If he had any aches or pains of his own, he kept it to himself.

That's what a medic does.

It couldn't have been easy for him, either. Not only was he a decade older than the rest of the guys, but Mendoza, who stood maybe five-foot-eight, was also a good twenty pounds overweight by infantry standards. Not that he was the only guy in the platoon with a thicker build, but most of us were fairly lean and fit. A few extra pounds on a twelve-mile hike, while carrying a full pack, could be exhausting. But I never heard Mendoza complain. It wasn't his nature.

A couple of days after that initial introduction, I went to Mendoza for some professional assistance. While showering I'd discovered a tick embedded high on my leg, close to my groin. I picked at it for a moment, unsure of it what it was, and quickly determined that not only was it alive, but it wasn't coming out without a fight. I tried to play it cool, but the truth was, having a tick doing its business so close to a part of my body that was really important to me . . . well, it made me more than a little uncomfortable. And when I mentioned it to some of the other guys, they treated the tick with more reverence and concern than they'd shown when I took a piece of shrapnel on the first deployment:

"Dude, those things carry Lyme disease. Don't fuck around with it."

"Yeah, and they burrow in. So don't just yank it out—its head will get stuck!"

"Better see the doc."

And so there I was, taking off my pants in front of a guy I'd just met, explaining my predicament. Mendoza was cool about the whole thing, although his treatment plan concerned me.

"No worries," he said. "We'll just burn it off."

"Umm . . . excuse me?"

"Yeah, that's the most effective way to deal with ticks. Light 'em up, and they fall right off. Don't leave anything behind."

I looked down at my package, and the tick just a few inches away.

"Maybe we should get a second opinion."

Mendoza shrugged.

"If it'll make you feel better."

So we consulted with another medic, who agreed with Mendoza's assessment. Next thing I knew, Mendoza fired up a handheld lighter, placed it on its side, and let the flame roast the surrounding metal components. When it began to glow, Mendoza picked up what was now essentially a miniature soldering iron and placed it lightly against my skin. I felt nothing, merely watched with amazement as the little black bugger released its grip and fell to the floor.

"Hey . . . nice job, Doc. Thanks."

"No charge."

Mendoza and I became friends; everyone considered him a friend. He was, for the most part, quiet and unassuming, and since he was significantly older than most of the guys, he shared my taste in music: classic rock. When we got back to Italy, he and I spent a fair amount of time together. Once, we spent a long night drinking in town; I was surprised to see that Mendoza could really put away the beer. And he was a happy drunk, which made him fun to be around. Although Mendoza was a perfectly capable soldier, I never got the sense that he had an angry bone in his body. He was not married; he did not have children. And yet, he behaved in a paternal manner, always asking how you were doing, how you felt, whether you needed any help. He sometimes talked about how he was going to be a firefighter when he got out of the Army.

That made sense to me. For Doc Mendoza, life was about trying to figure out ways to be useful; to give back.

———

Specialist Frank Eckrode was a SAW gunner on Brennan's Alpha Team. His father had been a career military man, so Eckrode grew up on the road, bouncing from base to base. When I first met Eckrode in Italy, I was struck mainly by his appearance. About five-foot-seven and 135 pounds, with sandy brown hair and traces of acne, he looked impossibly young. You hear the term "baby-faced" used to describe some people, and it certainly was applicable to Eckrode. There were a lot of "kids" in the Army, people who had signed on right after high school and thus looked like they weren't old enough to drive, let alone fight and die for their country. But Eckrode was on the far end of the spectrum.

Unlike Casey and Clary, Eckrode was quiet and introspective. Like Gangwer, he was fascinated by fantasy—books, movies, video games. You name it. If it involved dwarves and elves and wizards and warlocks, Eckrode was into it. He was the first person I'd ever met who collected figurines. He owned literally thousands of little plastic and porcelain goblins and trolls, many of which he had painted himself by hand. Nothing wrong with that, of course—we all have hobbies. But Eckrode had brought his entire collection to Vicenza, which naturally made him something of a target with guys like Casey and Clary. In garrison, Eckrode would hang out in his room all night, drinking Mountain Dew and playing video games. For some reason he liked to sleep in his chair rather than his bed, and he hardly ate anything.

Sometimes I'd walk into his room and see him sitting there, controller in hand, figurines out on the bed, and I'd wonder how the hell he was going to survive Vicenza, let alone deployment to Afghanistan.

"Dude, put those things away, all right?" I said the first time I saw the collection. "If they're important to you, that's cool, but pack them up and send them home."

Eckrode seemed hurt and confused.

"Why, what's the big deal?"

"Trust me, it's not going to go over well with some of these guys."

"Why not? Gangwer likes this stuff, and nobody says anything."

I laughed.

"Gangwer is six-three, two-thirty . . . he can do whatever he wants to do."

But here's the thing about Eckrode: When you put him in the field, he was every bit the soldier that any of us was. You could count on him, and that's all that mattered. What I hope to convey here is the sense that while virtually everyone in First Platoon (and probably everyone in Battle Company) possessed unusual traits and characteristics that might have made it challenging for them to fit in elsewhere, they were incredibly professional and courageous when called upon to serve their country in a combat situation. I really don't know whether this is more a reflection of the training we all received, or of the type of personality that is drawn to the infantry. I suppose it's some combination of the two. I do believe this: There are a lot of young men out there who by any reasonable definition would be considered more "normal" than the men with whom I served in Battle Company; guys who are smart and talented and successful in their own right. But I think damn few of them would have succeeded in the 173rd. The experience would have broken them; hell, it would break most people. You walk eight to ten hours in ninety-degree heat, with fifty pounds on your back, then you get into a firefight and watch one of your buddies get killed; you stand there watching the helicopter taking him away, knowing the entire time that you're going to do it all over again tomorrow.

That can break anyone's spirit. It can crush morale. For some reason, though, it never did. Not in Battle Company, not in First Platoon. I can't explain it. I don't know if there was a common denominator—some specific philosophical, moral, or psychological trait we all shared. I just know that when I looked around, I saw a bunch of guys who would not quit. They knew why they were there. They understood the price, and they paid it willingly. And for me, to be in a senior role or a leadership role and to watch these guys grow up and become an incredible fighting force was enormously satisfying. One day they're struggling to put on their night vision goggles, and the next they're behaving like a perfectly choreographed team in the midst of a firefight, taking care of each other, wiping out the enemy, and defending their country in a war most people don't understand or even care to know much about.

To me, that's the height of professionalism, and by talking about how quirky or unusual some of us might have been, I'm really talking about how much it didn't matter.

Normal?

I don't even know what it means anymore. Does it mean "typical" or "average"? If so, then I guess we weren't normal. Guys like Eckrode and Gangwer and Casey and Clary; guys like Brennan and Gallardo. All of them, really. I don't think they're normal at all. I don't think they're average and I don't think they're typical. I think they're amazing people who did their part to make this country great. I'm proud to have fought beside them, and I think it's worth noting that without the Army, many of them might never have had the chance to show what they could do.

I don't know why they signed up for the job. Maybe they wanted to make a difference. Maybe they just wanted to shoot someone. I do know that every one of these men accepted the hard times and the boring times and performed to the best of their ability. For some of them, maybe combat was the one thing in life they were truly meant to do, the one thing that gave them purpose and meaning. And they were fucking great at it.

There is a reason less than 1 percent of the country fights: because the vast majority of people possess neither the aptitude nor the inclination to fight. If you're out there with a gun in your hand, you hope the other 99 percent at least support what you're doing or appreciate the individual efforts of the men involved. But I can honestly say that it didn't really matter.

For the 1 percent, being there was enough. For them, for all of us, the world didn't exist beyond the Korengal Valley.

PART FOUR

Rock Avalanche

CHAPTER 14

October 6, 2007

Hey Baby,

Well today is a good day. It didn't seem like it was going to be but it all has worked out OK. I had the board today to become a sergeant and what do you know— they actually believe that I make a good leader! So next month I get paid like a hundred extra bucks per month for my four years. Then when I get pinned in December, I will make like another 200 on top of that, so that should be nice. It sounds like we don't have a bird to take us anywhere until the 9th, so I will be able to talk to you on your double-dozen birthday. Just think after today you will never be twenty-three again. Jeepers it looks like all you got left is a quarter of a century and then you are for sure old. I wonder if people will ask me who the hot older chick is in the pictures with me. Haha we can only hope.

I love you Jenny, and miss you tons.

—Sal

Funny thing about talking with the people you love when you're on deployment—whether by phone or email or snail mail. It's supposed to make you feel better, but it doesn't. It makes you feel worse. It makes you realize how much you wish you were somewhere else, and how much you've come to hate the work you do, and how much you've changed, and not necessarily for the better.

You can't really share much anyway. It isn't fair to share the gory details of combat with your girlfriend or wife, or with your parents. All they want to hear is that you are alive and well, and that you'll be coming home to them soon. I get that. I understand it. They shouldn't have to bear the burden of knowledge; it's enough that they spend all their time worrying. So you try to put up a front, keep the conversations light and superficial. But it's hard, so you end up making fewer phone calls, writing fewer letters or emails. You get stuck in your head, which isn't necessarily the best place to be.

So when I sat down at the laptop that afternoon to hammer out a quick note to Jen, I tried to focus on the good stuff, like the fact that I was relaxing in relative comfort and safety at Camp Blessing, having just passed my board and earned the rank of sergeant (although the official promotion would not take place for a few more months). I'd finally caught up with my buddies! That was a good thing, and worth sharing and celebrating.

What I didn't tell Jen is that less than two weeks earlier, on September 23, we had lost our platoon daddy, Sergeant First Class Blaskowski. I can't say that I was particularly close to Sergeant Blaskowski—he was well ahead of me in the chain of command and was not the sort of person who believed in informality when interacting with his troops.

Blaskowski was a serious soldier and a hard man. He'd grown up in Michigan, enlisted right after graduating high school, and been in the Army nearly ten years by the time I met him. Blaskowski was well regarded as a fierce and loyal leader. He'd been shot in the leg during a previous deployment to Afghanistan, in 2005, and was awarded the

Silver Star and Purple Heart in the process. The official Army narrative that accompanied the citation for that event read as follows:

> *Numerous times, Staff Sgt. Blaskowski placed himself at great risk while engaging the enemy positions and relaying directions to his machine gun crews. Blaskowski's unwavering valor and understanding of his mission fixed a determined enemy and prevented them from maneuvering in any direction, thereby allowing First Platoon to destroy 17 enemy in the orchard, breaking all resistance in the valley. Blaskowski fought with dogged determination even after he was wounded in the leg pulling a wounded soldier to safety, maintaining his position for another hour until he was able to help other wounded soldiers to safety.*

At the time of that incident, Blaskowski was a Weapons Squad leader in Chosen Company. We all knew he'd come by his reputation honestly, and we respected the hell out of him. Still, I have to admit that he was not the easiest guy in the world to get along with. Sergeant Blaskowski was rigid and demanding. He brought to Battle Company various methods of operation and attitude that he'd developed while in Chosen Company, and that naturally rubbed some of us the wrong way. It's a simple fact of life in the Army that every battalion finds itself superior to other battalions, every company think it's the best within a battalion, and every platoon believes it's the best within a given company.

And so on.

It's all a matter of pride.

In Battle Company, we were accustomed to doing things differently than they were done in Chosen Company. I'm not saying our way was the right way or the only way to accomplish a given task or mission; it was simply familiar to us. Blaskowski came into Battle Company, kicked a little ass (as new sergeants sometimes do), and it definitely got our attention. There was no questioning his expertise or experience—the guy had multiple deployments under his belt—so even if we weren't particularly fond of the suddenly accelerated pace at which we were expected to work, we couldn't use cluelessness or arrogance as an excuse for our griping. You don't get to be a platoon sergeant in the Korengal Valley without knowing your shit, and Blaskowski was clearly seasoned. The basics never change: patrolling the region, improving and upgrading bases (mending fences and HESCOs), pulling guard duty. Vigilance is paramount. When so much time is spent waiting around for the action to commence, complacency is problematic.

Not with Sergeant Ski, as we called him. He simply did not tolerate it. He insisted that conditions at Vegas and Little Rock be as safe and secure as they could possibly be, even if that meant working twenty hours a day, every single day. There was never a moment of downtime when Blaskowski was in charge of the platoon. He worked us to the freaking bone, but like any good leader, he did it for our benefit, not out of any sense of self-aggrandizement. Sometimes, when I was exhausted, I'd think back to the way Vegas looked when we first arrived, in a state of advanced deterioration, with no pride of ownership. It didn't look that way anymore. The place was safer, more attractive (as attractive as a mud hut on the side of a mountain could be, anyway), and generally well maintained. Its appearance spoke to us and it spoke to the enemy: *The people who live here are not to be taken lightly.*

The platoon sergeant's primary job is to make sure that every man under his command returns home alive, and Blaskowski did not take that responsibility lightly. In many ways he was one of the best leaders I've ever known. The sad irony is that almost all of the men in his platoon did in fact return home alive; Blaskowski did not. And he died in a way that surely would have pissed him off.

It happened on September 23, while Sergeant Ski was giving a reporter from Al Jazeera a tour of Firebase Vegas. They had strayed a short distance from the HESCOs, to a point not far from the base latrine, when a sniper's bullet punctured Blaskowski's neck. It still bothers me to this day that I was not at Vegas when this went down; I was at the Korengal Outpost with First Squad, taking our turn refitting, showering, getting a hot meal. I was sitting around with Tom Hunter when the news came squawking over the radio that Vegas was under attack. That's about the worst feeling in the world—to know that your boys are under fire, and you're not there with them. All we could do was listen to the fight as it played out in real time. We could hear the echo of mortar fire from Vegas, an epic response to what turned out to be nothing more than a simple but lethal sniper attack. We could hear it through the radio speakers, and then, seconds later, we could hear it echo through the valley.

Blaskowski died within a matter of minutes, bled out on the Medevac as they were taking him up. I couldn't help but think that if ever there was a guy who deserved better, it was Sergeant Ski. He was the consummate soldier; he'd survived a hellish firefight two years earlier; he was one of the more experienced combat veterans in Battle Company; and now he'd been killed by a single bullet from an enemy he never even saw. And he wasn't even fighting at the time. This was every soldier's nightmare, to take a bullet while simply going about your business. There is no good way to die, of course, but some are better than others. Like I said before: If you had to go, you wanted to go down swinging, looking your enemy in the eye, telling him to fuck off right before you drew your last breath.

———

The first time that I heard about Operation Rock Avalanche, I was actually still at Camp Blessing following my sergeant's board in early October. I was feeling pretty good about things, waiting for a ride back out to the KOP and then to Vegas, when I ran into some guy from the Asymmetrical Warfare Group, an Army unit established during the war on terrorism specifically to provide "observation, analysis, training, and advisory support to Army and Joint Force units in order to enhance their capabilities to predict, mitigate, counter, and defeat asymmetric threats and methods." That's the official company line, anyway. The AWG is an elite force of some four hundred personnel that supplies advice to commanders on tactics and strategy devised by the enemy, along with methods of countering those tactics. These guys are in the military, just like me, but their role is strategic. We work the front lines; they work behind the scenes. I can only presume that they are a lot smarter than I am.

And a lot more well-informed.

"So, where are you headed?" one of the AWG guys asked me one day.

He did not look like a soldier; thin and fragile, with a slight scruff of facial hair, he looked more like a scientist or a policy geek. I didn't know what to say, whether I owed him a response or not. The guy's uniform did not even reflect a specific rank.

"Uhhhh . . . back to Vegas," I finally said. "Battle Company, First Platoon."

The guy smiled knowingly and began nodding his head, like I'd offered some sort of secret code.

"Ohhhh . . . yeah," he said. "You guys are gearing up for Rock Avalanche, huh?"

I had absolutely no idea what the hell he was talking about, and frankly I found his demeanor to be kind of creepy.

"I'm sorry," I began. "Rock Avalanche?"

He kept nodding.

"Yeah, you know . . . the big mission."

"I don't mean to be rude," I said, "but I don't know anything about that."

The guy never stopped smiling.

"Okay," he said. "You will."

I put the whole thing out of my mind as soon as I left Blessing. To be perfectly candid, the guy seemed to be a few bricks short of a load, and despite the fact that he claimed to be working for AWG, I didn't find him to be a credible source of information, let alone intelligence. It wasn't until a few weeks later, when I heard about an actual battalionwide mission named Rock Avalanche, that I truly came to understand the way things work in the Army. Dissemination of information really is on a need-to-know basis. Everything works from the top down. The guys who hold the guns? We're usually the last to know. On this one occasion, though, I'd circumvented the chain of command, simply by being in the right place at the right time, and running into someone who couldn't keep his mouth shut.

The name "Rock Avalanche" had nothing to do with the specific goal or tactical plan of the mission. "Rock" was a reference to our battalion nickname, the Rock, and "Avalanche," as I noted earlier, was just a reference to a professional hockey team. But it sounded badass; it sounded like a mission designed to generate mayhem and a body count, and to discourage insurgent activity in the process. In that regard, it was an entirely appropriate name.

The most widespread and ambitious operation of the entire deployment, Rock Avalanche involved the simultaneous mobilization of Able Company, Battle Company, Chosen Company, and Destined Company—some four hundred heavily armed men, along with air support, and in conjunction with the Afghan National Army, moving aggressively into Taliban strongholds, looking for caches of weapons and trying to shut down popular routes of travel. A second goal of the mission was to establish peace and cooperation with the local civilians so that a road could be safely constructed in the region by the Afghan government. But we all knew that Rock Avalanche was primarily a combat mission. We were going to take the fight to the enemy in a very big way. Operation Rock Avalanche was about an entire battalion actively going out and pushing into areas that were known to be troublesome. In effect, we had decided to kick the biggest and nastiest hornet's nest in all of Afghanistan, and we could expect to get stung in the process.

Planning for Battle Company's portion of the mission was carried out at the Korengal Outpost, using the biggest damn sand table I've ever seen. We must have brought in four hundred pounds of sand by wheelbarrow and poured it onto the building's concrete floor, covering an area at least twenty feet long and ten feet wide. Sand tables, as I noted earlier, were a commonly used planning tool on deployment, but this one was uniquely large and detailed, depicting much of the Korengal Valley, with an emphasis on an area of roughly ten square kilometers and Battle Company's progression throughout the course of the operation. Every important landmark was noted—every mountain, every village, every outpost and trail. Model helicopters dangled from the rafters, hovering over potential hot spots and landing zones.

The sheer scope of the mission, and the number of people involved, practically guaranteed that the company would suffer casualties. This realization alone was enough to infuse the briefing with an unusually somber tone. We approached every mission with professionalism and seriousness, but Rock Avalanche promised to be especially dangerous and demanding.

Briefings for the operation stretched across three days. The actual mission began on the night of October 20. Right before we left, Captain Kearney pulled everyone together and offered his version of a pep talk.

"Good luck, boys," he said.

And that was about it.

It may not sound like much, but the thing is . . . Kearney had never done that before. We'd been through many missions and many patrols since we arrived in the Korengal, and the company commander had never wished us luck. To a soldier whose heart is racing, every detail, every word, takes on added importance. I'd never spent three days preparing for a mission. I'd never seen so many people higher in the chain of command gathered at the Korengal Outpost. For some reason, though, those few simple words from Kearney did the most to drive home the fact that Rock Avalanche was different. This one was a game changer.

Uncertain how long we would be out in the field, we packed an enormous amount of gear and waited for the helicopters to arrive. Battle Company was headed to the southwestern part of the valley, to a town called Yaka Chine. Although normally we walked when going out on patrol, this was too great a distance, carrying too much equipment and firepower, to safely travel by foot—we risked being exhausted before we even arrived at our destination. So we'd be traveling by Chinook, with Apache escorts.

First Platoon had never been to Yaka Chine before, but we knew from the briefing that it was located in a region where once there had been so much lumber that the townspeople enjoyed a very comfortable existence, and now they were hurting and unhappy. We also knew Yaka Chine was a Taliban stronghold, strategically located along a route by which weapons and money flowed into and out of the Korengal Valley. We believed strongly—and intelligence supported this viewpoint—that Yaka Chine was a hotbed of insurgent activity. If we could stop or at least strongly discourage the gun traffic through Yaka Chine, we could seriously disrupt the Taliban's grip on the entire Korengal Valley. My personal opinion—and soldiers do have opinions, although they are rarely expressed—was that the Korengal Valley kept us busy enough without venturing off to Yaka Chine. But the Army viewed Operation Rock Avalanche as a strike at the head of the serpent: Cut it off and the body will die. All this other shit, all the death and destruction across the breadth of the valley, will come to a swift and sudden end.

As was true with most military activity in the Korengal, our plans were contingent on gaining some cooperation from the local populace. Even under ideal circumstances, this was never easy, and Yaka Chine was far from ideal. The very first night in Yaka China we experienced small-arms fire. And we returned fire. It was an intensely hostile situation, and one almost guaranteed to result in casualties. On some level I understood the frustration of the locals. We'd tried to compensate for the loss of their lumber trade by offering bags of rice, and they resented it. It was charitable, but a short-term, ineffective solution—like giving a man a fish instead of teaching him how to fish.

And they were pissed.

The shooting began almost as soon as we arrived, the Apaches overhead dropping hot shells all around us as they swept the area of insurgent activity, trying to make it reasonably safe for us to camp for the night. Intelligence units had been spread across the area as well, and combined with surveillance drones they were able to track Taliban movement in our vicinity. Enemy fighters were quickly dispatched with an impressive display of force, using heavy artillery on the ground and B-1 bombers and Apaches from the air. It was a flexing of muscle designed not only to provide security for troops on the ground, but also to let the Taliban know we meant business.

We spent the first night roughly a klick from the village, high on a ridgeline, overlooking a farmhouse. We took turns pulling guard duty, trying to get a few minutes of sleep, but tension and anxiety made it difficult. I finally nodded off shortly before daybreak, only to be awakened by the sound of Gangwer yelling.

"Hey, you! Stop!"

My first reaction was one of annoyance—*Shut the fuck up, Gangwer!* When I sat up, though, I could see that Gangwer was not kidding around. A short distance away, no more than thirty meters, was an Afghan male with an RPG launcher slung over one shoulder and a bag, presumably filled with ammo, over the other.

Gangwer yelled again.

"Stop right there!"

The man did not respond. Instead, clearly surprised to learn that he had nearly stumbled across an U.S. Army unit, he began sprinting away. Gangwer, who already had the guy in his sights, squeezed the trigger of his rifle. Instantly, the man lit up like a sparkler, and then burst into a human fireball.

"Holy fuck!" Gangwer said.

I'd seen a lot of weird shit in Afghanistan, but never anything quite like this. The bullet must have hit the guy's ammo bag, which acted as a propellant. There was no explosion, but merely a quiet eruption of flames, like a book of matches igniting. And then he was gone, seemingly lifted off the side of the mountain by the force of fire.

Awe was quickly replaced by relief as we realized how close this guy had come to our position. It reinforced what we already knew: that Yaka Chine was literally crawling with insurgents.

We spent the next twelve hours sitting and watching. Waiting. At some point Sergeant Gallardo informed us that there was trouble in the village below. During the massive display of firepower the night before, a bombing raid had killed not only insurgents, but five civilians; nearly a dozen others, all women and children, had been injured, a tragedy that obviously heightened animosity.

This sort of collateral damage was in some ways the most difficult thing for me or any other American soldier in Afghanistan or Iraq to cope with. I mean, it didn't compare to losing a buddy, obviously, but no one wanted to be responsible for causing the deaths of women and children. But guilt and sadness weren't the only emotions I felt on these occasions. I also felt anger . . . rage.

If you're so damned concerned about what happens to innocent civilians, then why do you allow them to offer protection to the Taliban?

This was the primary conundrum when fighting in the Korengal Valley: distinguishing between the real enemy and the imagined enemy; between fighters and people who were aiding and abetting. It made a difficult war nearly impossible, and an ugly war almost indescribably brutal. Now, just a few hours into Operation Rock Avalanche, we'd been confronted with a scenario virtually guaranteed to complicate matters considerably. A meeting took place involving some of the village elders and Captain Kearney and Lieutenant Colonel William Ostlund, our brigade commander. I wasn't involved in those conversations, but it didn't take long for a virtual transcript of the narrative to work its way down the chain of command.

The elders were seriously pissed, and despite their best efforts at negotiation, it was clear that Lieutenant Colonel Ostlund and Captain Kearney were unable to assuage their anger. By the time we flew out of Yaka Chine, the elders had declared jihad against American forces in the Korengal Valley.

Things were about to get weird in a very different and more dangerous way.

———

We did not go back to Vegas right away. Instead, we moved on to the next phase of the operation, which would take us to a ridgeline of the Abas Ghar, where Battle Company's job was to offer support to Chosen Company as it checked villages in the neighboring Shuryak Valley for Taliban activity. Basically, we were looking for "squirters"—insurgents who might flee the villages during raids, and then try to reclaim the high ground.

Most of First Platoon stayed there for two days, watching and pulling guard duty, waiting for something to happen. We'd been out for nearly four days and had slept less than ten hours during the entire time. We were tired and on edge, but thus far the mission had not generated nearly as much contact as we had anticipated. That all changed on the morning of October 23, when gunfire rang out from a part of the Abas Ghar known as the Gatigal Spur, roughly in the vicinity of where Second Platoon was located. Specifically, it came from a spot known as Honcho Hill.

We were roughly a kilometer away, close enough to hear the gunfire, to feel the RPGs exploding, but not close enough to know what was happening, or to offer any assistance. Radio contact was chaotic and fragmented, and provided only snippets of information. It wasn't until the shooting stopped that we began to get some idea of what had happened. I was sitting on the ground at the time, bullshitting with Brennan, Eckrode, and Pistol Pete. Casey and Clary were nearby; Griego, as part of my team, would normally have been there, too, but he'd recently gone on mid-deployment leave and missed Rock Avalanche. We all knew there had been some sort of firefight, more intense than usual, but we were accustomed to the sound of bombs exploding in the valley and just sort of presumed that everything had turned out okay. We were wrong.

"We got KIAs," Gallardo said as he approached our group. "We got WIAs. The shit's hitting the fan down there."

I was stunned. KIA stood for "killed in action" and WIA for "wounded in action." We all jumped to our feet and grabbed our gear, ready to go to war. But there was no place to go, nothing that could be done, except to wait for orders and information. Slowly, over the next ten to fifteen minutes, news began to roll in. A scout team and a gun team had been overrun by enemy fighters. There had been casualties, including at least one fatality. When information about KIAs goes out over the radio, names are never given; a fallen soldier is identified by the first initial of his last name, followed by the last four digits of his social security number. In this case, the soldier's last name began with the letter R. We all silently began doing a mental checklist of everyone in Second Platoon who fell into this category. There were four possibilities—four men we knew well, and one of them was now dead. And we couldn't do anything about it.

Eventually we began moving in the direction of Second Platoon, and as we drew closer, the information became more concrete. The man who had been killed was Sergeant Larry Rougle, a scout team leader who proudly wore the nickname "Wildcat."

I did not know Rougle well, but I did know him. He was something of a legend in Battle Company, a strong, smart, good-looking guy who had grown up in New Jersey and had come to the 173rd from Ranger Battalion. Most of what I knew about Rougle I'd picked up from Sergeant Michael Gabel, who had been one of my team leaders when I was training up for my first deployment to Afghanistan. Rougle and Gabel were good buddies, so I heard a lot of stories about the two of them, most of which revolved around what a tough and experienced beast of a soldier Rougle was. I'd also spent a week with him and some of the other scouts while I was at Blessing studying for my sergeant's board, and they were uniform in their praise of Sergeant Rougle. Out of everyone in Battle Company, he was one of the easiest guys to admire, simply because he had such a laundry list of accomplishments. Everything a budding infantryman in the 173rd wanted to achieve, Rougle had already done. He was a decorated combat veteran who had served in both Iraq and Afghanistan. This was his sixth deployment since 2001. He had spent time with the Rangers and opted ultimately to serve in the 173rd. He was a big, muscular guy, fit as hell, but also quick and silent and sneaky, exactly the kind of soldier you want on the scout team.

In short, he was not the kind of fighter you could ever imagine getting overrun.

Rougle's death was almost incomprehensible. So, too, was the fact that the enemy had taken his M4 rifle. There was no way that this could have happened while he was alive, so the only explanation was that the gun had been pried from Rougle's body after he'd been killed. This realization was almost as shocking as the actual fact of his death: I could not, under any circumstances, imagine anyone touching the body of a soldier in the 173rd. This was sacrilege, and it made my blood boil.

The scope of the attack could also be seen in the wounds suffered by Staff Sergeant Kevin Rice and Specialist Carl Vandenberge. Rice was shot in the abdomen and required multiple surgical procedures to put his life back in order. He's a terrific guy who has since become a close friend and snowboarding partner of mine. Vandenberge was shot in the arm and shoulder, severing an artery; he nearly bled out on the Abas Ghar. I suspect Vandenberge's size—he was like a bigger version of Gangwer—might have helped save him that day.

Rougle, Vandenberge, and Rice were three strong and seasoned fighters, and yet their units were completely overwhelmed during the onslaught. Afterward, the Taliban took off with not only Rougle's M4, but Vandenberge's 240, Rice's M14 assault rifle, and two pairs of night vision goggles. Purely in military terms, this was a huge victory for the insurgents. Night vision goggles were one of the tools we had in our favor in the Korengal, and we certainly didn't want them falling into the hands of the enemy. And the guns represented a significant amount of firepower. Moreover, their acquisition represented great fodder for propaganda as the Taliban went about the business of recruiting young Afghan men to their cause.

So there was no time to grieve, no point in reconstructing what had transpired or what had gone wrong. That would all happen much later. For now, the nature of our mission immediately changed from capturing or killing bad guys to something else entirely. Something more personal and urgent:

We're going to get our stuff back.

CHAPTER 15

October 25, 2007

We were on the move well before dawn, somewhere between 2:00 a.m. and 3:00 a.m., under an iridescent moon that rendered night vision goggles almost superfluous. First Platoon had returned to the Korengal Outpost following the events of the previous day, but merely to refit and link up with Third Platoon. Now more than thirty of us were heading out again to provide support and security for Second Platoon, which had remained in the field throughout, pummeling the valley with mortars and bombs and trying to reclaim its missing gear.

It's hard to describe the collective mood as we marched that morning. It was a mix of anger and frustration and sadness, but I also think we were still in disbelief about what had happened: The thought of the Taliban overrunning not just an American position, but a 173rd position, a Battle Company position, was beyond my comprehension. And I'm sure I wasn't alone. This wasn't an IED blast or a single sniper's bullet. This was a much more impressive and disturbing show of military might on the part of an enemy that had not previously seemed capable of such feats.

The attack did not change the way we went about our business—it's not like you can march any harder or scan any better or listen more intently. But it did heighten tension through the company. On the surface, everything was businesslike. As a unit, as a team going about a mission, you can't let emotion interfere with the task at hand. Everyone needs to be focused and to understand the very specific nature of the job: *retrieve the goggles and the guns, and kill as many bad guys as we possibly can.* Getting pissed off and shooting people indiscriminately is not going to help the situation; it's not going to bring back Rougle (or Sergeant Ski), and it's not going to make up for the injuries suffered by Rice or Vandenberge. That's how soldiers sometimes end up in jail: by letting their emotions get the best of them in a combat situation. It's okay to feel the pain of loss; it's okay to get mad. But you have to put those feelings in the proper place. Hard as this might be to believe, emotion tends to get in the way when you're fighting. It clouds your judgment, and it can get you killed.

Every day in the Korengal Valley held the possibility of death. The sun came up every morning and the shooting started shortly thereafter. That's just the way it was. The fact that you might have to kill someone, or that you might be killed, did not burn through your head, because that was life in the valley. Yes, Rock Avalanche was different because it was a battalionwide mission, and yes this particular day was unique because it involved all of Battle Company, and because of what had transpired the day before. Really, though, it was just another mission, one that we hoped would play itself out the way we had planned.

We walked in a southwesterly direction for maybe two to three hours, down to the Korengal River Valley, passing Firebase Phoenix and Restrepo, and eventually crossing the river before reaching our assigned position on the Gatigal Spur. From this spot, on Honcho Hill, First Platoon was supposed to simply sit tight and watch over Second Platoon as it worked its way through the town of Landigal below, banging on doors and interviewing villagers. Third Platoon, meanwhile, went even higher and slightly to the northeast, so that they could hold the high ground and ensure that no one would attack us from above. In essence, then, First Platoon was overlooking Second Platoon, and Third Platoon was overlooking First. This was to ensure that we stayed within range of our weapon systems and didn't force too long or difficult a shot if one was required.

By 5:00 a.m. we had hunkered down, and we remained there for at least the next fourteen to sixteen hours, watching and waiting. This was some serious glassing, staring hard through the binoculars, not talking much, trying to remain vigilant. At some point word came across the radio that Second Platoon was conducting a shura with village elders—ostensibly a diplomatic meeting in which the primary objective is a fair and mutual exchange of information. Shuras occurred regularly in the Korengal Valley and typically were led by Captain Kearney in an attempt to improve relations with the populace. In this case, though, what Second Platoon really wanted out of the shura was the names and locations of insurgents in the region, especially those who might be in possession of stolen American gear. After the shura, Second Platoon would return to the KOP. And we would join them in the village for the walk home. Third Platoon would follow us down as well.

"Get your guys ready," Sergeant Gallardo said. "We're going down at dark."

By this point it seemed that the day would end quietly. It wasn't until much later that we realized what was actually going on—that, in fact, a group of at least a dozen enemy fighters had, at some point during the day, crept up behind us and sat patiently under cover, waiting for the moment that we would begin moving.

I can't stress strongly enough how big a role terrain plays in the Afghanistan conflict. It is a not a minor character in the ongoing drama of war; it is a major factor in every mission, and in every battlefield encounter. For example, the terrain dictated that on this day we had only one path back to the Korengal Outpost—unless we wanted to jump off the side of a mountain, which obviously wasn't a legitimate option, we were going to go out the same way we had come in. Any time you have few options for traversing a route, there is the possibility of encountering opposition force—directly in front of you. That's fine, though. We were trained to handle such conditions. We carried guns and grenades and we were proficient at using them. I'm not implying that we were treating the situation with a lack of respect. I'm simply saying it was what it was: a hike back home, at night, in the midst of a dangerous operation. It was inherently risky. But I don't recall feeling a lack of confidence, or a heightened sense of danger.

This is going to sound strange, but you almost had to admire the battle plan of the Taliban. If we were going to set up an ambush, we would have done it in exactly the same way: by forming an L-shaped barrier with our troops. One short line of soldiers (in this case somewhere between two and four men) directly in front of the enemy, a second, longer line (as many as ten to twelve men) on the enemy's left flank. It's a classic and effective military tactic, facilitating maximum carnage in the shortest amount of time. You can hurt or shoot almost everyone with the initial barrage; once the surviving members of the enemy force get in line to return fire, another portion of the ambush unit sweeps down on the side, flanking them before they even realize they've been attacked from two directions.

This is precisely what the insurgents did, and they did it extraordinarily well, and with shocking efficiency and precision. To this day, I still have trouble believing it happened. Typically, the insurgents we faced in the valley weren't capable of this type of tactical maneuver; they lacked the leadership and organization. They lacked the command control. In the valley you'd see random—and sometimes deadly—shooting, but nothing of this nature. Like the attack that had overrun the scout team a day earlier, this ambush bore the hallmark of a professional fighting unit. And I think that's exactly the case. I do not believe the men who executed that ambush were Korengalis; I believe they were fighters brought in specifically for that mission.

These guys were not farmers.

They were soldiers. They were pros.

There were eighteen of us, walking single file, a distance of perhaps ten to fifteen meters separating us. You keep a distance when marching so that a grenade or RPG injures only one or two people. Sergeant Brennan, as Alpha Team leader, was out in front, walking point. Next was Eckrode and then Gallardo. I was fourth. Behind me were Casey and Clary. A little farther back was a headquarters element led by First Lieutenant Bradley Wynn, and including Tyler Gangwer and Doc Mendoza. Also in the group were Private Michael Burns, Staff Sergeant Curtis Brouthers, Specialist Christopher Izell, Private Oliver King, Specialist Brett Parry, Sergeant Nathan Reilly, Staff Sergeant Chris Reyes, Sergeant Roberto Sandifer, Staff Sergeant Chris Shelton, Specialist Drew Talley, and Staff Sergeant Joshua Valles.

From my vantage point, what happened in the ensuing five to ten minutes was utter chaos, a classic example of hell breaking loose on the battlefield. What we later learned, after statements were taken and the entire event pieced together by military investigators, was that when the Taliban opened fire, Sergeant Brennan and Specialist Eckrode were immediately hit by multiple rounds. All I knew, though, was that we were under massive fire, like nothing I had ever seen or experienced. And the enemy was shockingly close, maybe ten to twenty meters away.

There was no time to think, no room to move, no place to hide. We were standing in the open, and they were under cover, behind rocks and trees. I couldn't believe the firepower! From the front—not more than a few meters from where Brennan and Eckrode had been walking, as it turned out—they were using modified AK-47s, getting off two hundred rounds or more before reloading; on the flank were belt-fed machine guns, with even greater killing firepower. RPGs crashed and burst into flames in the surrounding trees and mountainside. That proximity actually turned out to be a blessing, because we were too close for most of the RPGs to be effective. RPGs are basically handheld rockets, and they require distance to be safely deployed. Unless you want to kill yourself in the process.

In any firefight, there is an instinctive, knee-jerk reaction that immediately follows the first crack of gunfire. Everyone responds differently, but training and experience helped us deal with the initial shock, to resist the body's natural urge to flee—which sounds like a better idea than it really is, since you're likely to get shot in the back. Instead, we learned to seek out the position from which the shot had been fired, to use our ears and eyes to determine the proximity of the enemy's position, and to ascertain whether we were in a reasonably safe place. All of this would happen in a matter of seconds.

But this was different. The opening burst of gunfire mushroomed almost immediately into something far more disorienting and lethal— a hailstorm of bullets and tracers and explosions illuminating the night sky.

Luck and advancements in technology, combined with poor marksmanship on the part of the enemy, allowed us to survive the initial ambush and begin fighting back. Within the first fifteen to twenty seconds—I can't say for sure, because time really does blur in moments like that—I had been shot in the rib cage. In any other war, that bullet would have produced a sucking chest wound and I would have died on the battlefield. This time, though, the impact was absorbed by my protective vest, and it didn't break through to the skin.

It was the strangest feeling—he vest plate actually displaced the force of the bullet as it came roaring in at two thousand feet per second. It didn't feel like I got hit in one spot, but rather across the width of my torso. The small amount of air trapped between my body and the plate instantly was squeezed out, producing a blast of air across my face and throat. It was the oddest sensation, sort of like getting hit in the chest with a baseball, but it didn't really hurt. Not that I noticed, anyway. Another bullet, which I did not even discover until later, went through the assault pack that was slung over my shoulder.

My initial concern, after the world essentially exploded in our faces, was the two guys under my charge: Casey and Clary. I tried to make sure they were alive and firing their weapons. I wouldn't have been the least bit surprised if I had turned around and seen that both of them were dead. But they weren't. They were on the ground, gathering themselves, no doubt trying to figure out what the hell was happening, just like the rest of us.

"Keep firing!" I yelled over the constant crackle of gunfire. "Don't stop shooting!"

I needn't have said anything, because Casey and Clary had already begun doing exactly what they were supposed to do, laying waste to the long side of the L-shaped ambush, Clary readying his M203 grenade launcher and Casey firing his SAW to the point of going cyclic, a rate of nine hundred to one thousand rounds per minute. Ordinarily, you wouldn't want to risk cyclic fire, since the barrel of the SAW might melt and be rendered unusable. This, however, was an extraordinary circumstance and called for extraordinary measures. And Casey responded heroically.

We had been in regular contact with the enemy over the preceding six months, so it wasn't like we didn't know how to handle ourselves in a firefight. It happened every day. What made this unique was the intensity of the battle, and the proximity of the enemy. It was almost like we were dancing with each other through a hailstorm of bullets.

In the initial moments following the onset of the ambush, I squeezed the trigger of my M4 assault rifle perhaps five times. That's all. Just to put some bullets on the muzzle flashes. Casey and Clary had more powerful weapons, so I wanted to be sure they could do their jobs; I wanted to be sure they were all right. Seconds later, though, I looked ahead and saw Gallardo get hit. His head twitched oddly, jerking to the side, and he fell to the ground maybe ten meters in front of me. My heart sank. I'd seen people get shot before, and when their head twitches like that . . . well . . . it's not a natural thing; the consequences are usually grave. Instinctively, I stood up from a crouch and began to sprint forward, simply because it felt like the right thing to do. I don't know how many bullets were flying, but enough to know I'd probably get hit, enough that it seemed as though there wasn't room for a fly to pass through the traffic.

I didn't care. I knew Gallardo would have done the same for me. Hell, any of them would have.

Gallardo was on his back when I got to him, but I could see right away that he was still very much alive and fighting. As I dragged him by the handle of his vest, Gallardo kicked at the dirt with his boots, back-pedaling with all his might. After a few seconds he flipped himself over, pushed my hand away, and scrambled to his feet; we ran back together and jumped into a shallow ditch. The bullet, as it turned out, had indeed hit Gallardo in the helmet, but it had merely grazed his skull.

So there we were, pressed against the ground, side by side, in position, trying to figure out what to do next.

"Grenades!" Gallardo said. "Let's throw the fucking grenades and move up."

And that's what we did. Clary, Gallardo, and I began heaving grenades while Casey, who had the biggest and most potent weapon, kept firing his SAW, lighting up the entire forest. Throwing and running, throwing and running . . . until we came to Eckrode. He had been shot twice in the leg and twice in the chest. Fortunately, the two bullets to the chest had been stopped by his vest.

"My weapon is jammed!" Eckrode said. He seemed more pissed than hurt.

Gallardo knelt beside Eckrode, assessed the situation, and dressed his wounds; he remained at Eckrode's side, absorbing constant fire, until the battle waned.

Clary and Casey were not far behind, still heaving grenades and discharging their weapons. My job, at that point, was to keep moving. We still needed to link up with Brennan, who was farthest away and, since he had been walking point, perhaps in a world of trouble. There was no sense stopping. Gallardo and Eckrode were okay, and the continued gunfire and explosions made staying in that position an unwise option. It would have taken only one grenade at that point, and Gallardo and I both would have died.

It's important in a battle to maintain spacing. And it's not important to do someone else's job when they are already doing it. There is no need for two people to be on the same step. You need to make sure you are accomplishing a task that has not already been undertaken by someone else in the unit. It's about teamwork and training, and acting as a unit, rather than a collection of frantic, scared individuals. You may, in fact, be scared, but that can't get in the way. Somehow, you have to keep doing your job, and that's all I did. That's all any of us did.

Eckrode was in good hands. Gallardo had that situation under control. They didn't need me. So I kept running on the path I was traveling.

Movement was crucial. The heaviest fire occurred in the opening thirty seconds of the ambush, when we were essentially standing still. Once we began returning fire and running—once we made it risky for the enemy to continue shooting—the accuracy of the attack diminished; every one of us took a bullet at some point. The rucksacks belonging to Casey and Clary were literally shot to pieces, shredded by gunfire. But I don't think any of us got hit after we began running.

The grenades had paid off. They're loud and they're scary and they make things blow up. It's hard to keep firing an AK-47 on target with grenades blowing up all around you. Within a matter of seconds, Gallardo, Clary, and I had tossed three grenades each, and the resulting concussive force seemed to have given the enemy pause.

I kept moving, running, firing my M4. I wanted to find Brennan, make sure he was okay, and try to do a battlefield assessment. But I couldn't find him. He seemed to have disappeared. I then ran a little to the left, more toward the shooting. That might sound crazy, and maybe it was, but in an ambush, when the enemy is so close, there are only a few options. One is to charge the ambush line, to put them in chaos, and to try to get in behind them and around them. If you can make it through the line of fire, you have a much better chance of survival. It's a desperate, almost suicidal approach, for sure. At some point, though, if the enemy does not retreat, you have to try it.

And anyway, I figured that's what Sergeant Brennan had already done.

Fuck! Josh just ran alone into the shit.

So I followed him there. I thought maybe we'd break the wall together. I don't know. It's not logical; it just happened.

Finally I reached an area of foliage, past the concentrated fire, and suddenly things quieted down.

Holy shit! I made it.

Then I saw them: three figures off in the distance, walking away from me. I didn't know what was happening at first. I couldn't imagine that anyone in my unit had passed me, so these had to be what we called "unfriendlies." And they were. Two of them, anyway. They were both wearing dark, camo-colored man-dresses, with AK-47s slung over their shoulders, and they were carrying something between them. I kept running, and as I drew closer I could see that it was an American soldier, and I knew it had to be Brennan. The gravity of the situation was overwhelming. They had him bound by the hands and feet, toting him like a hog on its way to a roast.

Much later, as we pieced together the narrative of the ambush, it was determined that I hadn't actually broken through the front of the L-shaped ambush. More likely what happened was this: The two men carrying Brennan were the same people who had manned the short end of the L; in order to grab him and his gear, and attempt to get away, they had to abandon their position at the apex of the L. In effect, by getting shot, Brennan had broken down the ambush. His efforts, as much as anyone else's, saved lives.

I wish I had processed the image sooner; maybe then I could have killed them both. As it was, I killed one—he dropped on the spot—and hit the other. The wounded man limped away and then disappeared—it looked as though he leaped off a cliff or at least rolled down a steep embankment; either way, I hope he was dead by the time he reached bottom. I ran to Brennan, grabbed him by the vest, and dragged him back beyond what would have been the front of the ambush line.

"It's Brennan!" I screamed to Gallardo. "They were fucking taking him!"

Meanwhile, the fighting went on, tracers whizzing overhead, grenades blasting all around. Above us, looking on impotently because of the intensely close nature of the contact, were Apache helicopters and a B-1 bomber. At this point, since our unit had been fractured and displaced, the danger of being killed by friendly fire may have exceeded the possibility of being hit by the enemy. It was chaotic, and at the center of the chaos was Sergeant Brennan, on the ground, badly wounded. In addition to having sustained multiple gunshot wounds, it looked like an RPG had exploded near him—shrapnel had taken off the bottom left side of his jaw.

"There's something in my mouth," he moaned.

The "something" was his teeth, floating and wandering rootless in what was left of his mouth as he gasped for breath and tried to talk. It was a horrible wound, but I figured he'd be okay in the short term if I could keep his airway clear. A bigger problem was the fact that he had been shot at least a half dozen times. He held my hand and asked for morphine. I had none to give him.

I kept calling for medical help, but none was forthcoming, which made me wonder what had happened to Doc Mendoza. This wasn't like him; short of a serious injury, nothing would have kept Mendoza from being at Brennan's side.

I was helpless. All I could do was assess Josh's wounds, wait for a medic, and try to talk with him, comfort him. That's what you do in those situations—you talk about the best things in life, about friends and family, and how you'll be home soon, rather than on some shitty mountain in Afghanistan, with a bunch of ungrateful fucks shooting at you.

"You'll be okay," I said. "You're going to get out and tell your hero stories."

Josh tried to smile.

"I know . . . I know."

The entire ridge shook as a pair of bombs fell from the B-1 overhead, erupting with such force that most of the shooting stopped and the enemy began to scatter. With American forces and insurgents now clearly identifiable and separated by sufficient space, the Apaches unleashed a torrent of fire, allowing everyone to move forward and regroup.

Eventually a medic from Third Platoon arrived, along with Staff Sergeant Brouthers, who was not only a medic but a registered nurse. Brouthers performed an emergency tracheotomy to help Josh breathe. I pumped the bag and stayed with him until the Medevac helicopter took him away. He still had a pulse, and I honestly thought he was going to make it. Josh was a strong fucker. He'd been hurt before and come back quickly. He'd get through this one as well.

"You're lucky, dude," I said before he left. "You're gonna go home and get a parade for this one."

———

It wasn't until that night that the full impact of the battle was revealed, when Captain Kearney called us together and told us that Sergeant Brennan had died following surgery. Doc Mendoza had been shot in the femoral artery and bled out in a ditch; Eckrode, Reyes, and Valles had been airlifted out with injuries.

It's hard to describe what you feel at a time like that. Josh was my closest friend in the military. We had come up together, fought side by side, been promoted at roughly the same time at every stop along the way. Brennan was supposed to have gotten out of the Army a month earlier. He should have been home, preparing for his new life as a police officer. But stop-loss had forced upon him a change in plans; his contract had been extended. Now he'd never see home again.

Mendoza's death was in some ways harder to comprehend, as I hadn't even realized he'd been shot. One moment he'd been with us, and the next he was gone. I was sitting next to Gangwer when Kearney delivered the news. Gangwer had been near Mendoza during the ambush, and I think he was instantly struck by a wave of survivor's guilt. Pain and anger were etched into his face. Was there something more he could have done to help Mendoza? Of course not. He had done everything he could, just as we all had. But you can't watch a buddy die and not experience some gnawing sense of responsibility.

I don't know how to describe it, except to say that the pain is deep and profound. It's a feeling of sadness and loss, but also a feeling of inadequacy, of not being good enough. I'll use wrestling as an analogy, because it's the sport I know best, and one in which I think the competition is uniquely personal and intense. When a wrestling match ends, there is no debate about who is better or who is victorious. One hand goes up, the other does not. Everything is settled—no discussion, no excuses. You have no one else to blame. It's just you and the other guy, and when the other guy beats you, he takes something from you, something very intimate and private. And afterward, you know the truth: You aren't the best and you aren't the baddest.

You're merely human.

In combat, when you hear that one of your brothers has been wounded or killed, it's like that sense of loss and shame, only multiplied a hundredfold. It's exponentially worse because the stakes are not comparable. The sadness is overwhelming. The sadness of knowing you will never see your friend again; of knowing you were there and supposed to help, and now it's on you that he is gone. It doesn't fall on his family back in the States, or on the president or Congress. It doesn't fall on anyone other than the men who were there with him on the day he passed; the brothers who were by his side in battle, who were supposed to protect him, and who somehow let him down.

That's a hell of a weight to carry around for the rest of your life.

When you hold a buddy in your arms and watch his skin turn gray, when you can feel his life slipping away, it's impossible not to walk around afterward in something of a stupor, asking yourself repeatedly:

How did this happen? Why wasn't it me?

But you have to let it go. If you think about it for too long, and too hard, your head will explode. I mean, it's war—horrible shit happens every day. People die, and sometimes there's not a damn thing you can do about it. But that doesn't make it any easier to accept. In that moment, outside the KOP, neither Brennan's death nor Mendoza's death seemed real, and the enormity of the loss was clouded by the fact that we all were utterly and completely exhausted. Days pass in wartime before reality sets in. Sometimes months pass . . .

Or even years.

CHAPTER 16

October 29, 2007

Hey, Babe:

How are you doing today? I have been trying to call you all day. The phones here for some reason aren't working but the Internet is so I guess this will have to do. I am going to try and order that external hard drive because now I met a dude who has like two hundred movies. I am also going to call up Josh's dad and let him know my take on the situation. Josh is a good friend to all that he ever met and an honest-to-God hero if I have ever seen one. With the phones down it is making this stuff that I don't want to do even more daunting on me. I don't really know what to say. My day has been very uneventful and I have been watching the TV show Prison Break. *From the sounds of things here I will be heading back to the place that I did the board at and just sitting and chilling out for a week, and I know that for sure they have phones so hope you can handle me calling and bullshitting every day. I got the pictures you sent me of the marathon and Damn girl I am proud of you. You are for sure the toughest woman that I have ever seen, and still so damn hot, too. I love you with all of my heart, Jenny. I know I tell you that all of the time but I don't want to miss a chance to let you know how much you mean to me.*

I will try to give you a call tomorrow and if the phones are still down I will just write you again. I love you babe.

Your man in the Stan,
Sal

For the first few days following the ambush I spent most of my time at a small observation post located a couple of hundred meters above the KOP, along with Gallardo, Casey, and Clary. We'd been sequestered there while the Army conducted multiple interviews in an effort to assemble an accurate narrative of what had transpired on Honcho Hill. This was standard procedure following any mission in which casualties were sustained, although obviously the job of investigating a particular incident became more difficult when multiple troops were injured or killed. Everyone sees things differently when the tracers and bullets are flying and the bombs are falling, and memory is not always flawless; therefore, the accurate reconstruction of any battle presents a formidable task. Add to that the pressure associated with having to inform relatives that someone they love has been killed or wounded and to do it in a timely fashion, and you can see how mistakes are made. Sometimes I wonder how they ever get it right.

The four of us stayed up there together, pulling security, talking, decompressing. We'd come down to the KOP whenever the investigators needed more sworn statements, or just to grab a hot meal and maybe use one of the laptops to write emails back home. If that sounds as though we were in some way being treated indelicately, well, it didn't feel that way at all. I think the manner in which things were handled was entirely appropriate and precisely the way they should have been handled. We were with the people we needed to be with: our buddies, the guys who knew what had happened. All four of us were in shock. Eckrode would have been there, too, had he not been airlifted out and brought to a hospital.

How could Brennan possibly be gone? And Doc Mendoza? It still didn't seem real, and the best way to cope with their absence, and the disorientation and sadness that came with it, was to simply spend time together, doing what we always did.

Being with your boys at a time like that does not make the pain go away, but it does make it slightly more tolerable.

Phone use was always limited at the KOP, but eventually I was able to call both Jen and my parents. Jen already knew about Brennan, Mendoza, and Rougle; she knew I was hurting emotionally, but okay otherwise, so we didn't talk about the ambush at all.

In fact, it was several years before I shared with Jen the details of what happened on October 25, 2007. And Jen was awesome about that, never pressuring me, always giving me space and time, letting me deal with things in my own way.

My parents had heard some things as well, and I know they were both curious and concerned. I had shielded my parents from the grotesque realities of war in Afghanistan both during and after my first deployment. On the second deployment I shared even less. This time, though, I knew they'd hear or read stories about Rock Avalanche, so I wanted to give them the basics as I knew them to be true. They got on the phone together and I told them I was okay, but that we had lost Rougle and Brennan and Mendoza, and how they were three of the best soldiers I knew.

And that was it.

Or so I thought. My father was quiet on the other end of the line, but Mom started asking questions, probing for details about the mission and the ambush. I found myself getting agitated. I didn't want to talk about it; I didn't want to relive any of it. It was bad enough that we had to keep telling the story to investigators. Every time I went back there in my head, it made me sick and sad.

I took a deep breath. I knew that my mother's curiosity came from a place of love, not from some strange need to know the grisly details. As hard as it was to serve in Afghanistan, and in the Korengal Valley in particular, I don't doubt for a moment that it was equally hard for my parents—or at least hard in a different way. Like parents of soldiers everywhere, I'm sure they worried and fretted incessantly about what was happening to their son. Was he alive or dead? Was he safe? Had he killed anyone? When I communicated with my parents, by phone or email, I resisted the urge to share any information beyond the merely superficial.

It sucks here and I'm tired and hungry . . . but I'm doing just fine. Love you both. Can't wait to see you.

That was it. And they accepted that tidy little summary of life, probably because it made things easier on them. It was like an unwritten contract: *I'll stay alive and come home to you; just don't ask me what it's really like.*

This time, though, was different. Hearing that three of my colleagues had been killed provoked some serious anxiety in my mother.

"Mom," I said. "Please don't ask."

"I'm just worried."

There was a long pause.

"Okay . . . I'm going to tell you what happened, but only this one time," I said. "Please don't ask me a single question. Please don't interrupt, and please don't ask me to explain."

"All right, Sal."

Over the course of the next few minutes, I told my mother and father, in a very guarded and careful way, what had transpired on the Gatigal Spur. It was not a blood-and-guts rendition, more a simple and quick recitation of the facts. I did this to protect them and to protect myself. When it was done I told them again how much I loved them, and they said the same back to me.

That was a hard phone call, but not the hardest.

The hardest call was the one Gallardo and I made together to Josh Brennan's father, Mike Brennan. Our rationale for the call was simple: We wanted to fill in the blanks for Josh's dad, and to let him know how much we cared about his son. You never know exactly what the families are told in these situations, or how the news is presented, but we could be reasonably sure that someone wearing the uniform of the U.S. Army had knocked at Mr. Brennan's door and calmly presented the news of Josh's death. I have nothing but respect and admiration (and sympathy) for the men and women who do this job, which surely is one of the most difficult and important in the armed services. But I also knew the practical reality of the situation: that whoever this person might have been, he did not know Josh Brennan. No matter how professional and polished he might have been, no matter how apparently empathetic, he was not connected to Josh in any tangible way.

Mike Brennan deserved better than that. He deserved to have an opportunity to speak with the men who had served with his son, who had fought with him and bled with him. It seemed reasonable that he might have questions, since the initial narrative of the event, cobbled together very quickly so that families could be notified, was not completely accurate. It was reported, for example, that Doc Mendoza had died while trying to save Brennan's life, when in fact they never saw each other after the first crack of gunfire. There were other mistakes as well, people misplaced, doing things they had not done. This does not in any way diminish the sacrifice of either man; we all gave everything we had on the battlefield that day, and it was mainly luck or the grace of God that allowed some of us to survive while others did not. But the fact remains that the story unfolded in pieces, changing shape as it developed. We knew that some misinformation had been presented to families, so we weren't sure exactly what the Brennans had been told, and we wanted them to hear the story as we knew it to be true. More than anything else, though, we just felt an obligation to let Mike Brennan know that in the eyes of everyone in Battle Company, First Platoon, Sergeant Joshua Brennan was one amazing soldier and friend.

How do you talk to someone whose son has just died? What do you say? I'd never done that before, and now here I was trying to express my feelings to a man I'd never met, a man in almost incomprehensible pain.

And yet, he was incredibly strong, appreciative of our reaching out to him from halfway around the world, sympathetic to what we had been through.

I can't say exactly what Mr. Brennan felt; I don't want to put words in his mouth or thoughts in his head. He was generous and warm, and I believe he was grateful that we had called. My emotions were so raw at the time that it was difficult for me to gauge what anyone else was feeling; it was hard enough just to talk through the tears.

———

Within a couple of days, after all the sworn statements had been collected and the investigation was nearing an end, Gallardo told me that something big was in the works.

"The captain wants to speak with you," he said. "They're talking about putting you up for the Medal of Honor."

I had no reaction whatsoever, no flush of pride or excitement. If anything, I felt utterly bewildered by the very mention of such a prestigious award, and all that it implied. The events of October 25 were still too raw and painful. I had no desire to be part of any sort of celebration of that day, the worst day of my life. Gallardo understood, but he made it clear that the wheels had been set in motion, and that there wasn't really anything I could do about it.

When I met with Captain Kearney, he told me the paperwork had already been submitted. As company commander, he was the person primarily responsible for the submission. I didn't know what to say . . . how to respond.

As I said before, the first words that came out of my mouth were "Fuck you."

Captain Kearney, solid man that he is, did not take it personally. He understood my reluctance. I didn't mean to be ungrateful; I was just confused. It didn't make any sense that so many things had gone wrong on that day—that two people had been killed—and somehow we were going to celebrate. And that I was going to be the focus of that celebration. If the Army wanted to recognize the performance of First Platoon, well, I guess I could accept that.

But why me?

Nearly twenty men were out there on Honcho Hill, all doing their jobs to the best of their ability under extraordinary circumstances. What I did was just one thing. I contributed one small brushstroke to a giant, sprawling canvas. If you asked me how many rounds I fired, I'd probably estimate somewhere in the vicinity of thirty to forty, but other people fired hundreds of rounds. I threw grenades while running into fire, but so did Gallardo and Clary. I got shot, but so did everyone else. The only reason I got to Brennan is that my fellow soldiers provided cover. We all did our part—every one of us.

I know for sure that every man in First Platoon—shit, probably every man in Battle Company—would have done exactly the same thing if placed in the same position, under the same set of circumstances. A series of boxes required checking, and we checked each one of them, simply because that is what we were trained to do, and because people's lives depended on it.

My actions have been described as "heroic," but I don't really even know what that means. I did what I was supposed to do, and I know for a fact that others behaved just as courageously. All I know is that if you put anyone in First Platoon in my shoes, he would have done the same thing. Maybe he would have lived; maybe not. There is a lot of luck involved, that's for sure. But to pluck me out of the group, to recognize my contribution with such a prestigious award . . . it just seemed ridiculous on some level.

It felt wrong.

"Don't worry about it for now," Kearney had said. "This will take some time anyway."

I didn't worry about it. I didn't even think about it. I put it in the rearview mirror, figuring the image would diminish with each passing day, until eventually it disappeared entirely.

———

Grief, they say, is a moving target. Everyone experiences it differently. Personally, I hate going to memorial services, or even to gravesites. I always have. I don't like seeing Americans in caskets covered with flags. So, unless I'm obligated for one reason or another, I don't do that. I don't need that. It's not going to make me feel better. I know what happened. I was over there. I get it. If a soldier is killed, it happens for a reason, and that reason is fundamentally simple: *He was doing a job to the best of his ability, competing against someone else doing a job to the best of his ability. For whatever reason, he lost.* End of story.

Deep in my heart, I still feel that way. Time and distance and maturity have helped me to understand the importance of pageantry, of standing up and recognizing the men and women who give their lives, or pieces of their anatomy, in combat thousands of miles away. It's important for their friends and their families, and for the United States of America. But it does not bring closure for soldiers. I know where things close. When life seeps from the body and the last breath is taken—that's closure. I don't know how to make that feel better. Some people think talking about your battlefield experiences—confronting the loss by recalling it—will ease the pain. I wish that were true, because if it were I should feel great by now. But I don't. It makes me feel sick and terrible every single time. But I do it anyway, because it means so much to others.

On November 2, 2007, dozens of men assembled at Camp Blessing for a memorial service in honor of the three men who had been killed during Rock Avalanche: Staff Sergeant Larry Rougle, Sergeant Joshua Brennan, and Specialist Hugo Mendoza. The ceremony was held outdoors, in a field splashed with shade. A memorial devoted to the memory of the three fallen soldiers had been constructed along traditional lines: Each man was represented by a pair of boots, an M4 rifle with a bayonet flipped upside down and planted into the ground, dogtags hanging from the pistol grip, and a helmet perched on top.

A disembodied soldier, distilled to his fighting essence.

At the foot of the memorial were photographs of the three men, in uniform, prideful, almost smiling, maroon-red berets tilted perfectly to the side.

This is the way you say good-bye in the Army. It isn't possible to send everyone back home for funeral services—there is still a job to do, after all—so you put something together in the theater of combat. You make the best of a tragic situation. You honor the dead for their courage and sacrifice. You talk about who they were, and what they might have grown to become.

Rougle, someone said, was a devoted father who left behind a young daughter. Mendoza was a man of immense heart and warmth who found true purpose in his work as a medic. And Brennan was remembered as not only the embodiment of everything a soldier was supposed to be, but a good friend as well, and a lover of music. Everyone from First Platoon took turns writing messages of condolence on the face of a six-string acoustic guitar, the very same one Josh used to play when we were hanging out, a memento that would later be presented to his family.

There were speeches and eulogies, both formal and personal, and all the time you could hear in the background the continuing sounds of war: gunfire and cannon blasts, and helicopters rising and landing. Life in a combat zone does not stop—not even for death.

Most of us stood quietly, somberly, absorbed in our own thoughts. Of all the people who spoke that day, the greatest impact was made by Rougle's old buddy, Staff Sergeant Michael Gabel. It was Gabel who stood up and spoke from the heart, his voice at times breaking, but always strong and proud, and occasionally rising to a shout.

"I will not be bitter," Gabel said. "I will not shed any tears of sorrow. I'm proud to have known such a good man and a warrior to the bitter end. Until we see each other again, sky soldiers!"

I had admired Gabel when he was my team leader before my first deployment, but I'd sort of lost touch with him over the last couple of years, following his transfer to Second Platoon. To this day, I've never seen anyone work harder than Gabel. He was a fascinating guy, with a background so unusual that you just couldn't figure out how he wound up in a combat zone, fighting for his life. But I think Gabel was the kind of man who could adapt to almost anything through sheer determination and force of will.

Gabel was a native of Baton Rouge, Louisiana. Before joining the Army he had studied culinary arts in France and become an accomplished sous-chef. Then, in 2000, he dropped everything and enlisted in the military. Clearly this was a guy who had other skills and other talents, who had a lot going in his life. He didn't need the Army. But he wanted to make a difference. He truly believed that there was no higher purpose for him than to represent the United States of America. He wasn't married; he didn't have kids. And maybe because of that, he didn't mind putting his life on the line. He was, in fact, one of the most aggressive and tireless soldiers I've ever met.

If you were on Gabel's team, even in garrison, you could expect to be worked to the bone. At any given moment Gabel was capable of pulling his guys out of the barracks and leading them through an impromptu, hour-long class. We'd stand there as he lectured, thinking, *Holy shit! This wasn't even in the schedule.* Then, when he was through, he'd tell everyone, "Meet me back here in forty-five minutes, right after lunch." The implication, of course, was that you weren't supposed to take the full forty-five minutes, and that in fact Gabel would be sitting there the entire time, probably bypassing lunch completely. But that was Gabel. He wasn't trying to be mean or antagonistic; he was simply enthusiastic. The guy's head was filled with knowledge, and he couldn't wait to share it.

Gabel was the ultimate hard-charger, but he did not believe in taking unnecessary risks. He believed in preparation and training, and he was meticulous in every aspect of his life. Once, for example, he invited me for dinner at his house in Vicenza. What an amazing experience! He never stopped moving around the kitchen—cutting and dicing and sautéing and broiling, bringing everything together at exactly the right moment, choreographing the entire meal with perfection and making the whole thing look deceptively simple—even as he provided a narrative of the meal and his own culinary experiences. He kept talking about how much he had learned in France.

"You work in a restaurant in America," he said, "and you'll see cooks wearing dirty aprons. That would never happen in France. Wouldn't be tolerated. Everything has to be clean and precise."

That was Gabel—clean and precise. Every spill had to be mopped up immediately, so that there was no trace of a mistake having been made. But if a mistake was made, you filed it away; you learned from it. And you did better the next time. I suppose it's no surprise that Gabel did well in the Army—the military is all about organization, detail, and staying on top of twenty different things at once, especially if you are in a leadership role. My own personal culinary experience was limited to those few months behind the counter at Subway—oh yeah, and that brief, sickening period on the assembly line at Krispy Kreme—so I'm certainly no expert, but I would think that running a kitchen involves corollary skills.

Shortly before we deployed to Afghanistan in 2005, Gabel was promoted to staff sergeant and shifted over to Second Platoon. I didn't see him too much after that, but we tried to stay in contact. By the time I ran into him at the Camp Blessing memorial service, Gabel was a highly decorated soldier with multiple deployments to Iraq and Afghanistan under his belt. He'd seen a lot of shit in his time—a lot of death and destruction—but none of it had discouraged him in the least, or even dissuaded him from his usual aggressive tactics.

We talked a little at the memorial about how things were going in Gabel's sector. In mid-September he had been reassigned to the First Platoon, Delta Company, First Battalion, and they were working primarily in a less mountainous region of Afghanistan. In that area mechanized travel was more feasible; it was also more dangerous, thanks to a proliferation of IEDs and roadside bombs. There had been numerous close calls involving his unit, but given the size of the area they patrolled, and the access to passable roads, there was no choice but to load up the trucks with human cargo on a regular basis.

"Man, I don't see why you guys feel the need to do all that driving," I said. "That's so dangerous."

Gabel shrugged, as if to say, *That's the job, dude.*

He approached life and his work in the military with passion and fearlessness, and his philosophy about the whole experience came tumbling out when he delivered the eulogy for his friend. This was exactly how Rougle would have wanted to go, Gabel said. He was a warrior to the end, and he would have been proud to die for his brothers.

Maybe Gabel was right. I don't know. I have to admit that as I sat there listening to him, I was taken aback.

Man . . . this is your best friend. Can't you just say that you miss him? Do we have to celebrate his death?

When I think back on it now, I realize that this was Gabel's way of dealing with the loss of his buddy. But I also think he meant every word of it. And maybe he was right. Maybe Rougle would have agreed with every word of it.

That was the last time I saw Gabel. A little more than a month later, on December 12, 2007, while traveling in the lead vehicle of a convoy in southeastern Paktika Province, he was killed by an IED blast. On the day I got the news, I was briefly overwhelmed by sadness. Then I remembered what Gabel had said about Rougle, and I couldn't help but feel comforted by the thought. I'll never know whether Rougle wanted to die for his country, or whether he would have approved of Gabel's eulogy. But I do know this: It was exactly the exit Gabel would have chosen for himself, because I heard the words come out of his mouth, and I know the kind of man he was.

And I know the Army now has one less amazing soldier.

——

Everyone gets a little squirrelly as the end of a deployment draws near. First Platoon made it through the next six months without losing another man. There was another long, cold winter, and more fighting in the spring, contact escalating predictably with the rising temperatures. We were lucky, though—there was nothing like Rock Avalanche on the agenda, no mission that compared to it in terms of scope, intensity, and casualties. We simply went about the business of patrolling and fighting, trying, with little success and diminishing enthusiasm, to gain favor with the populace. Day after day, week after week, month after month. Just grinding away.

By the end of June we'd all become obsessed with the idea of getting out of Afghanistan and returning to Italy. Fifteen months is a long deployment regardless of where you're stationed; in the Korengal Valley, it's an eternity. The Fourth of July brought another round of fireworks, more somber than the previous year as the parachute mortars lit up the valley, commemorating the lives of Battle Company soldiers lost in the name of freedom and the war on terrorism, and offering a hearty "Fuck you" to the Taliban as they wafted down, once again illuminating our position, basically challenging insurgents to launch an attack on such a personal and important occasion.

That's right—we're still here. Now go ahead . . . give us a reason to return fire.

It didn't happen. Independence Day passed with no greater contact than we saw on any other typical day.

The countdown to departure continued. And believe me, that's exactly what it was. Despite the fact that we did not know the exact date that we would be leaving the Korengal, we knew it would happen roughly sometime in late July, and as we approached that point on the calendar, it began to mess with our heads. This is not a unique phenomenon in the annals of military history. Everything begins to take on added significance for the short-timer; superstition takes root in even the most sensible and grounded soldier. You find yourself looking over your shoulder more frequently on patrol; you become more reluctant to take chances; and you find yourself questioning the wisdom of virtually everything you might be doing on a given day.

Simply put, you begin to suspect that your luck is running out.

Much of the work we did in those final weeks involved helping our replacements, the soldiers of Viper Company, transition to deployment in the Korengal Valley: showing them around, introducing them to some of the village elders, familiarizing them with the safest routes of travel. According to protocol, we would leave behind all of our water and ammunition, along with some of our more potent weapons and various other supplies. Much of the personal crap we'd accumulated over the previous fifteen months would be burned. Basically, we'd be leaving with little more than the clothes on our backs.

And yet, throughout this period we had to remain vigilant. The enemy could not possibly have cared less whether we had two weeks or two months or two years remaining in our deployment. We wore the uniform of the U.S. Army, and that alone was cause for them to hate us and to try to wipe us off the face of the earth, regardless of how long we'd been in their country. We needed to look no further than the town of Wanat, a few miles to our north, for clear evidence that the Taliban, far from being discouraged or tamed by the presence of the American military (which numbered more than thirty thousand by this point), had in fact become increasingly brazen and lethal. Their ranks swollen on any given day by the recruitment of villagers and farmers and young boys, the Taliban would attack with a couple of hundred soldiers, all willing to give their lives if it meant they could kill just a small handful of "infidels."

Like those of us in Battle Company, the men of Chosen Company were within weeks of concluding their deployment in the Korengal Valley. But on that day in Wanat, they became involved in one of the deadliest firefights the valley had seen. Some three hundred insurgents had amassed near the town and mounted a ferocious attack on the forty-five men of Chosen Company (who were aided by another two dozen Afghan soldiers). The assault went on for hours, and in the end nine soldiers had been killed, another twenty-one wounded.

It was a tragic and catastrophic loss, and a reminder that none of us, at any time, was completely safe. Not even in the fading days of a deployment.

Hell, especially not then.

———

One night in mid- to late July, shortly after the sun had gone down, an insurgent slipped between our positions at Vegas and Little Rock and opened fire. There had been a lot of kinetic activity throughout the Korengal in recent weeks, so the shooting in itself wasn't a big deal. The point of origin, however, was a very big deal. We took great pride in ensuring that our bases were highly fortified and guarded, with walls of HESCOs around Vegas and massive coils of concertina wire protecting Little Rock. With only a couple of hundred meters separating the outposts, and guards always standing vigil, the odds were stacked against any insurgent sneaking between the two.

Somehow, though, it happened.

Technically, they had split us up, and we did not know at the time whether those first few shots represented merely the work of a lone sniper or the opening volley of a well-coordinated attack. Like Chosen Company, it was possible that we were on the verge of being overrun by a few hundred well-armed insurgents ready, willing, and even eager to meet Allah. Practically speaking, even a much smaller group, if it gained control of Little Rock, could turn our own weapons on us, aiming downhill and wiping out most of Vegas in a heartbeat.

So this was not a small matter.

"Fuckers!" Gallardo yelled. "Let's go!"

Within seconds we were on the run—me, Gallardo, Griego, Casey, and Clary, sprinting past the HESCOs, throwing grenades as far as we could. Someone came out with a big case of grenades, and we all stood there, picking them off the pile as quickly as possible, throwing one after another, until the whole valley seemed to shiver at once. I don't know how many grenades we threw that night—I must have heaved at least thirty by myself. Was it overkill? I have no idea. And I didn't really give a shit. No one from First Platoon was hurt that night, and that's all I really cared about.

———

On July 25, 2008, I boarded a helicopter at the KOP. Our platoon had been departing in waves over the course of four or five days, and now it was my turn to say good-bye to the Korengal Valley. I rode with Eckrode, Gallardo, Roberts, Casey, Clary, and maybe a couple of guys from the gun team. I don't remember exactly how many of us were on the chopper that afternoon, but I do recall looking over at Casey and shaking my head in disbelief as the bird lifted its nose and pulled away from the KOP, chasing rubble and dirt in its wake.

There had been no words exchanged as we tossed our gear onto the chopper and climbed aboard, but now, as the Korengal faded from view, and the certainty of our departure began to settle in, we loosened up.

"Hey, Sal," Casey said, "I don't think I've ever seen you smile like that."

Was I smiling? Was I happy? I hadn't even realized it.

"You know why, Casey?" I said. "Because I'm never coming back to this shithole again."

He laughed. We all did. It was a sentiment that resonated for countless reasons. There had been so much pain and misery in the preceding fifteen months, so much death and destruction. Only the camaraderie and the perverse thrill of combat (when it didn't end badly) had made it tolerable. I fucking hated the Korengal Valley. I hated every rock and tree stump, every goat and scorpion and snake.

And, yes, I had come to hate the people, whether they were Taliban or not.

Within a year the Army would begin pulling out of the Korengal, and by the summer of 2010 there would be no American military presence in the region. More than forty U.S. soldiers gave their lives, and hundreds more were injured in that corner of the war on terrorism. (By the summer of 2012, the number of American soldiers killed in Afghanistan during Operation Enduring Freedom reached two thousand.)

Was it worth it?

I don't know. I prefer not to think about it. We did everything we could to make the Korengal a better place than it was when we arrived, and I guess that has to be enough.

I looked out the windows of the chopper and watched the valley recede, knowing there was no way I'd ever set foot there again.

And that was okay by me.

EPILOGUE

Post-traumatic Stress Disorder (PTSD):
   A mental health condition triggered by a terrifying event. Symptoms may include flashbacks, nightmares and severe anxiety, as well as uncontrollable thoughts about the event.

—The Mayo Clinic

I'd be lying if I said that I adjusted quickly and easily to life without combat. I don't think that's possible. The feeling of exhilaration we all experienced upon leaving the Korengal Valley was soon replaced mostly by disorientation. The entire trip from Afghanistan back to Vicenza stretched out over four days, and after that we were dropped back into a semiordinary world, one run by the military, yes, but not one in which we were expected to use our guns or fight for our lives. Seemingly overnight we went from being shot at ten times a day and told that it was okay to kill people—in fact, instructed to kill people—to being told that none of these things was normal or acceptable.

We were all excited to get back, of course, but I don't know that any of us were prepared for the transition. It all happened so quickly, and the immersion was so complete, that you couldn't help but feel uncomfortable. All the rules had changed. We had led a violent, almost tribal existence for the previous fifteen months, one in which anger was not to be squelched, but rather used as fuel for survival. Now we were expected to throw a switch and behave like polite, rational members of civil society.

And that is not who we were.

We were fighters. We were soldiers.

I was thrilled to be out of Afghanistan, but there were moments in those first few days at home when Jen and I would be sitting on the couch, talking and watching television, when I'd excuse myself in this way.

"Hey, babe . . . I have to use the bathroom. I'll be right back."

Jen would smile politely and say, "You don't have to tell me every time you go to the bathroom, Sal."

Habits die hard, especially when they've been forged in a setting where habitual behavior—and communication—can mean the difference between life and death. On deployment in the Korengal Valley, there was not a moment of privacy. You lived in a small space, surrounded by twenty or thirty other men. If you had to pee or check the perimeter, you damn sure told someone of your plans, because if you didn't come back right away, it usually meant something bad had happened.

As was the case following our first deployment, we had all forgotten how to be alone. I had some time off when I got back, and while it was great to spend time with Jen, I'd feel anxious and nervous the moment she stepped out the door to go to work, or to run some errands. In the previous fifteen months I hadn't experienced more than a few minutes of isolation. Suddenly there were all these great blocks of solitary time that needed to be filled, and I didn't know how to do that.

Nor was I completely comfortable with the notion that I no longer had to walk with my head on a swivel. If you wake every morning for more than a year knowing that you're going to be shot at, and that each day might be your last, you grow accustomed to the idea that the world is a very dark and dangerous place. You adjust accordingly. Neither Vicenza nor Caserma Ederle was particularly threatening, but there were times when I'd forget where I was.

One day, not long after we returned, I was walking on a sidewalk on the base when a motorcycle drove past and suddenly backfired.

Bang!

To a normal person, that sound produces a startled response and perhaps an inappropriate word or two. To me, it sounded like something exploding, and I responded in the way I had been trained to respond. I dropped to the pavement, arms spread out, stomach pressed against the ground, heart racing, eyes scanning the perimeter for the source of the threat. I went from walking normally, like everyone else on the base, to a prone position. Instantly I was thrown into combat mode.

And as I lay there, trying to process what had happened, trying to regain my composure, I could hear someone laughing. I looked to my left and there was a young kid in uniform, maybe in his late teens, early twenties, doubled over in laughter.

"Dude," he said with a condescending smile. "You okay?"

I stood up, and in that moment I could feel the rage coursing through my veins. I'd already gone into warrior mode, a sensation I recognized well. In my life, that sound was like the opening bell of a boxing match. It did not mean that it was time to run or hide or negotiate. Any loud noise, any explosion, was a sign of something threatening, and my body and mind instantly became focused on eliminating that threat. And the threat was not the motorcycle; it was the asshole standing in front of me, laughing at my response.

I took two big steps toward the guy, fully intending to rip his head off. It required every bit of restraint I had to stop short and simply put my chin near his and tell him how I felt.

"Listen, you little piece of shit. The reason I feel this way is that I spent the last fifteen months fighting a war. What have you been doing?"

He froze, obviously scared, and managed a weak "Sorry, man," and then said nothing else. I walked away as quickly as I could.

I don't know that I've ever been so angry with someone. Here was another soldier, someone who should have known better. But he didn't, because he'd not yet spent any time in a combat zone. He was clueless, and I was ready to kill him for that. I mean that quite literally. I didn't want to punish him or scold him or reprimand him. If I had gotten my hands on him, I don't know that I could have stopped. In my mind's eye, I could see his head being driven into the sidewalk and cracking open like an eggplant. I could feel it in my hands.

Yeah, I know how that sounds: horrible, barbaric. The thing is . . . I am not by nature a fighter. As a civilian, I had never gone looking for trouble. I was a laid-back, happy, levelheaded guy, more adept than most when it came to reasonable discussion. I'd never felt the need to prove myself in that way.

I still don't.

But in that moment, I could have killed. Just as effectively and assuredly as I'd done it in the Korengal. More so, actually. I could have done it with my bare hands. I don't say that with pride; I say it with a sense of relief, for I know the consequences would have been life-altering. No question about it. But it's a very difficult line we draw for our soldiers. When we're over there, the United States of America tells us, *Words do not work; we're going in to fight it out.* But when we come home, the message is completely different: *Talk it out. Articulate yourself. Violence is not the answer.*

On an intellectual level, of course, I understand this. It's the way things have to be. On an emotional level, though, it's agonizing. There is an age-old problem faced by every soldier returning from war: the challenge of adapting to a society that needs trained fighters to protect its interests, but whose citizens may not necessarily want those fighters to live in their neighborhoods; at least not if they're going to behave as though they are still on deployment.

It's a tricky thing, and every returning soldier I know has experienced at least some difficulty adjusting to those expectations. And I'm not even talking about the guys who have suffered serious physical trauma: For them, the adjustment to civilian life is enormously challenging on a multitude of levels. For me, it was mainly just . . . confusing.

The definition of PTSD is so broad that virtually any soldier returning from a combat deployment would likely receive a positive diagnosis after meeting with military physicians and psychiatrists and counselors, which is something we all went through upon returning to Vicenza. I resisted the label. As I had following my first deployment, I went through the motions, quietly accepting the after-care requirements established by the Army. I underwent precisely one session with a counselor, and while he was a nice enough guy and tried to be empathetic, all I could think of while we were in his office was *You can't possibly understand what I've been though.* At the end of the session he asked if I was okay, and I told him I was.

And that was it for me. I had no desire to endure sessions on a shrink's couch, and I certainly wasn't going to embark on a pharmacological regimen to cope with my problems. Counseling? Talking? Trying to get outside your head? I can see the benefit in that. But I did not like the idea of medication that would screw with my brain chemistry and alter my personality. I'd seen too many of my friends go through that, and I can honestly say that I have serious doubts about whether any of them benefited from the treatment.

In all honesty? I knew exactly what my problem was: I'd just spent more than a year in one of the most violent places on the planet—the Korengal Valley. I'd been at war. I had killed people, and I had seen my buddies get killed. That was my problem, and I just needed time to deal with it.

————

I've been luckier than most guys. Believe me, I know that. Not everyone has a caring, supportive family waiting for them when they get home from deployment. Not everyone has a girlfriend who is willing to move halfway around the world just to be with you, and then spends the better part of three years waiting for you to come home . . . worrying about the possibility that you won't come home at all, or that you'll come home as something less than you were when you left.

If you're fortunate enough to find someone like that, you don't let her get away without a fight.

On July 4, 2009, Jen and I got engaged. She'd been dropping some not-so-subtle hints for a while about the future of our relationship. I understood that. No woman wants to waste too much time on a man who can't or won't make a commitment. Jen was smart, beautiful, ambitious; it wasn't like she didn't have other options. At the same time, I couldn't just pop the question right after she inquired about my plans. I mean, I was a decorated war veteran . . . a tough guy. I couldn't let her break me down that quickly, right? It was supposed to take years for that to happen. But I'm not stupid, either. No way was I going to risk losing her; I just had to figure out how to do it right.

On July Fourth, 2009, we went snorkeling on a little island off the coast of Italy. It was a beautiful day filled with sunshine and easy conversation and crystal-blue water; a perfect day. That night we grabbed some pizza and grappa and headed back to the beach for a casual dinner under the moon. Now, I don't even like grappa, but I needed something to calm my nerves. There are very few things that get me riled up, but a commitment of "forever" is one of those things, as is the possibility that my offer to share "forever" might be rejected.

You never know.

I had it all planned out. I wanted to propose on the Fourth of July so that we'd always be able to celebrate our anniversary on what was, to me, the most important of American holidays. Of course, I'd completely forgotten the fact that no one celebrates the day they got engaged; they celebrate the day on which they were married. What can I say? I wasn't thinking straight. At least this way, when we watched the fireworks each year, it would have a unique and profound impact.

Shortly before midnight, as we walked on the beach, holding hands and watching the stars, I began talking to Jen, trying to tell her how much I loved her, and how I wanted to spend the rest of my life with her. But I don't actually even remember what I said, because the words kept getting all screwed up. My voice broke, and I could feel the tears welling up in my eyes.

Oh, come on, man. Pull yourself together!

Nothing was going quite the way I had anticipated. I had planned on getting down on my knees, but now the tide was rolling back in and we were sinking into the wet sand. It was too late now to get a hotel, and we were covered with sand and salt, anyway. The perfect moment, it seemed, was falling apart. I'm a pretty good talker, and I'd always been particularly comfortable with Jen. But now, for some reason, I was a mess.

We stopped walking and Jen looked into my eyes. She seemed scared. Not exactly the response I had hoped for.

"What are you trying to say to me, Sal? Are you leaving me?"

I shook my head, said, "Not a chance," and then fumbled over words that sounded like "Will you marry me?" although I can't be sure exactly how they came out, for the next thing I knew Jen was leaping into my arms and crying.

"Does this mean yes?" I asked.

She laughed.

"Yeah, Sal. It means yes."

We hung out on the beach for a while longer, then walked the five blocks back to where our car was parked, in a lot overlooking the ocean. We unlocked the doors, reclined the two front seats, and lay there together all night beneath the moon and the stars, listening to the ocean waves as they crashed against the shore.

———

The craziness began on September 9, 2010.

By that time I had settled in Italy and accepted a desk job in rear detachment. I was in charge of deployment for Battle Company, a job that involved handling questions and concerns from the spouses of soldiers, solving expense and payroll problems, and generally just ensuring that the guys in the field could focus on the dangerous work at hand without worrying about what was happening back home. I'd extended my contract by two years and gotten married to Jen. I considered myself to be among the most fortunate guys on the planet. My life was happy and quiet, until five o'clock that afternoon when the phone in my office rang.

On the other end was a man who identified himself as a colonel based at the Pentagon.

"Am I speaking to Staff Sergeant Salvatore Giunta?"

"Yes, sir."

"Staff Sergeant Giunta, you're about to receive some very big news."

For three years the possibility of this call had been hanging over my head. Most days I didn't think about it at all. Other times I'd wake up in the middle of the night, anxious and sweating. As I said, I'd been told shortly after the incident in the Korengal Valley that I had been submitted for the Medal of Honor, an award I felt unworthy to receive, and preferred to not even think about. The Medal of Honor, after all, went to heroes. I was no hero. To this day I believe rather emphatically that my role in that encounter was no greater than the role played by any of my comrades. We each had a job to do. I didn't fire the most shots, I didn't make the greatest sacrifice. So to think that I would be singled out was almost incomprehensible.

Now, though, it seemed that the incomprehensible was about to happen.

"I can't tell you what it is," the colonel continued. "Just make sure you are at your desk tomorrow afternoon, at precisely this same time. When the phone rings, pick it up."

"Yes, sir."

"Staff Sergeant, Giunta?"

"Yes."

"Don't let anyone else answer the phone. And don't tell anyone about this."

"Yes, sir."

I hung up the phone, went straight home, and immediately told

Jen what was happening. There was a chance, of course, that I was going to receive some other award—a Distinguished Service Cross, for example—but the Medal of Honor discussion had been out there, on the back burner, for three years now. Nearly four decades had passed since any living soldier had received the award. If I was to be the first, I wanted Jen to know it. I wanted her to share in the news, and to help me bear the weight of it. The Medal of Honor had long felt like this big thing that I had no control over. It would be a life-changing event, and it might happen, or it might not. The best way I could deal with it was to just not think about it. I was never a big public person. I liked to go out and drink beer and hang out with the guys. I didn't like to get dressed up and talk fancy. And that was pretty much guaranteed to happen with the Medal of Honor. With the award comes a forfeiture of privacy; your life is no longer your life. You get a Wikipedia page and television appearances; people suddenly know more about you than you ever wanted them to know.

It's a lot to handle.

"I want you to come to the office tomorrow," I said to Jen. "Just be there by five o'clock."

I was sitting at my desk when Jen arrived. Right away the other guys in the office knew something was up, because Jen never came to visit me at work. (It wouldn't be work if she was there.) I knew the phone call would be right on time, and it was. It was the same colonel calling. After verifying again that I was indeed Staff Sergeant Giunta, he put me on hold. Within seconds I was transferred to a woman who identified herself as a secretary at the White House.

My heart raced.

"Is this Staff Sergeant Salvatore Giunta?" she asked.

"Yes, it is."

"Please hold for the president of the United States."

I looked at Jen, who was sitting next to me. I took her hand in mine. Suddenly there was a voice on the other end of the line.

"Staff Sergeant Giunta, this is President Barack Obama."

I have trouble remembering exactly what followed, but I do know it was a fairly short conversation and that it included the president saying, "I'd like to congratulate you. The packet recommending you for the Medal of Honor has crossed my desk, and it's been approved."

I didn't know how to talk to a president. I mean, who does? But I did my best.

"Roger, Mr. President."

He went on to thank me for my service. He told me that my country was proud of me. Two or three minutes after it had begun, the conversation ended. When I looked up, the room was packed with close to fifty people (there were only five of us who actually worked in that space), some of them looking at me with utter disbelief, like I had a dick growing out of my forehead.

"Mr. President?" one of my buddies said with a smile.

I nodded.

"So, I guess we're going out for beers tonight, huh?" he said.

"I guess so."

———

Two months later I found myself at the White House, listening to President Obama talk about me like we were old buddies. By that point I had met with generals and been feted at the Pentagon. My whole world had been turned upside down. I tried to handle it as gracefully as I could, but usually I felt like I was screwing up somehow, or that someone, someplace, had made a huge mistake. As much as I expected my life to change, it changed even more.

The juxtaposition of the world I knew, a world of enlisted men and foot soldiers, and the world I had been tossed into, one populated by elected officials and military officers whose uniforms were adorned with a blinding array of brass, was extremely jarring. Nothing demonstrates the craziness of their intersection more vividly than the night before the Medal of Honor ceremony, when we had dinner at the home of General

George W. Casey, who was then chief of staff of the United States Army. It still seems almost surreal for me to write these words, and to think that I had done anything that merited an invitation to General Casey's house.

I was a kid from Iowa who just a few years earlier had been slapping together sandwiches at Subway. I was a staff sergeant in the Army who had merely done his job, just like everyone else with whom he served. It was humbling, to say the least.

A small, private bus brought us back to our hotel following the dinner with General Casey. There were fewer than a dozen of us on the bus—just my family and some other military personnel. As we approached the front door of the hotel, we passed slowly through a large group of men. They surrounded the bus and began beating on the walls and the doors. They shouted and chanted. And then they began rocking the bus back and forth.

I looked out the window and immediately recognized several of my buddies. And then several more.

Holy crap! They're all here.

And so they were, nearly fifty soldiers with whom I had served in Italy and Afghanistan, all members of Battle Company. I had known that some of them were planning to attend the ceremony, but I hadn't expected this sort of turnout. Some of these guys I hadn't seen in two or three years. And while I knew they'd be a raucous group, I hadn't figured on them attacking the bus.

As the bus came to a stop, I could tell everyone else on board was a little nervous. Someone suggested I go outside and ask the guys to stop banging on the side of the bus.

I laughed.

"Yeah, like they're going to listen to me."

I stepped off the bus and did not even touch the ground. They were right there at the door, waiting for me, grabbing me and tossing me above their shoulders, passing me from person to person, slapping me and yelling at me. I surfed along the top of the crowd, smiling and laughing like a little kid. These were my boys! It felt so good to be among them again.

At the back of the pack some big guy grabbed me and tossed me over his shoulder, carrying me like a rucksack. He started bouncing up and down, yelling, "Giunta! Giunta!"

Holy shit! I don't even know this guy!

Then he set me down and looked me in the eye.

"How you doin', bro?"

It was Michael Mason, the man at least partially responsible for my having met Jen. I honestly didn't recognize him. Although tall, he'd always been a semi-lean and wiry dude, but now he looked like a mountain man. He'd put on probably seventy-five pounds and the added weight, combined with a thick beard and a biker jacket, gave the impression of a man who had been completely transformed. I had to look hard to see the Michael I remembered.

"Mason!" I said. And I gave him a big bear hug. Or he gave one to me. I guess it really doesn't matter.

I like to remember Michael the way he looked that night, or the way I remember him in Italy or Afghanistan. Always happy and upbeat.

A few weeks after the gathering in Washington, D.C., Mason was seriously injured after leading police on a chase through Santa Clara, Oregon. I don't know what Michael was thinking that day, or what led to the final showdown. I know only what I heard from friends and what I read in media reports: that Michael had fired his gun several times while sitting in his car outside a shopping mall. When police arrived on the scene, Michael fled. Eventually his car was stopped, there was another standoff, and he was shot several times.

Michael survived the incident, but his wounds were severe enough that he no longer has the ability to walk. It hurts to even think about him that way, as someone whose heroism and service might now be lost forever in the shadow of something that happened afterward; something terrible and tragic; something probably triggered by PTSD.

The truth is, not everyone comes back from war in one piece, and the wounds aren't always visible. Out of all the men with whom I served, I'd say probably 50 percent are living relatively normal, productive lives. The other 50 percent are struggling, some quite severely. They're falling below the average standard of living, maybe drinking too much or using drugs to self-medicate.

It pains me so much to see these guys, and to know how much they're suffering, because I know for a fact that they make this country great. What's remarkable is that they can handle combat—they can survive, and even thrive, under the most hellish of circumstances—but they can't necessarily handle the normal, everyday world. They come home to discover that life has not been put on hold; things are not the way they were when the deployment began. Friends have gone to college and now hold jobs. Children have grown up. In some cases, wives and girlfriends have lost interest and moved on.

Meanwhile, the skills these men have acquired, so vital in the military—and in combat in particular—seem not to translate readily to the civilian world. But that isn't really true. I think too many veterans wear blinders; they become self-limiting, convinced that they are qualified only for jobs in law enforcement or security. Those are fine professions for those who choose to enter them, but if you look at the guys who are doing well, across a remarkably diverse range of fields, you know that vets, given the opportunity and resources, can do almost anything.

———

The Medal of Honor ceremony itself was at once exhilarating and awkward, standing on that stage, the center of attention in a room thick with soldiers and politicians and family members. To have so many legitimate heroes, so many men of accomplishment and valor right there in the front row (the eight living Medal of Honor recipients). To see the families of Brennan and Mendoza. I tried to hold it together, even as a stew of conflicting emotions boiled within me. This was a good thing. I knew that. But it still hurt—to know that two people had died and others had been wounded, and I was the only one up there onstage, a living example of the cost of war.

That is something I struggle with to this day: the fact that people think October 25, 2007, in the Korengal Valley of Afghanistan, was a good day for the U.S. Army; that it showed our might and our will and our spirit. In my mind, October 25, 2007, was a loss. We could kill every member of the Taliban and it still wouldn't bring back Brennan and Mendoza. Every time the Medal of Honor comes up, I get patted on the back and thanked for my service, and all I can do is politely say "Thank you" and swallow what I really feel.

How can I be so great if I allowed two of my friends to get killed?

That comes with the territory, I guess. It is part of the responsibility of accepting the Medal of Honor and all that it represents.

I understand more as time goes on that the medal stands for something much larger, something incredibly important, but it doesn't obscure the reality of what happened. I can accept the accolades, but every time someone says something about the medal, my mind goes back to that firefight, and to the two people who will never see another day. The award is symbolic of something greater than any individual soldier—it is symbolic of pride and honor and patriotism. I get that.

But to me it's something much smaller and something much more personal.

———

In the two years since receiving the Medal of Honor, I've gotten better at handling my emotions and juggling the responsibilities that come with it. Jen and I have a baby girl, and much of my professional life, now that I've left the Army, is devoted to public speaking engagements and working with various veterans' groups, which I find incredibly rewarding.

I met a man named John Wordin at a Medal of Honor event a while back; in the course of our conversation, he asked if I enjoyed riding bikes. I told him that I did, and John asked if I might be interested in participating in Ride 2 Recovery, a program for wounded veterans that he founded following a career as a professional cyclist. Ride 2 Recovery is produced by the Fitness Challenge Foundation (also founded by John), in partnership with the military and the VA Volunteer Service Office. The group's stated mission is to support "mental and physical rehabilitation programs that feature cycling as the core activity."

I liked the sound of it, but admitted to John that I was at best a casual cyclist.

"What are the requirements?" I asked.

"Just be yourself."

Sounded simple enough.

I never dreamed Ride 2 Recovery would become such an important part of my life, but it has. The organization provides adaptive bicycles for soldiers who have lost limbs, endured traumatic head injuries, or suffer from PTSD, and the vets who benefit are some of the most extraordinary people I've ever met. My first event with Ride 2 Recovery was the "Texas Challenge," which consisted of riding six days straight from San Antonio to Arlington. Upon completion of the ride, we all went to a Texas Rangers baseball game.

It was an amazing experience. After so many traveling and dinner events I'd gotten a little thick around the middle, and it had become increasingly difficult to keep calling myself "one of the boys." With Ride 2 Recovery, though, that's exactly the way I felt. I got at least as much out of it as they did—riding 450 miles, sweating, working, and meeting people who treated me as just another vet trying to figure out the next step of my transition.

Ride 2 Recovery is a program aimed at vets of all branches, and open to servicemen and women both active and no longer in the military. The commonality is that we all seek something more in our lives. People get involved with Ride 2 Recovery for all sorts of reasons. Some are newly postoperative and just want to get out of the hospital for a little while; some have undergone several surgeries and want to feel the breeze on their faces again; others have lost limbs and are now looking for a new form of exercise, an outlet for all that energy and athleticism they once had (and still have!). As for me . . . I'm part of this program not just because I get such a charge out of seeing these men and women break through barriers, but also because of the camaraderie we all experience. I have met several people on Ride 2 Recovery whose personalities would mesh neatly with those of my buddies in the 173rd. Some of these guys are Marines or Air Force or Navy vets, but we're all like-minded people who served our country to the best of our ability. And in some cases paid a heavy price along the way.

Now we just want to get together and support each other, to laugh and bond over the course of a week and several hundred miles. I joined Ride 2 Recovery to help wounded vets, but I do it for myself as well. I like working hard, hanging out with my new buddies, hearing their stories, and seeing their progress. And with seven weeklong rides each year, there's plenty of opportunity.

Another group that means a lot to me is the Congressional Medal of Honor Society (along with one of its branches, the Medal of Honor Foundation). I first had a chance to meet a Medal of Honor recipient at the White House, when I was presented with the award. Since then I've had the privilege of meeting many more recipients at different events. The society gathers a few times a year around the United States. It is truly amazing to be able to interact with these men and to hear their stories—not just war stories, but deeply personal stories involving family and friends; stories about the places they've visited and the things they've been able to do because of the medal. These are men who have influenced the course of history on battlefields around the world—from World War II to Korea and Vietnam. It feels strange to be introduced at events with such extraordinary soldiers, and to stand alongside them. I have been given lots of good advice over my lifetime, but most of it has been common sense (which, admittedly, I lacked at times). The advice I receive from the other Medal of Honor recipients is different; it's larger, born of experience and lessons learned through a lifetime of representing the men and women in uniform. It is priceless.

Admittedly, it's odd to have so much in common with men who are thirty-five to sixty-five years my senior. But it's comforting, too. Through the Medal of Honor Foundation we meet with schools, Boys & Girls Clubs, and other organizations to share stories of citizenship, patriotism, loyalty, duty, honor, and integrity. Things that can help anyone, really, but the schools provide a perfect forum: an eager (or at least interested) audience of young people. It's one thing to hear your mother say, "Treat others as you would like to be treated," but it's something else entirely to hear stories from men who have been willing to sacrifice their very lives to help a buddy, and who often have the battle scars to prove it.

I am conflicted sometimes when I meet other recipients and get to know them well, not only because I am unaccustomed to having so many older friends and mentors, but also because they tend to be in and out of the hospital with health problems, and often in the waning days of their journey. I find it sad to meet these great men, and to get close to them, only to lose them so quickly. But of course I'm better for having had the opportunity to spend time with them, however brief it might have been, and my life has been enriched by their friendship.

They are the best of the best.

————

It's fair to say that even though I am no longer in the Army, the Army remains a vital part of my life and my history, and because of the Medal of Honor that will never change. I can accept it more graciously now, largely because I see the effect it has on people. It inspires them and moves them. It helps them believe in something bigger than themselves. But I don't get caught up in the idolatry or the use of the word "hero," especially when it's directed at me.

I talk about the award because I want the names of my brothers to be heard. I want to stand up and say that what I did was not unique or special, and certainly not amazing. How could it be special if everyone in the Korengal Valley that day responded just as admirably, and with just as much professionalism and courage? I want people to understand something: that if that's how you define "amazing," then amazing things are happening every day in Afghanistan and Iraq, on battlefields half a world away.

I use my public appearances to talk about my friends, who are nothing less than the best this country has to offer. I want people to know that the life we have in America—a life of freedom and opportunity, a life largely free of violence and suffering—is not without cost. There are people out there fighting for it every day. Soldiers on the ground do not have the luxury of political opinion—it's irrelevant to their existence and their mission. They do what they are told, regardless of how crazy it sometimes seems. Soldiers do not make big decisions; they do not have choices, other than those that are made in the blink of an eye and have life-and-death consequences.

And they accept this responsibility willingly. They seek it out. They fight so that others don't have to fight.

It's remarkable, really. In this country, you turn eighteen years old, and you have the right to vote. You have a say in how your government is run. You have a voice in the process. I think it's acceptable to remind people once in a while that these privileges, given as a birthright, are preserved and maintained by men and women in uniform, and that these people are doing extraordinary and courageous work under unbelievably difficult circumstances. In return, they expect . . . nothing.

I hope my daughter grows up in a world without war, a world without hate and bloodshed and pain. But I know that's a practical impossibility. So I will make sure she understands what freedom really means, and the price that is paid in its name. I will encourage her to embrace some type of public service, because I think it's a healthy way to express patriotism, and to share some of the burden of a free and democratic society. Do I want her to put on a uniform and carry a gun? Do I want her to know combat, or to see the horrible things that I've seen? No, of course not. What father wants that for his child?

But you know what? If she chooses to join the military, I will support her one hundred percent, because I know in my heart that there is no more noble path.

I think about my daughter often when I'm out traveling around, giving speeches, shaking hands, talking about my friends in the military. I want her to be proud of me, and to know that what I'm doing is important. I want her to know that I accept the Medal of Honor not for myself, but because it provides a forum for talking about my brothers and the job they are doing, and the sacrifices they've made.

Those men and women who do the fighting—too often, they don't get to talk.

I want their voices to be heard.

ACKNOWLEDGMENTS

I have thought about this long and hard, agonizing over the inevitable oversights and omissions that occur when you try to recognize everyone who deserves to be thanked for the role they have played in your life. I can say with complete assurance that there has been a person (or persons) helping me become a better "me" around every corner and on every step of the journey. Whatever I've accomplished, whatever I've achieved, I haven't done it alone. So . . . I guess I'll just start at the beginning.

Thanks to Mom and Dad for always believing in me, even if I didn't always believe in myself.

Mario and Katie: I could not have asked for a cooler brother and sister.

To all my cousins, aunts and uncles in the Giunta, Judge, Lackermann, Bentley, Ernzen, Parks, and Dunham families. Thanks for allowing me to grow up in a loving and caring family environment.

To the teachers who put up with me through all grades and subjects. School was never really my thing, but with the help of caring, dedicated professionals like you, I have passed and can now say with certainty, "knowledge is power." Thank you for giving me the power to experience life to the fullest.

To the friends I grew up with: my golf buddies, teammates, and party companions.

I am grateful to the terrific folks at the Washington Speakers Bureau for helping me share my experiences in a positive and professional manner.

A thanks to Jack Jacobs for putting me in contact with the right people to help me tell my story, including Frank Weimann of The Literary Group and Ivan Kronenfeld.

Thanks to the folks at Simon and Schuster for publishing the book and working through the details of it all. A special thanks to my coauthor, Joe Layden. If not for his ability to be not only a great writer, but also a keen listener, this story would have fit in a pamphlet instead of in a book.

I have had the great fortune since receiving the Medal of Honor to be mentored, guided, and counseled in a positive direction by men who know the responsibility that comes with it. Thanks to all of you, I can wear the medal and not get sick to my stomach or feel embarrassed for having it on; thanks to you, I know I can continue to serve the great country of the United States of America.

Last and certainly not least, this is for "The Boys," the fighting men of the 173rd. I have never been led by an incompetent commander at any level in the 2-503. I have never had a leader lead me down an immoral or unethical path in the military. I have never been pushed harder or asked to do more with less than I was in the Rock, and for that I thank all of my brothers who fought, shivered, huddled, sweat, and bled with me.

If not for all of you, I would not be here today. The Men of Battle Company will forever be my brothers.